The Politics of Orientation

SUNY series in Contemporary Continental Philosophy

Dennis J. Schmidt, editor

The Politics of Orientation

Deleuze Meets Luhmann

HANNAH RICHTER

SUNY
PRESS

For information, contact State University of New York Press, Albany, NY
www.sunypress.edu

Library of Congress Cataloging-in-Publication Data

Name: Richter, Hannah, 1990– author.
Title: The politics of orientation : Deleuze meets Luhmann / Hannah Richter.
Description: Albany, NY : State University of New York Press, [2023] |
    Series: SUNY series in contemporary continental philosophy | Includes
    bibliographical references and index.
Identifiers: LCCN 2022062172 | ISBN 9781438495064 (hardcover : alk. paper) |
    ISBN 9781438495071 (ebook)
Subjects: LCSH: Senses and sensation. | System theory. | Democracy. | Society.
Classification: LCC BF233 .R498 2023 | DDC 152.1—dc23/eng/20230623
LC record available at https://lccn.loc.gov/2022062172

10 9 8 7 6 5 4 3 2 1

To Waltraud and Peter, and to Sascha

"Would you tell me, please, which way I ought to go from here?"

"That depends a good deal on where you want to get to," said the Cat.

—Lewis Carroll, *Alice's Adventures in Wonderland*

Contents

Acknowledgments

To those readers who know me, it won't come as a surprise that I am compelled to start these acknowledgments with the acknowledgment that I found writing them quite possibly more difficult than writing the actual book. Making the author speak in such a personal manner implies more direct attention on their persona, not the conceptual but the actual one, than seems warranted to, certainly than is comfortable for, this particular author. Throughout this book's long germination process, I have continuously wavered between either writing this section in a tone of self-mockery, or not writing it at all. Now that the time has come, I am compelled to resist both impulses. The people to be acknowledged here deserve better than a humorously inverted thank you.

This book started life as a doctoral dissertation at the University of Kent, where it was born from a moment of puzzlement, and a theoretical hunch that followed. Reading Niklas Luhmann's discussion of sense in *Theory of Society*, it seemed strangely familiar to me. Turning to Luhmann's footnotes to discover where I could have encountered it before, the answer they offered was surprising, and immediately intriguing: Deleuze's *The Logic of Sense*. Luhmann read Deleuze—on sense. Following both thinkers down the rabbit hole of their shared theory of sense, I discovered the theoretical hinge that my ideas had been lacking up to this point. For years I had been thinking about states of exception, crises, and the generally evental logic of public political engagement, but with the dissatisfied feeling that I was stuck at the level of symptoms. I was analyzing what was being produced, not how it was being produced, or why. Deleuze's and Luhmann's sense offered me a pathway to explore exactly this what and why at a time when it felt, and still feels, particularly urgent to understand why some political forces and positions, namely those of the political right, seem to be set up so much better for winning in the contest for popular support. While this book certainly spends time in the heights of conceptual abstraction, these lofty explorations always take place in the service of eventually returning to the ground of politics, better equipped. I thus first and foremost hope that this book will be politically useful to those reading it, whatever this might mean for the individual reader.

I would like to thank Iain MacKenzie for supporting my free and wild conceptual explorations in their badly founded early stages, and Stefan Rossbach for supporting me in bringing them to a preliminary doctoral thesis conclusion. This preliminary conclusion turned out to be only one stop in this book's long journey toward completion. Its traveling ideas benefited from stops in many ports, and from the feedback, interrogation, and support that they—and their author—received from many they have met along the way. For their friendship, mentorship, and often both, I would like to thank Greg Bird, David Chandler, Dee Goddard, Hollie Mackenzie, Martijn Konings, Gavin Rae, Sara Raimondi, my forever office-wife (regardless of our respective institutional positions) Elisa Randazzo, Jemima Repo, Lina Soukara, and Tom Watts. Special mention deserve my fantastic University of Hertfordshire colleagues Francesca Batzella, Ben Nutt, Pierre Parrouffe, Ivor Sokolic, and Ignasi Torrent for their comradeship in the face of adversity, and in battling what Hannah Arendt so aptly described as tyranny without a tyrant. I would like to thank my acquisitions editor Michael Rinella for his always swift replies and excellent editorial guidance, and the two anonymous reviewers for their incredibly generous engagement with what I still think of as my weird little book. Thank you to my parents, Waltraud and Peter, without whose love and support neither my lengthy academic apprenticeship nor this book would have ever been possible. And finally, thank you to Sascha. Both Luhmann and Deleuze have written on love, but to anyone who has read both it will be obvious why I choose to quote from the latter on this occasion. For Deleuze, falling in love means discovering a multiplicity of worlds from the signs emitted by the beloved. Thank you, Sascha, for your worlds, which make my life and my writing so much richer every day.

Introduction

"That which cannot be conceived through anything else must be conceived through itself" (Luhmann, 2012a, p. 7). Niklas Luhmann's *magnum opus* of sociological systems theory, *Theory of Society*, is curiously prefaced by the second axiom from Spinoza's *Ethics*. Curiously, because Luhmann, usually read as a positivist structuralist in the tradition of Talcott Parsons, is not known for his Spinozist predilections. Luhmann's Spinozist epigraph hints at a secret, a hidden philosophical depth and playfulness, a concern with immanence, contingency, and multiplicity only superficially concealed by the dry formalism of his systems theory. The arguments developed in this book will unfold from a journey into the hinterland of Luhmann's thought. Placed at the beginning of *Theory of Society*, Spinoza's second axiom seems to be both the declaration of a theoretical program and an analytical call to action: start on the inside, for it is only from the inside that we can begin to understand anything. This theoretical program is immediately reminiscent of Gilles Deleuze and Félix Guattari's call to "see things in the middle, rather than looking down on them from above or up at them from below, or from left to right or right to left" (Deleuze and Guattari, 1987, p. 23), repeated insistently in the opening pages of *A Thousand Plateaus*. "[T]ry it," they urge the reader, and "you'll see that everything changes" (p. 23). How could a book on Luhmann and Deleuze then not follow the calls of both of its protagonists, and indeed start from the middle, from the inside of the arguments it develops?

This book employs the theories of Deleuze and Luhmann to develop a political theory of twenty-first-century democratic politics. The book generates a novel Deleuzian-Luhmannian lens to explore how contemporary democratic politics operates at the intersection of institutional processes, citizens, and their perceptions and needs, how this functioning is conditioned by the

1

capitalist societies which situate democratic politics, and which continuities and changes mark the socio-evolutionary history of modern democracy. An obvious discontinuity that has recently received much attention from political theorists and public commentators alike is the rising popularity of right-wing populism in many established democracies, from the United States to the United Kingdom, Germany, and Italy, often fueled by conspiracy theories and counterfactual claims to an extent that has earned it the label of "post-truth" politics. The Deleuzian-Luhmannian political theory developed in this book hopes to provide valuable insight into the contemporary appeal of this post-truth populism, and to unpack the underlying shift in the functioning of contemporary politics it signals. But it also draws out its functional continuity with a modern politics whose operational hinge has always been, and is still, the provision of collective steering.

Following Luhmann's and Deleuze's shared theoretical programs, this book explores politics from the middle, from the inside of its own operativity. It draws out how the *raison d'être* of modern politics lies in authoritative worldmaking against a complex multiplicity of alternative worlds—in the expression of power that shapes the social world inhabited and experienced by subjects. While Luhmann (2002) uses David Easton's (1957) classical political science definition of collectively binding decision making to capture the steering function of politics, Deleuze and Guattari, in *Anti-Oedipus* (1983), describe political steering as the overcoding centrally performed by the despotic machine of the modern state. Deciding on the particular world to be produced allows politics to reproduce itself as the authoritative center of the political community. But when neoliberal capitalism, with its deterritorialized flows and atomized, functionally differentiated systems, becomes the dominant mode of social organization, it alters social conditions away from the hierarchical centralization that the political system's despotic machine requires to operate. Politics, under these conditions, can no longer adequately understand, let alone control, the social flows it is supposed to govern (Deleuze and Guattari, 1983, pp. 222–228; Luhmann, 2002, p. 110; 1990, p. 102). As Deleuze writes in his "Post-script on the Societies of Control," the institutional centers of modern society, including those of democratic politics, "are finished" (1992a, p. 4).

This lack of directly effective steering capacity constitutes a lethal threat for a contemporary democratic politics, which sustains its claim to power by continuously demonstrating the former. The consequence, however, is not the end of modern democracy, with recent populist upheavals heralding its disintegration. On the contrary, viewed through this book's

Deleuzian-Luhmannian lens, the rise of post-truth populism must rather be understood as the symptom of democratic politics' functional adaptation. Under conditions of neoliberal capitalism, which the "post-mortem despotism" (Deleuze and Guattari, 1983, p. 228) of liberal democracy can no longer effectively control, it becomes a *politics of orientation* that continues modern politics with different means. This book introduces the idea of a politics of orientation to describe a form of democratic politics in which authority and legitimacy rest not on whether and how political actors shape or propose to shape society through effective decision making but on the means of "contingency control" (Luhmann, 2002, p. 68) and "uncertainty absorption" (Luhmann, 1993b, p. 530) they offer the citizens of complex, deterritorialized democracies.

Orientation is here used in a manner similar to Kant's understanding of orientation as a grounding *intuition* that allows individuals to locate, fix, and distinguish objects, and thereby determine their own position in the world (Kant, 1992, pp. 382, 403).[1] However, beyond Kant, complexity-reducing orientation does not only condition spatial distinctions but performs an ontological condensation and placing that allows subjects and societies to perceive themselves and the world they inhabit in a more general sense. Orientation, in this book, is further not an intrinsic capacity of the human mind but rather the dedicated objective and product of psychic and social processes that evolved for the very purpose of ensuring that subjects and societies are steadily supplied with orientation. Twenty-first-century democratic politics will in the following be unpacked as one such processual apparatus.

A politics of orientation sustains its position as society's steering authority by guiding subjects on how to make sense of this world, and of their own position within it, by offering problem diagnoses, value systems, narratives, and explanatory frameworks. Populism, post-truth politics, and conspiracy theories thrive under these conditions because they are particularly effective in offering complexity-reducing orientation for sense-making. While there is no easy way out of a democratic politics that social conditions have geared toward the provision of orientation, such a politics is not exhausted in the post-truth populism that currently shapes its appearance. The challenge this Deleuzian-Luhmannian political theory will leave the reader with is that of imagining a democratic politics of orientation.

Having covered the middle, it is time to return to the beginning. To readers of both Deleuze and Luhmann, the above sketch of the book's political theory might seem similarly foreign. In order to develop it, it is first necessary to embark on the conceptual and ontological journey of reading Luhmann and Deleuze together. While this book certainly contains comparative moments, its aim is not a theoretical comparison between the philosophical worlds of Deleuze and Luhmann that reveals hitherto unexplored parallels and common grounds. The book certainly renders visible multiple points of contact between Luhmann and Deleuze, but only as they are already being put to work in a process that Andreas Philippopoulos-Mihalopoulos, in his work on both thinkers, describes as theoretical "folding" (2013, p. 60). Folding aims at neither comparison nor synthesis but rather at the creative genesis of a theoretical third no longer purely Deleuzian or Luhmannian. "The encounter itself defines the point of view, the perspective" (p. 60) established in a process of folding which, for each theory enfolded, takes place "inside, in the system, yet draw[s] space *from* outside, from the environment" (p. 60; original emphasis).

The theoretical folds this book generates around concepts central to the works of both thinkers—time, the event, difference, and multiplicity/complexity—are held together by a hinge: the concept of sense. Of all the concepts discussed and enfolded in the following, their theories of sense are where Deleuze and Luhmann come closest.[2] Both thinkers conceptualize sense as the medium and mechanism of worldmaking. Subjective selves and worlds are continuously made and remade in sense. Again, inside and middle are of vital importance here. Sense-making is thoroughly immanent; it has no ground outside of always-already made relations of sense and expresses nothing but new sense, which can then once again serve as the conditioned ground for future sense-making. While sense-making always draws on both material and epistemic constituents, their shaping power is here secondary to their synthetic enfolding in sense. Sense-relations thus charge their own reproduction against the co-constituted potentiality of nonsense or not (yet) actualized sense. Self-production in sense oscillates between emergent order in time, which allows for the making of stable selves and worlds, and a perpetually returning evental rupture, from which sense is remade in identical or changed fashion. Order in sense thus functions self-productive only insofar as it constantly renders itself precarious.

With Deleuze, and even more explicitly with Luhmann, this theory of self-grounding, self-rupturing, and ultimately self-reproductive sense must be thought not only as ontology but also as social theory. Not only subjective consciousness, but also the mechanisms, structures, and interactions of social life are sense-based. Capitalism's machinic logic has created societies that are subject to a dense network of multiple disjointed flows, populated by subjects and social systems which can only be understood from the inside, or the middle, of their own sense relations. Subjects and social systems operate and reproduce themselves within their own logic of sense. They cannot conceive of anything outside of themselves other than as threatening, deterritorialized complexity, but are yet forced to continuously expose themselves to this complexity to fulfill the multiple demands these societies place on them. It is under these conditions, which Luhmann terms functional differentiation, and Deleuze describes as societies of control, that collectively steering politics becomes a politics of orientation—both because it cannot sufficiently understand the workings of the economy, law, or the nonhuman environment to produce effective governance, and because the public demand it responds to is one for complexity-reducing re-territorialization and re-coding more than it is one for effective social steering.

The Critical Luhmann

The arguments and explorations developed in this book rest on the assumption that an enfolding of Deleuze's and Luhmann's ideas is not only theoretically productive, but, more fundamentally, plausible in the first place. This founding assumption is already contentious. From the time of Luhmann's early publications in the 1960s and 1970s up to the contemporary reception of his thought, the relationship between his writings and the tradition of critical theory, in which Deleuze's work is situated, read, and applied, has been marked by tension and mutual rejection (Kim, 2015, pp. 356–357). In his lifetime, Luhmann encountered critical theory primarily in the form of the Frankfurt School, and in Jürgen Habermas more closely than any other of its representatives. Luhmann and Habermas were the two grand social theorists of postwar German academia. Their dislike for the respective other's theoretical project is obvious. However, they nevertheless mutually and amicably recognized the scope and quality of the other's work. As a contemporary observer notes, the Habermas-Luhmann debate was "far from being the kind of trench warfare that the Adorno-Popper controversy certainly was" (Sixel, 1976, p. 185). Indeed, Habermas and Luhmann made "every effort to listen to and learn from what the other" (p. 185) had to say. Luhmann himself respectfully acknowledges the "pointed, nuanced and very differentiated" (1971b, p. 291; my translation) character of Habermas's critique.

Early on in their respective careers, Luhmann and Habermas even co-authored a publication, *Theorie der Gesellschaft oder Sozialtechnologie: Was leistet die Systemtheorie?* (1971), which unfolds a debate on the merits and limitations of a systems theoretic account of society. Against the background of his own critical theory of communicative action, Habermas, in his contribution to the volume, accuses Luhmann of a functional determinism that eradicates individual agency. Because Luhmann's systems theory removes the category of the subject from the creative process of communicative expressions, his theory, according to Habermas, renders deliberative emancipation and social transformation categorically impossible (Habermas, 1971, pp. 238–278). All communication can do, in Luhmann, is uncritically reproduce the constructions of its own making. Ultimately, Habermas cannot accept that Luhmann's theory "need not and does not sell itself to praxis via legitimation nor does it reflect on it" (Sixel, 1976, p. 194). Habermas's matter-of-fact critique remains mainly focused on the workings Luhmann's systems theory. The criticism Luhmann received for his technocratic mannerisms and apparent aloofness toward pressing social issues from other Frankfurt School thinkers, and their students, was often harsher, more personal—and did not stop at *ad hominem* attacks, both figurative and literal (Brunkhorst, 2012; Brunczel, 2010, p. 220). Friends and colleagues recall the empty classrooms Luhmann was teaching to in the politicized early 1970s, an incident involving flour and eggs thrown at the lectern, as well as enduring gossip about the supposed right-wing political sympathies of Luhmann, who avoided party-political affiliations throughout his lifetime (Kruckis, 1999).[3]

More contemporary critics draw out parallels between Luhmann's society of functionally differentiated systems and the emergent, self-regulating neoliberal economy to brand Luhmann as a theoretical apologist, if not herald, of neoliberalism (Malowitz and Selk, 2015; Bröckling, 2016). Other scholars focus on how Luhmann's theory remains "up to its ears stuck in the covert which is the problem of subjectivity" (Ternes, 1999, p. 131) and other Enlightenment remnants, but chooses to ignore the questions of power, legitimacy, and resistant agency associated with these (see also: Ashenden, 2006; Lange, 2005). In its general academic reception, Luhmann's work remains framed as analytically positivist and politically conservative. Luhmann himself certainly did not help himself here. His published works and public speeches include frequent mocking remarks on critical theory, above all directed at the "confident provinciality of the Frankfurt School" (Luhmann, 1992, p. 51, quoted in Dammann, 1999, p. 27; see also Luhmann, 1991a). With the exception of Habermas, Althusser, and Marx, Luhmann dismissed critical theory as analytically simplistic and overly moralizing (Lauermann, 1999; August, 2021, p. 355). Even more gravely, he suggests that the normative certainty and superiority underpinning (Frankfurt School) critical theory should be regarded as the true hallmark of conservativism (Luhmann, 1991; Esposito, 2017, p. 23). It reproduces notions of ontological essentialism and universal moral judgment which, for Luhmann, have no place in a social theory fit to provide insight into the particular society it is embedded in.

For Luhmann, such theorizing can happen only from the inside, and thus requires a recognition of its epistemological perspectivism and limitations. Luhmann's rejection of the normative certainty underpinning Frankfurt School critical theory echoes criticisms put forward by poststructuralist thinkers, including Foucault's and Deleuze's discussion of Marxist theory in "Intellectuals and Power" (1977). Luhmann, on the surface, advocates for abandoning the notion of critique in favor of the analytically more "useful" theory of second-order observation (Luhmann, 1991a, p. 4) in a manner reminiscent of Bruno Latour's infamous "Why Has Critique Run Out of Steam?" (2004). However, at a closer look, Luhmann does in fact not reject the theoretical project of critique altogether but rather seeks to replace the Frankfurt School's narrowly defined, normative critique with a more encompassing, postfoundational critical analytical attitude. Luhmann comes closest to defining what his own critical project could look like at the very end of *Theorie der Gesellschaft oder Sozialtechnologie?*

By way of a concluding remark, he suggests that "the better option" for social theory was always "to keep hold of theoretical insecurity in terms of approach and methodical proceedings" (Luhmann, 1971b, p. 404; my translation). This theoretical insecurity, for Luhmann, "might be the condition for all possibilities of controlling political implications" (p. 404). Reflecting on his methodological remarks, as if to correct Habermas's reading of his theory, Luhmann stresses that he does "regard them as critical" (p. 405), even if it is unclear whether such a methodological and political "function of insecurity" (p. 405) will prove theoretically durable. Luhmann makes a case for a mode of theorizing that embraces contingency and ontological insecurity to capture, and retain, an open-ended potentiality that safeguards against political oppressiveness. It is in this sense that Elena Esposito identifies Luhmann's theoretical perspective as a project of *critical observation* that

> looks for the contingency (improbability) of what evolution led us to regard as normal and not surprising [. . .]. What is familiar to us could not be there or be different, depending on social conditions that can themselves be observed. Critical observation, which looks for the conditions that make these improbabilities

> normal . . . is observation of society within society. From this
> perspective, sociological systems theory could be seen somehow
> provocatively as the most accomplished form of the critical
> attitude—a reflexive form of critique. (Esposito, 2017, p. 24)

In recent years, a small but significant body of scholarship has taken on the task of exploring, rendering visible, and making use of the critical potential of Luhmann's theory. Under the label of "critical systems theory," a number of scholars are leading "Niklas Luhmann's unmanned flying object back to earth after its blind flight above the clouds and the volcanoes of Marxism" (Fischer-Lescano, 2012, p. 10), drawing out synergy effects between Luhmann's theory of functional differentiation and Marxist critiques of neoliberal automation and alienation (Amstutz and Fischer-Lescano, 2013; Siri and Möller, 2016; Dias Minhoto, 2017; Overwijk, 2021; Daly, 2004; Procyshyn, 2017; Cordero et al., 2017). The larger part of this new critical Luhmann scholarship, which seeks to free Luhmann's ideas from the shackles of their conservative-positivist canonization, however rereads his theory as a postfoundational critique (Wolff, 2021; August, 2021; Konings, 2018; Kim, 2015; Opitz and Tellmann, 2015; Moeller, 2017, 2012; Borch, 2005; Teubner, 2001; Rasch, 1997, 2000; Philippopoulous-Mihalopoulos, 2011, 2013; Stäheli, 2000).

This book will use the label "postfoundational" to qualify both Luhmann's and Deleuze's scholarship as well as the theory produced from their speculative enfolding. Postfoundationalism is here not used to signify membership of a particular "school of thought" but rather to qualify a philosophical line of investigation. For the context of this book, postfoundationalism will be understood in Oliver Marchart's sense as characterizing scholarship where "the primordial (or ontological) absence of an ultimate ground is itself the condition of possibility of grounds as present" (Marchart, 2007, p. 15). In other words, this book presumes that absolute grounds are impossible in the works of both Luhmann and Deleuze, but that the question of how and in which form the contingent grounds of the social that fill this ontological void are made and remade is of central concern for both thinkers—as it is for the political philosophy that the author draws from their scholarship.

Many of the existing works dedicated to a "postfoundational Luhmann" unpack relations of kinship between Luhmann's ideas and the thought of Foucault, Derrida, Lyotard, or Laclau. This book starts from the presumption that a particularly productive Luhmannian encounter is so far missing from this list: the one between Deleuze and Luhmann.[4] This absence is peculiar insofar as a number of Luhmann scholars seem well aware of the "virtually unresearched" (Müller, 2012a, p. 268) congruence of Deleuze's and Luhmann's conceptual worlds, which evolve around ideas of creative differentiation, sense, and time (Müller, 2012b, p. 74). While I have made it clear what kind of Luhmann will encounter Deleuze in the following—Luhmann, the postfoundational philosopher—the *conceptual persona* of Deleuze that will meet Luhmann has yet to be characterized. I believe that three of his general "character traits" should be made explicit here, which every chapter will flesh out further through the concept that forms its theoretical hinge—sense, self/world, time, event, and politics. First, the work of this book's Deleuzian conceptual persona is not only an ontology with political implications but also a political theory (Widder, 2008, 2012; Connolly, 2014; Patton, 2000; Lundborg, 2009; Buchanan and Thoburn, 2008).

Deleuze, as read here, does not only help us to envision a world in which we think and act differently, but is chiefly concerned with how power and control can prevent or facilitate living otherwise. While most of his political readers, such as Nathan Widder, Paul Patton, and William Connolly, turn to Deleuze for a contribution to radical democratic thinking, this book, with the help of Luhmann, employs Deleuze's thought for a critical analysis of the political present. This book's Deleuze is thus secondly an analyst of structural continuity as much as he is a thinker of revolutionary change (Lundy, 2013; Zourabichvili, 2012, 2017; Patton, 1997). Finally, the Deleuze of this book dwells on the surface of sense, not in the depth of matter—he reads more Nietzsche than he does Bergson or Spinoza. This book aligns itself with scholarship where Deleuze's philosophy does not unfold from an ontological source but is postfoundational in a "thick" sense, undoing any notion of ontological primacy (Zourabichvili, 2012; Clisby, 2015; Widder, 2008). The surface philosophy of this Deleuzian conceptual persona unfolds through sense, time, and the event. Matter, bodies, and their affective responses make and shape productive relations but hold no privileged position or relevance for creative becoming, which sets this book's Deleuze apart from—broadly understood—materialist readings of his work (DeLanda, 2006; Massumi, 2011; Braidotti, 2006; Grosz, 2017).

In reading Luhmann and Deleuze together, this book hence enters a theoretical terrain which, while not completely unmarked, has so far remained largely untreaded. Before its journey can even begin, this book hence needs to find a way around the obvious distance between Luhmann's sterile, highly formalistic account of a society comprised of functionally differentiated systems and Deleuze, the postfoundational philosopher who postulates the benefits of being "a little alcoholic, a little crazy" (Deleuze, 1990, p. 157) to escape the socioeconomic confinement of thought, and whose philosophy—especially in his collaboration with Guattari—unfolds in obscure images, colorful narratives, and the occasional vulgarity. This distance will be bridged here with an emphasis on Deleuze's sobriety and Luhmann's humor.

Deleuze's Sobriety, Luhmann's Humor

Various passages of Deleuze's work with Guattari stress the value of sobriety for critical-transformative thought. In *A Thousand Plateaus*, Deleuze and Guattari insist that linear, arborescent social and epistemic structures cannot be distorted through mere "typographical, lexical or even syntactical cleverness" (1987, p. 6). To stimulate transformation, a dynamic multiplicity "must be made, not by always adding a higher dimension, but rather in the simplest way, by dint of sobriety" (p. 6). "Sobriety, sobriety" is thus "the common prerequisite for the deterritorialization of matters, the molecularization of materials and the cosmicization of forces" (p. 344). Deleuze and Guattari detect such a methodological use of sobriety in the writings of Franz Kafka and Samuel Beckett (1986, pp. 19–34). Here, sobriety is used as a literary means of de-personalization. It prepares the ground for a becoming-other that can escape capitalism's machinic subjection to socioeconomic production (Bogue, 2003, pp. 10–11).

    What could be more apt to describe Luhmann's writing than the term sobriety? On the one hand, there is Luhmann's public persona, recounted by his contemporaries in the retrospective *Gibt es eigentlich den Berliner Zoo noch?* (1999). They paint the picture of a theorist who works with "assiduity beyond every tiredness" (Souto, 1999, p. 55; my translation) but who "was not one of those figures who made it easy for their environment to find, beyond their professional role, access to a more personal background. On the contrary. Great personal distance and aloofness, the consistent narrowing of conversations to more general topics characterized his nature" (Kieserling, 1999, p. 45; my translation). The Luhmann who emerges from these and similar accounts is dry, technocratic, always friendly but strictly professional in his exchanges with students and colleagues. One of his former colleagues recounts an episode where Luhmann was evidently appalled at the insinuation that his writings contained "funny examples" (Rammstedt, 1999, p. 19; my translation). "Where are they?" (Luhmann, quoted in Rammstedt,

1999, p. 19), he is recalled to have responded, "Something like this must be removed immediately" (p. 19).

This public persona fits well with the style of Luhmann's writing, infamous for its lifeless technicality. In *The Radical Luhmann*, Hans-Georg Moeller dedicates a whole chapter to the question of why Luhmann "wrote such bad books" (2012, p. 10), unpacking Luhmann's "extremely dry, unnecessarily convoluted, poorly structured, highly repetitive, overly long, and aesthetically unpleasing texts" (p. 10). The central explanation that Moeller offers "for the forbidding nature of Luhmann's style" (p. 12) is the peculiarity of his theoretical project. While explicitly formulated as a sociological theory,[5] Moeller (pp. 12–14) argues that Luhmann's work is in fact intended as a philosophical super-theory in the tradition of Kant and Hegel, whose stylistic formalism and propensity for length and theoretical heaviness Luhmann therefore adopts (see also: Rasch, 2013). I would like to propose a different, more Deleuzian, explanation for Luhmann's "bad" writing: a methodological sobriety that functions in combination with Luhmann's rupturing humor.

Most accounts of Luhmann's personality and his writing are of a certain schizophrenic quality. They illustrate the aforementioned dryness but in combination with reporting Luhmann's humor, his "enjoyment of political incorrectness or even joyful cynicism" that spanned "the complete scale of humorous communication from the mocking of classical references that require an educated audience to the merciless dullness of the corniest jokes" (Kruckis, 1999, pp. 48–49; my translation). An example famous amongst Luhmann scholars is the research plan he produced upon request when joining the newly founded faculty of sociology at the University of Bielefeld in 1969: "the theory of society; term: thirty years; costs: none" (Luhmann, 2012a, p. xi). It seems as if the theorist Luhmann deliberately endowed his social systems theory with a matching author persona that bracketed other parts of his personality, but from which he occasionally distanced himself through humorous remarks. Such remarks make regular appearances in Luhmann's writing, calling into question how serious the outrage was that Rammstedt recounts above.

Often hidden in footnotes or made in passing, Luhmann's humorous interjections reveal him as a sharp, critical observer of philosophical trends and social conditions who anarchically ridicules dogmatic in an almost Nietzschean fashion.[6] On one occasion, Luhmann chooses to begin an invited talk on business ethics with the words: "I have to say it right at the beginning: I did not succeed in finding out what I am actually supposed to talk about. The thing has a name: business ethics. And a secret, which is its rules. But I assume that this phenomenon is similar to the *raison d'état* or the English cuisine, which appear in the form of a secret because they need to hide the fact that they actually don't exist" (Luhmann, 2008a, p. 196). On the topic of religion, Luhmann observes that in order to achieve a social ordering system of similar effectiveness, "it would be necessary to combine Marxism with drug addiction but attempts at this have not turned out convincing so far" (2000, p. 127).

Against the background of Luhmann's humor, the dry aloofness of his writing and public persona appear consciously crafted—an artificiality that renders apparent the contingency behind its own, and thereby all, constructed order. Such a reading of Luhmann's stylistic sobriety fits well with how Luhmann's contemporary André Kieserling describes his style of lecturing. According to Kieserling, Luhmann "cultivated the artificiality of his whole project so clearly that nobody would be deterred from disagreeing by the lecture itself" (1999, p. 57). Reminiscent of Bertolt Brecht's epic theatre, where the action on stage is made to seem distant through a range of dramatic devices, from a lacking display of emotion by the actors on stage to encouraging the audience to smoke and talk during the play, deployed to make the tragedy played out on stage seem contingent and thus avoidable, I suggest that Luhmann's stylistic sobriety performatively reveals the artificiality, contingency, and variability of all social order, which lies at the heart of his theoretical project. To use a Deleuzian term, it functions dramatizing (Deleuze, 1967). Dramatization in Deleuze begins with distinct concepts and explores the dynamic problems that lie behind and exceed them. Uncovering "the dynamic spatio-temporal determinations (the differential relations) that constitute the terrain of the Idea" (MacKenzie and Porter, 2011, p. 489), dramatization reveals not only that the world we inhabit could be actualized in very different ways but also recovers the potentiality to perform such divergent actualizations. Together with his rupturing humor, Luhmann's sober *conceptual persona* dramatizes the concept of order.[7] Nothing in Luhmann's society of autopoietically closed but functionally unstable systems is ever essential or determinate. All order is contingently self-produced against the background of a chaotic multiplicity of alternatives, and temporary; things could always be radically otherwise.

While it takes a second glance to recognize the humorous quality of Luhmann's work, Deleuze explicitly mobilizes the rupturing purchase of humor in his critical philosophy. In "Coldness and Cruelty," Deleuze opposes the humorous, productive contractualism of the masochist to the ironic, dissective legalism of the sadist. Both seek to overcome the realm of conventional law. But due to its ironic inversion of the law, the anti-legal anarchy that the sadist desires ultimately functions as a constitutive outside which only reproduces the law's validity. "Sade often stresses the fact that the law can only be transcended toward an institutional model of anarchy," Deleuze writes (1991, p. 87). The issue is that "anarchy can only exist in the interval between two regimes based on laws, abolishing the old to give birth to the new" (p. 87). On the contrary, the logic of masochism is humorous, chaotic, and creative. "[I]nseparable from an attempt to overturn [. . .] authority" (Deleuze, 1991, p. 130), humorous masochism does not just invert the dialectic relationship between master and slave while leaving its logic intact. Its dramatizing enactment rather dissolves the dialectic itself by creatively opening up alternative relational connections.

For Deleuze, irony operates on the basis of an accurate common sense, ridiculing false diversions through exaggerated inversion to, in the end, arrive at a reproduction of this common sense. Humor, on the contrary, does not require or contain assumptions about "rightness." It opens up the rupturing intensity of chaos, freeing singularities from their representative confinement by distorting the dialectic opposition between sense and nonsense. "[I]f irony is the co-extensiveness of being with the individual, or of the I with representation, humor is the co-extensiveness of sense with nonsense" (Deleuze, 1990, p. 157). The philosophical opponent whom Deleuze targets with his humorous philosophy is Hegel, and his synthetic resolution of contradictions. For Deleuze, dialectic synthesis reproduces the philosophical—and political—status quo and eradicates every possibility for divergent creative production.[8] Deleuze opposes the dialectic annihilation of difference with a humorous philosophy that "does not attempt to resolve contradictions, but to make it so that there are none, and there never were any" (p. 11; see also: Deleuze, 1994, pp. 171–189). Humor dismantles the dialectic functionality of philosophical, economic, and political order to open up the chaotic multiplicity of alternative relational connections. If brought into contact with epistemic or social relations, this creative potentiality can bring about actual change in the order of the world we inhabit (Ionica, 2016).

That both Luhmann and Deleuze employ a combination of sobriety and humor to expose the contingency of order, and the chaotic multiplicity behind it, does, however, not mean that order and chaos have exactly the same status in their theories. Luhmann seems content to highlight the unlikeliness and contingency of order through humorous cracks in the sobriety of his writing and his public persona. He neither targets a particular social order nor implies that a different kind of order should be made following his deconstruction of the ordering principles that make the world as it is. Luhmann is not a revolutionary, and while the idea that things do not have to be the way they are is central to his work, they never amount to the demand, or political call to action, that things should be different. Deleuze, on the contrary, weaponizes humor and sobriety to actively challenge and disrupt the doxa of philosophy and the machinic workings of capitalist society.

Following the example of the "writing machine[s]" (Deleuze and Guattari, 1986, p. 32) of Beckett, Burroughs, and Kafka, Deleuze's philosophy aims to "plug into" (p. 48) systems of order to rewire our understanding of them, and to encourage readers to challenge the status quo upheld by their public acceptance. Different from Luhmann, Deleuze's ideas are intended to function as revolution. Acknowledging this difference in philosophical intent, this book suggests that much can nonetheless be gained from exploring the common ground of Deleuze's and Luhmann's work: an ontology and a social theory in which chaos is the norm, and order the contingent, fragile, and laboriously upheld exception.

Structure of the Book

The Deleuzian-Luhmannian political philosophy of this book will be developed through an exploratory enfolding of both theories intended to push each "deeper into its creative potential" (Philippopoulos-Mihalopoulos, 2013, p. 60) and unlock ideas and arguments that remain inaccessible through their isolated engagement. For Luhmann, this enfolding aims to recover his work from the theoretical "ossification" (Philippopoulos-Mihalopoulos, 2013, p. 63) to which its positivist-analytical reception, especially in the Anglo-American academy, has led. While most of the recent critical writings on Luhmann focus on laying out the analytical program for a critical Luhmannian systems theory, this book aims to go one step further, and politically apply the critical Luhmannian theory unlocked through the unfolding with Deleuze. Equivalent to what Esposito (2011; Esposito and Stark, 2019) and Konings (2018) have performed for the context of a financialized economy, and Philippopoulos-Mihalopoulos (2006, 2011, 2014) for the realm of law, this book aims to make Luhmann's thought useful as a lens for critical political analysis.

The critical potential of Deleuze's work of course requires no unlocking. It is the central driving force behind Deleuze's writing as well as behind the reception of his work. For Deleuze, the creative potentiality unlocked through the enfolding with Luhmann is hence not political critique but rather sociopolitical analysis.[9] In Deleuzian scholarship, the political potential of his theory is, for the most part, utilized for abstract theoretical explanations of where political potentiality is located within contemporary societies stratified by capitalism (Widder, 2012; Buchanan, 2008; Patton, 2000), of how resistance can generate or access it (Braidotti, 2006; 2013; Massumi, 2002, 2011), and of how we are to create a more radical, more open democracy from doing so (Connolly, 2014; Patton, 2005; Schrift, 2000).[10] Rarely does Deleuze's theory inform a detailed sociopolitical investigation of whatever forms the focal point of the political critique put forward. Where such a Deleuzian political analysis is developed, it is highly specific, both in terms of the aspects of Deleuze's work made use of, and regarding the social phenomenon under investigation, for instance algorithmic governance in Deleuze's digitalized societies of control (Celis Bueno, 2020; Galloway, 2004, 2012; MacKenzie and Porter 2019) or the machinic stratification of events through media coverage (Lundborg, 2015, 2009; Patton, 1997).

Through the enfolding with Luhmann's systems theory, which offers a meticulously detailed account different social systems in their particular functioning and social couplings, this book renders Deleuze's critical philosophy useful as a lens for sociopolitical analysis, and applies the former to the functioning of twenty-first-century democracy. While such an overarching Deleuzian analysis of contemporary democratic politics covers new ground for Deleuze scholars, I hope it will also showcase how analytically well-equipped, powerful, and practically useful the "tool box" (Deleuze and Foucault, 1977, p. 208) of Deleuze's philosophy is to a wider audience of political theorists and social scientists that might have so far dismissed the former as (nothing but) abstract, jargon-heavy postfoundational ontology.

This book's enfolding of Deleuze's and Luhmann's theories is not completely even, and cannot be performed without some tearing and bending. The following chapters will not draw on Deleuze and Luhmann to an equal extent. Some folds might be more Deleuzian than Luhmannian, some vice versa, and some require the abrupt departure from the trajectory of one theory to refold toward the other. To smooth the process, this book will enfold not only the thought of Luhmann and Deleuze but also the works of thinkers who have directly informed, or echo in, the writings of both: Leibniz, Husserl, Nietzsche, Whitehead, and Marx. The process of enfolding Deleuze's and Luhmann's already in themselves unwieldy, and in many ways radically different, works nevertheless requires a certain amount of theoretical force, some speculative pushing, and interpretive pulling of both theories. As Philippopoulos-Mihalopoulos suggests, the "effect might be one of estrangement for both Luhmann and Deleuze scholars" (2013, p. 61). The creative potentiality uncovered in both theories through this enfolding, I hope, justifies the occasional use of theoretical force. Such use of force is at least not foreign to the scholars on whom it is being exercised. Luhmann adopts the conceptual framework of Talcott Parsons's systems theory but turns it on its head to produce a postfoundational social philosophy that bears little resemblance to the former. Deleuze, on his part, considered himself a traitor to the authors who inspired his work (Kedem, 2011; Bryant, 2008) but argues that such treacherous philosophizing is preferable to acting as the "interpretive priest" (Deleuze and Guattari, 1987, p. 114) of the philosophical canon. For new philosophical habits to be formed, old ones must be broken first.

This book is split into two parts. The first part develops a Deleuzian-Luhmannian ontology that identifies ungrounded, self-grounding relations of sense as the mechanism and medium that makes subjects as well as the social worlds they inhabit. The second part unpacks the functioning of politics against the background of this social ontology as self-reproduction through collectively steering decision making. In neoliberal capitalism's functionally differentiated societies, the only steering that politics can provide for its citizens is orientation for sense-making, which allows populist forces and conspiracy theories that are solely focused on the provision of complexity-reduction to flourish. Chapter 1 will begin the enfolding of Luhmann and Deleuze with the concept on which it is hinged: sense. The first chapter unpacks how both Luhmann and Deleuze, whom the former references directly, conceptualize sense as immanently creative. Sense-relations are ungrounded insofar as they are composed of material and epistemic constituents but exceed them to produce something new that only becomes actual on the surface of sense. The motor of immanently creative sense-making is the complexity or multiplicity of nonsense. Marking the excess of sense rather than its absence, nonsense is the constitutive outside co-produced in every process of sense-making.

Chapter 2 develops an ontological application of immanently creative sense as the mechanism and medium of self- and worldmaking. It argues that self and world emerge as the two sides of one and the same process of open-ended sense-making, which must be directed to be able to generate stable selves and continuous worlds. Chapter 3 unpacks how Luhmann and Deleuze both identify time as the emergent ordering framework that ensures productive continuity in sense. Because the order of time is, however, also without stable ground, like sense, it requires an in-built reproductive mechanism that keeps it moving. Ordering time is continuously ruptured by the event that allows for its continuation. Chapter 4, which marks the transition from ontology to political theory in the book, shows how this rupturing event functions as the source of both continuity and change, depending on which pathway of sense is actualized from it. In the context of society's sense-relations, the decision on this actualization marks the function of modern politics.

Chapter 5 explores the functional dilemma that a self-reproductive politics focused on this steering provision faces in a capitalist, functionally differentiated society where governmental access to the social realms that require political steering is severely limited. Under these conditions, politics becomes a politics of orientation. A politics of orientation steers societies not through direct worldmaking in sense, but by offering citizens guidance for sustaining their processes of self- and worldmaking, which complex digitalized societies have rendered increasingly precarious. Chapter 6 then unpacks the rise of post-truth politics and populist forces within twenty-first-century democracies as an effect of this functional shift toward a politics of orientation. Beyond existing analyses of post-truth politics, which emphasize their radical break with modern democracy, the Luhmannian-Deleuzian lens of a politics of orientation sheds light on the underlying social-functional continuity between both. However, the shift to a politics of orientation benefits those political forces whose simplistic messages offer the most radical complexity-reduction and thus the most effective orientation—which are, as it stands, the political voices of the populist right.

Chapter 1

The Immanent Creativity of Sense

Sense exists only as sense of the operations using it, and hence only at the moment in which it is determined by operations, neither beforehand nor afterward. Sense is accordingly a *product* of the operations that use meaning and not, for instance, a quality of the world attributable to a creation, a foundation, an origin.[1]

—Niklas Luhmann, *Theory of Society, Volume 1* (p. 18)

[A]ll meaningful operations always reproduce the presence of what has been excluded, for the world of sense is a complete world, which can exclude what it excludes only itself. Non-sense, too, can therefore be thought and communicated only in the medium of sense, only in the form of sense.

—Niklas Luhmann, *Theory of Society, Volume 1* (p. 21)

[S]ense is always an effect. . . . There is no reason to repeat that sense is essentially *produced*. It is never originary but is always caused and derived.

—Gilles Deleuze, *The Logic of Sense* (pp. 70–95)

[N]onsense does not have any particular sense, but is opposed to the absence of sense rather than to the sense that it produces in excess . . . Nonsense is that which has no sense, and that which, as such and as it enacts the donation of sense, is opposed to the absence of sense. This is what we must understand by "*nonsense.*"

—Gilles Deleuze, *The Logic of Sense* (p. 71)

The hinge for this book's creative enfolding of Luhmann's and Deleuze's theories is the concept of sense. Deleuze's and Luhmann's theories of sense are their exact mirror image. For both, sense is productive but at the same time always itself produced. Creative sense is without absolute ground or outside; its only limitation is the underside of nonsense co-produced in every act of sense-making. Rather than forming the genuine opposite of sense, nonsense is only its temporary boundary, and always remains connected to sense as both constitutive outside and creative reservoir. This book, like many years ago the philosophical journey that led to its writing, begins with the puzzle of Deleuze and Luhmann's unexpected convergence on the notion of sense. It was Luhmann who facilitated its discovery: his own systems theoretic discussion of sense in the first volume of *Theory of Society*, quoted above, contained, hidden in his footnotes, references to the equivalent passages in Deleuze's *The Logic of Sense*.

"One can't help . . . but two can": Sense and Paradox in Deleuze and Luhmann

Deleuze picks an unusual reference point to unfold his theory of sense: the writings of Lewis Carroll. Deleuze justifies this unusual choice at the very beginning of *The Logic of Sense*'s first chapter, or series, as Deleuze titles the thirty-four sections of the book. Carroll's *Alice* and *Through the Looking Glass*, Deleuze suggests, gives us insight to "a category of very special things: events, pure events" (1990, p. 1). The special quality of a pure event lies in its paradoxical nature: it affirms both sides of a distinction at the same time. Alice's growing in the present means that, at the same time, the previous Alice is shrinking. "She is larger now; she was smaller before. But it is at the same moment that one becomes larger than one was and smaller than one becomes" (Deleuze, 1990, p. 1). Early on, Deleuze here provides the reader with a key to unlock his theory of sense: the paradox.

Carroll's tales of Alice's adventures are steeped in paradoxes. Alice's absurd dialogues with the inhabitants of the wonderland make sense only as nonsensical exchanges, affirming both sides of the distinction of sense. When Alice observes that "one can't help growing older" (Carroll, 2001, p. 70) to Humpty Dumpty in *Through the Looking Glass*, he replies with: "ONE can't, perhaps . . . but TWO can. With proper assistance, you might have left off at seven" (p. 70). Carroll, the mathematician turned surrealist children's book author, was well aware of the conventional role and treatment of the paradox in logic and analytical thought. Whereas ancient Greek thinkers used paradoxes to teach logic, early twentieth-century analytical philosophy sought to escape the paradox because it risked undermining the absolute validity of theoretical paradigms. The paradox reveals how any such validity always requires a foundational distinction or exclusion. To use Epimenides's famous Cretan liar paradox as an example, in the face of a Cretan proclaiming that "all Cretan's are liars," one must decide whether to accept the paradigm by believing this one Cretan, or to reject the paradigm by accepting its validity in this one instance.

Carroll's interest, against Gottlob Frege and Bertrand Russell, lies in using the paradox to reveal exactly this contingency of all theoretical paradigms. As Alwin Baum puts it in his analysis of Carroll's semiotics of paradox, "Alice's dream friends go to non-Euclidean schools" (1977, p. 101). Carroll illustrates his subversive use of the paradox in his take on the paradox of Achille and the tortoise, a variation of Zeno's paradox. In its original form, the paradox concerns the infinite expansion of space in time that follows when we understand movement as a series of spatial segments transitioned in a particular time. The fleet-footed Achilles, confronted with the supposedly easy challenge to race the slow tortoise, grants the latter a head start. The paradox unfolds when Achille discovers that, because the tortoise had been allowed to start first, it is impossible for him to ever catch up, regardless of how fast he runs. By the time Achilles will have reached the position of the tortoise, the tortoise will have moved again by exactly the same distance it had crossed while Achilles was waiting (Sainsbury, 2009, p. 19). In Carroll's version, the unlucky warrior does not lose the race because of its ever-receding finishing line, but rather loses an argument about the ultimate contingency of logical propositions because of the ever-recurring foundational decision that conditions theoretical validity, as in the example of the Cretan liar. Here, the tortoise draws attention to the fact that "[i]f A and B and C are true, Z must be true" is nothing but "another hypo-thetical" (Carroll, 1995, p. 692). If one "failed to see its truth" (p. 692), one "might accept A and B and C, and still not accept Z" (p. 692).

Carroll's paradox reveals that, for every proposition, any attempt at finite grounding reveals nothing but an infinite regress of prior propositions. The sense of a proposition is not charged by, and therefore anchored in, any external source. Instead, sense emerges from a moment of distinction demarcating the boundary between sense and nonsense from the inside of the sense-relations that this distinction will *deparadoxify*, and thereby continue, in one way or another. The distinction resolves the paradox by drawing a line between sense and nonsense, which separates the sense that is accepted as the ground for further sense-making from what it is not, an outside multiplicity from which alternative lines of sense could be drawn. The creativity of sense, which unfolds from the continuous distinction between sense and nonsense, is the pure event that Deleuze seeks to understand in *The Logic of Sense*.

Sense is the radically immanent medium of worldmaking. Deleuze develops an interest in the ontogenetic function of sense early in his career, when he suggests that the philosophical project must be understood as "an ontology of sense" (1997, p. 191) in his 1954 review of Jean Hyppolite's *Logic and Existence*. Sense is necessarily productive, perpetually moving. Any attempt to determine the source or original quality of sense—is Alice growing larger than she was or smaller than she will be?—can only take place as a contingent decision within sense itself. It takes the form of further sense expression, and thus moves farther away from what it was intended to capture. Following Deleuze, this paradoxical immanent creativity of sense comes to the fore once we remove sense from the doxa of *common sense* and *good sense*: the idea that sense is based on a stable distinction between being and nonbeing and teleologically pre-directed to represent this being accurately (Deleuze, 1990, pp. 75–77). Good sense and common sense make their first appearance in *Difference and Repetition* as characteristics of the "dogmatic image of thought," the orthodox way of doing philosophy that Deleuze seeks to overcome. Understanding and unlocking the immanent creativity of sense beyond the dogmatic image of thought is the project of *The Logic of Sense*, published only one year later.

Interestingly, Luhmann draws exactly the same link between paradox, foundationalist common sense, and teleological directedness in his essay "The Paradoxy of Observing Systems" (1995b). Here, Luhmann identifies the rhetorical function of paradoxes as that of deframing and reframing "the frame of normal thinking, the frame of common sense" (1995b, p. 39). Like Carroll and Deleuze, Luhmann suggests that the eternally regressive or self-undermining nature of the paradox ultimately subverts the possibility of fixed essences and ends in favor of a perpetually recurrent openness. The paradox must thus be understood as "an autological operation, infecting itself with whatever is a paradox" (Luhmann, 1995b, p. 40). Sense is of this *para-doxical* quality—it momentarily keeps at bay absolute openness, but only insofar as it undermines any notion of fixed ground. As the medium of worldmaking, sense is positioned between world and truth. It both precedes and outlives any particular representation of the world, meaning that any such truth is merely a contingent distinction in sense (p. 41).

The contingency of this decision, and the possibility of an otherwise, is carried forward in every expression of a particular truth in sense, like the tortoise's lead in Achille's race. For Luhmann, this paradoxical contingency renders the medium of sense immanently creative and thus allows it to function ontogenetically. A world made in sense "is observable because it is unobservable" (Luhmann, 1995b, p. 46)—worlds come into being only insofar as they are the contingent, and temporary, products of sense-expression. Worldmaking in sense involves a selective decision about the particular world that is being observed. But at the same time, every such decision carries with it its own foundational insecurity, as the original, grounding distinction withdraws in an infinite regress and remains "indistinguishable" (p. 46). Just as in Deleuze, this is the case in Luhmann because any such "first" distinction can be observed only through yet "another operation" (p. 46) of sense-making. Sense can "distinguish only by using itself, in other words 'autologically.' It is the absolute medium" (Luhmann, 1995a, p. 26). Luhmann develops his very own take on the Cretan liar paradox in the preface to *The Science of Society* to indicate, in Luhmann's usual veiled self-irony, that even his status as an author and theorist is nothing but a contingent distinction in sense: "It remains only to say, as usual, that any remaining errors are chargeable to me—with the exception of errors in this sentence, obviously" (Luhmann, 1990c, p. 10; see also: Moeller, 2012, pp. 40–41).

Both Luhmann and Deleuze employ the figure of the paradox to illustrate how sense functions as a medium of creative genesis. Worldmaking in sense *is para-doxical* insofar as it is charged by a continuously becoming, regressively moving sense without external foundation or direction, free from *common sense* and *good sense*. This chapter will zoom in on Luhmann's and Deleuze's respective theories of sense to explore how sense unfolds a creativity that exceeds any external source charging it, and is therefore thoroughly immanent. Deleuze theorizes sense as the "excluded forth" of idealist, materialist, and logical-analytical philosophy, which Luhmann's theory of sense smoothly folds into. But on the other hand, Luhmann expands the philosophical horizon of a theory of immanently creative sense beyond ontogenesis in the mind of the subject. Luhmann shows that not only subjects, but also societies and the different functional realms they are composed of, produce the world they inhabit in a way that is intelligible to them in sense. Both subjects and societies thus rely on the creative force of paradoxical sense. But at the same time, they must constantly conceal the paradoxical quality of the sense that makes their worlds in order to prevent them from crashing into the groundless abyss of infinite regress that lies beneath its immanent paradox.

Deleuze's Sense: Stoic Bodies and Chaotic Nonsense

Deleuze's philosophy is most commonly associated with the concepts of difference and becoming, with war machines and lines of flight that open up ways to think and act differently. The concept of sense is missing from this standard Deleuzian vocabulary. Sense plays an important role in Deleuze's review of Hyppolite, and then becomes the focal point of Deleuze's own philosophy in *The Logic of Sense*, published in 1969, but is glaringly absent from his subsequent writings. As Jean Jacques Lecercle notes, sense "does not seem to have been productive" (2002, p. 99) in Deleuze's work—a philosophical dead end, recognized as such and abandoned without second thoughts. For Lecercle, Deleuze's philosophical experimentation with the concept of sense thus constitutes an unfortunate "accident" (2008, p. vii) tarnishing "an otherwise distinguished career" (p. vii). Deleuze, the argument goes, had simply not quite found his philosophical field and voice yet when he wrote *The Logic of Sense*. Adding to the theoretical impasse of sense, the work is still strongly influenced by linguistic structuralism and psychoanalysis. Deleuze will later distance himself from both and, through the influence of Guattari, become explicitly critical of the apolitical nature of psychoanalytic thought.

The comparative neglect of *The Logic of Sense* within Deleuzian secondary literature supports Lecercle's dismissal of the book as a preliminary, outdated version of Deleuze's philosophy. Despite some recent interest (Widder, 2012, 2008; Bowden, 2011, 2010, 2014; Voss, 2013a; Williams, 2008; Dejanovic, 2014; Collet, 2016; Świątkowski, 2016), it remains one of Deleuze's infrequently discussed books.[2]

What sets this book apart from these recent explorations of *The Logic of Sense* is first and foremost that it is not primarily aimed at unpacking Deleuze's philosophy of sense as such, but rather seeks to draw a novel theoretical perspective from the encounter between Deleuze and Luhmann, which is hinged on, but certainly does not exhaust itself in, their respective theories of sense. On the side of ontology, Sean Bowden unravels the paradox of immanent creative production from the side of the event. This book, like Widder's (2008), proceeds in the opposite direction, beginning with sense. Different from Bowden's event, sense does not hold absolute ontological priority as a creative force that is always deeper, and always more forceful than any particular actuality it generates. Rather, it will be shown how creative production in sense does away with any meaningful notion of ontological priority precisely because it unfolds through continuously self-grounding relations.

The second difference concerns the political application of Deleuze's arguments from *The Logic of Sense*. The productivity of Deleuze's theory of sense for a critical political theory has been drawn out convincingly by Widder (2008, 2012),[3] but the political role of sense remains abstract here: understanding how ontogenesis in sense draws and ontologizes contingent boundaries makes it possible to conceive of a "micropolitical domain of ethical negotiation where what matters is not the ability to construct an identity but rather the capacity for revaluations that move us beyond crude oppositions" (2008, p. 188). Beyond Bowden and Widder, through the link to Luhmann, I suggest that Deleuze's immanent creativity of sense offers a perspective for critical political analysis. It can tell us something about how the very particular stratifications of contemporary democratic societies are produced and reproduced at "the frontier, the cutting edge" (Deleuze, 1991, p. 28) of sense. The innovative moment of Deleuze's philosophy of sense is that it re-organizes the relationship among truth, world, and sense to arrive at a creativity *sui generis* that operates by continuously exceeding the products that ground further creation.

In different ways, Western philosophy has identified sense as the liminal space between meaning systems and referent objects. Sense is the passive vessel through which ideas make the world, through which the world imprints itself on human understanding, or through which the stable relations between both are kept intact and become intelligible. Sense is here passive, not creative. In Deleuze's *The Logic of Sense*, sense is instead the active medium of ontogenesis to which both world and truth are secondary (Voss, 2013a, pp. 4–6). Importantly, however, sense functions only creatively insofar as it is also expressed. It does not have absolute ontological priority and thus, as Bowden notes, must not be confused with "an already given condition like the Kantian transcendental" (2011, p. 185). Peculiarly, this makes creative sense "an event which is immanent to itself" (p. 185). Deleuze's ontogenesis in sense can take place as immanent "all the way down" because of two distinct qualities of sense. First, sense is the always excessive "fourth dimension of the proposition" (Deleuze, 1990, p. 19) whose creative capacity goes beyond what is drawn from speaking subject, referent object and the meaning of the proposition that is being expressed. Creative sense is "an incorporeal, complex, and irreducible entity, at the surface of things, a pure event which inheres or subsists in the proposition" (p. 19). In Widder's words, sense is neither "body nor Idea, sense is . . . relating concept and thing at and through the surface" (2008, p. 109). Second, sense is able to continuously function creatively without an external source that charges this creativity because there is an uncontained multiplicity on the inside of sense that is reproduced in every act of sense-making—nonsense. In Deleuze's philosophy of sense, nonsense does not signify the absence of sense but rather the immanent driving force behind the *perpetuum mobile* of ontogenesis in sense: "nonsense expresses its own sense" (1990, p. 67) and thereby "enacts *a donation of sense*" (pp. 69–70).

To understand why it is so important that Deleuze characterizes sense as the "fourth dimension of the proposition," it is necessary to take a closer look at how Deleuze's theory differs from other philosophical accounts of sense. The other three dimensions that Deleuze dismisses as inadequate for capturing the creativity of sense are (1) the idea expressed, formed in the mind of the rational subject, (2) the material referent that a proposition is designated to describe, and (3) the logical relationship between both, set up by the proposition itself. It is certainly not accidental that these three dimensions represent the focal points of the three perspectives on sense that dominate the canon of Western philosophy. Hence, the consequence of Deleuze's dismissal is more far-reaching than it seems at first glance. Deleuze shows how existing philosophies of sense explain sense-making by projecting their ontological stance onto their respective account of sense in the form of the external source that drives creative production in sense. As a consequence, each perspective offers a reductionist account of sense that can shed light on its creativity only if we accept the validity of its particular foundational claim.

The first philosophy of sense that Deleuze dismisses grounds sense in the ideas formed by the rational speaking subject. Present in the pre-Socratic philosophies of Parmenides and Anaximander (Palmer, 2013), it comes to full fruition in Plato's idealism. Plato acknowledges the vital character of materiality for sense-making as sensory experience, a vital "instrument" (1997, p. 204) that helps the mind gain access to the quality of things. However, only the contemplative mind is able to order the resulting chaos of sensory impressions to form and express an accurate representation of the world experienced. Ideas, not objects or propositions, drive and direct sense-making (Silverman, 1990, pp. 157–158; Kirk, 1951). The philosophical lineage of grounding sense-making in the ideas of the rational mind finds various expressions in Enlightenment philosophy but is maybe most explicitly formulated by Descartes. In his *Meditations on First Philosophy*, Descartes famously uses the example of a piece of wax melted to a liquid state of aggregation to point out the inadequacy of sensory information for understanding the real nature of things (Descartes, 1968, pp. 6–7). Because material objects reveal their true nature only when sensory information is mediated and decoded by the rational mind, sense-making must be understood as guided by the "mind's faculty of judgment" (p. 7), not the object perceived or discussed. Regardless of the form it takes, or the words we use to describe it, the rational subject knows that wax remains wax.

Kant's transcendental philosophy then continues this rationalist account of sense, but also turns it inward—toward an in itself productive domain of sense located in the mind of the subject. In the *Critique of Pure Reason*, Kant initially offers an account of sense as relational and synthetic. The "inner sense" produced in thought and the "outer sense" that emerges when human sensibility is physically affected by a material object are equally necessary conditions for making sense. Kant dissolves the domain of sense from the idea that sense-making is pre-directed by a particular faculty that ensures that the representation of produced is accurate. The world, as it can be known to us, emerges from the free interplay of inner and outer sense (Schmitz, 2015; Roche, 2010). We are able to catch a glimpse of Deleuze's creative sense uncurtailed by an ontologically fixed *common sense* in Kant.

As Voss puts it, "Kant's revolutionary move is to make truth dependent on sense . . . for something to have a sense, that is, to be an object for us, it has to be related to the transcendental conditions that constitute sense" (2013a, p. 6). Creative sense is thus, as Deleuze points out, "the characteristic discovery of transcendental philosophy" (1990, p. 105). However, Kant forecloses the radical implications of his twofold concept of sense with a turn to the transcendent. Metaphysical objects such as God can be made sense of accurately even though we exclusively have inner sense available to do so (Kant, 2008, pp. 37–38, 98–108). Ultimately, it is the *a prioris* of the rational mind that orient sense-making and ensure its accuracy in Kant (Jansen, 2016; Roche, 2010). The theory of sense-making focused on the rational subject ultimately captures the creativity of sense as secondary to the mind's capacity to produce accurate ideas of a worldly being that is firmly distinct from nonbeing.

The second philosophy of sense, which does not fair better for Deleuze, is comprised of those theories that ground sense in the material world that it

is intended to capture. Where Plato points to the heights of ideas to understand the origin of sense, Aristotle returns to the richness of the material
ground. For Aristotle, the sense we make of the world is ultimately a trace
of the material objects that affect our sensory organs, comparable to the
imprint left behind by a signet ring in a block of wax (Aristotle, 1976, pp.
187–188; Magee, 2000). Sense-making is here charged and directed by the
referent object experienced and described. Hume's *Treatise of Human Nature*
similarly suggests that we must think of sense as anchored in the material
reality of the world. Like Kant, Hume introduces a distinction between the
physical sensation generated by a referent object and the rational idea we
attach to the former. Here, ideas are merely copies of sensory impressions,
while these sensory impressions do not copy anything. More explicitly than
Kant, Hume acknowledges the arising issue that, if creative sense ultimately
unfolds in the free connection between material impression and ideational
representation established in the mind of the subject, we can never be sure
that our ideas of the world depict it accurately (Butler, 2009). However,
because the driving forces behind this process of interconnection are, for
Hume, our sensory impressions of material objects, these empirical data
about the material world are the most reliable anchor for sense we have.
For this reason, "men are carried, by a natural instinct or prepossession,
to repose faith in their senses" (Hume, 2004, p. 133). To avoid facing the
threatening possibility of an ontogenetic creativity fully immanent to sense,
Hume pragmatically suggests that we should trust our senses.

  Husserl's account of sense then reveals any such attempt to contain the
productivity of sense in a sensed referent object as futile. Similar to Hume,
Husserl identifies sense-making as the linking of two distinct domains,
perception of matter and meaning, within the consciousness of the subject.
For Husserl, the material world presents itself to consciousness in the form
of a multiplicity of possible, not yet actual perceptions. Their actualization,
from which the world, as it can be known, emerges for the subject, takes
place in sense. Importantly, this ontogenetic actualization follows a logic
that is thoroughly immanent to sense itself (Knodt, 1995; Hopp, 2008;
Mulligan, 1995). Sense is the product of rational ideas applied in a way that
fits the material context perceived. The idea of a feather evokes a particular
sense when we look an at individual white feather, but has a very different
sense when this single feather is perceived as an indistinguishable part of
a seagull's feathering. In order to make sense in a way that is appropriate
for a particular context, subjective consciousness must draw on a reservoir
of past experiences stored as sense, which then become the ground for the

production of new sense. Sense makes sense. In his account of sense-making, "Husserl aims at describing the process of sense making not as an empirical process but *the process as such*" (Arnoldi, 2010, p. 29; my emphasis), which unfolds independently from the external influence of sensory impressions. What Husserl discovers here is thus precisely the paradoxical nature of self-grounding sense on which both Deleuze and Luhmann center their theories of sense. It is thus not accidental that both acknowledge their indebtedness to Husserl (Deleuze, 1990, pp. 97–99; Luhmann, 1995a, pp. 69, 145–146).

A theory of sense-making as grounded in nothing but the "resemblance between the appearing object and other perceived or otherwise presented objects" (Husserl, 2001, p. 637), established through links in sense, sets up "an infinite regress" (p. 637). While Husserl thus comes even closer than Kant to a theory of open-ended creativity in sense, like the former, he eventually conceals this possibility through the ordering faculties of the rational mind (Dejanovic, 2014). In the end, Deleuze argues, the emergence of sense is, for Husserl, not a " 'paradoxical' instance, which, properly speaking, would be 'non-identifiable' (lacking its own identity and its own origin)" (1990, p. 97). On the contrary, Husserl's sense emerges from a "faculty of common sense, responsible for accounting for the identity of an object in general" (p. 97.) and is pre-directed by a good sense that ensures that its representations are accurate and consistent. The origin of creative sense that Husserl reveals is in fact nothing but the foundational presumption of his phenomenological philosophy projected into the analysis of sense undertaken. In Deleuze's words, Husserl offers us yet another theory of sense that "conserves the essential" (Deleuze, 1990, p. 98) and "is satisfied with raising to the transcendental a mere empirical exercise in an image of thought presented as originary" (p. 98).[4]

The third and final philosophy of sense, which for Deleuze fails to capture the immanent creativity of sense itself, is the proposition that sets up a formal relationship between idea and referent object. The analytical philosophy of Frege and Russell seeks to unravel sense-making from the side of the proposition. A proposition "expresses its sense, stands for or designates its reference" (Frege, 1993, p. 27). Whatever creativity is unfolded in sense-expression, according to Frege, finds its origin in the propositional link between idea and object. Where a proposition can be formulated in a generalizable manner, the creativity of sense unfolds in a predictable and context-independent fashion. Despite the contextually varying signs used to describe objects, this is possible because the immobile, ontologically stable nature of the referent object grounds the proposition (Speaks, 2013; Makin, 2000). "Morning star" and "evening star" have the same sense despite the varying signs used to label the referent object. The formal-analytical philosophy of sense avoids the iterative regress of sense that Kant and Husserl encounter but choose to conceal, and which Deleuze and Luhmann embrace, because the truth of a proposition is here anchored in the referent object on the outside of sense (Voss, 2013a, pp. 2–3).

However, this stability collapses once the analytical gaze is shifted from the sense of a proposition to its emergence in sense-expression. The failure of Russell's set-theoretical attempt to capture sense in its processual quality illustrates this issue poignantly. While a given proposition can be anchored in a stable referent object, this referent object is displaced perpetually in every expression of sense. The sense *of* the proposition "morning star" is not identical with the sense expressed *by* the proposition "morning star." Every attempt to ground the sense of the proposition can produce only new sense, creating a novel demand for ontological anchoring, which is then again doomed to fail. Instead of a delineable master set, the ground of sense-expression is an infinite regress (Makin, 2000, pp. 25–27; Livingston, 2011, pp. 22–23). As Wittgenstein notes, every attempt to determine the truth of a proposition thus constitutes a case of the Cretan liar paradox. " 'Very well, but which proposition do you mean?'—'Well, *this* proposition'.—'I understand, but which is the proposition mentioned in *it*?'—'*This* one'—and so on" (Wittgenstein, 1981, pp. 119–120).

The formal-analytical philosophy of sense retraces the productivity of sense to exactly the source that foundationally grounds its theoretical assumptions—the stable relationship between a signifier and a referent object. Once this foundation crumbles, sense is revealed as a creative force *sui generis*. Sense becomes "a pure event which inheres or subsists in the proposition" (Deleuze, 1990, p. 19; see also: Voss, 2013a, p. 7). Its creativity exceeds the ideas of the rational mind, the material object designated and the proposition expressing it, and thus cannot be said to find its ontological source in either. This is precisely what Deleuze means when he identifies sense as "the fourth dimension of the proposition." Sense emerges when the three dimensions come into contact with each other; it is "never originary but always caused and derived" (Deleuze, 1990, p. 95). Yet, the creative interplay that unfolds is "unconditioned" (p. 19) and genuinely immanent to sense. Deleuze explores the paradox of immanently creative sense by turning to Stoic philosophy, which he credits with its discovery (p. 19.). For the Stoics, ontogenesis is never the product of external causes, such as

Platonic forms. Instead, what functions creatively are the "quasi-causes" of mixed bodies: *incorporeals*. Stoic philosophy maintains that the only things that exist and have the capacity to act are bodies. However, this is not to be confused with contemporary ideas of material agency, as the Stoics have a very particular general understanding of bodies. Here, not just physical objects but also souls and ideas are bodies (Voss, 2013a, p. 15).

These existent bodies are distinguished from a second category that makes up the realm of being, incorporeals. Different from both ideas and matter, incorporeals are not existent bodies, but rather "a way of being, an effect resulting from the interaction of bodies" (Voss, 2013a, p. 15). For the Stoics, corporeal causes interact and thereby produce something new, an incorporeal that is more than the sum of its corporeal parts. It is these relational incorporeals, and not their bodily causes, that create, shape, and change the world that surrounds us in its particular state (Butler, 2005, p. 132; Widder, 2008, p. 102). For the Stoic, it is neither the corporeal of the knife nor that of the criminal idea, but the incorporeal of being cut emerging from their interaction that causes the wound. The consequence, Deleuze argues, is that the Stoics dismember our conventional understanding of causality to impose an entirely "new distribution . . . on beings and concepts" (Deleuze, 1990, p. 6). Incorporeals are only "quasi-causes" (p. 6) insofar as they always result from the synthesis of bodies. However, at the same time, the synthetic incorporeals function as causes because they are what brings forth actuality. Stoic philosophy thereby opens up a "cleave of causality" (p. 6) between the external causes that provide the necessary conditions for something to happen, and the quasi-cause that actually makes it happen.

Ontogenetic causality in Deleuze's logic of sense follows the Stoic epistemology of incorporeal quasi-causes (Widder, 2008, pp. 106–107; Bowden, 2014, p. 232). While sense can function creatively only because objects, language, and ideas interact to "make sense," the productivity of sense is a novel, independent effect of their interaction, which is immanent to this interaction in sense itself. Ontogenesis is hence "no longer a question of Dionysus down below, or of Apollo up above" (Deleuze, 1990, p. 132), as both realms are merely composed of bodies, which themselves never cause actual effects. Instead, it must be explored with a focus on "Hercules of the surface, in his dual battle against both depth and height" (p. 132)— the interplay of bodies on the surface of sense. Deleuze offers a theoretical account of ontogenesis in sense that has no external cause but is charged by a free interplay of bodily singularities that is immanent to sense. This free interplay is re-opened in every instant of sense-making, so that sense always carries with it something "unconditioned," rendering ontogenesis in sense genuinely open-ended.

The second paradox that *The Logic of Sense* is hinged on allows us to understand this "unconditioned" underside of excessive, expressive sense better: the relationship between sense and nonsense. For Deleuze, sense and nonsense are not simply opposed. Nonsense has no sense, but should yet not be understood as the absence of sense. Rather, nonsense is the productive force "which animates the ideal game and the impersonal transcendental field" (Deleuze, 1990, p. 116) from which sense is derived. For Deleuze, nonsense fulfills two functions in the process of sense-making. First, nonsense is the constitutive outside of sense. Sense-making takes place as a movement of expressive creation away from nonsense, which produces a sharp delineation between a particular, expressed sense and its nonsensical outside. Nonsense is the "empty square" (p. 47) to be filled with sense—but this filling should rather be understood as an act of cutting or condensing; the empty square is not actually empty. Rather, it is an intense multiplicity of mixed bodies, incorporeality, not yet distinguished into signifier and material referent (p. 80). Intense nonsense is then secondly the excessive, uncontained element that "enacts the donation of sense" (p. 70) from the inside of its relations. "Nonsense and sense have done away with their relation of dynamic opposition in order to enter into the co-presence of a static genesis" (p. 140). As Widder puts it, it is the "disjointed . . . nonsense of difference that constitutes sense in terms of divergence" (Widder, 2003, p. 471).

Within contemporary Deleuze scholarship, the role of intensity in Deleuze's writings has received increasing interest (Mader, 2014, 2017; Roffe, 2017; Widder, 2008, 2021). This recent scholarship aims to overcome the prevailing focus on the virtual/actual dynamic, which has dominated readings of Deleuzian ontology since the 1990s. While the movement from virtual to actual can tell us something about how ideas and species come into being through the respective processes of differentiation and differenciation, this remains a technical account of ontogenesis in the abstract (Widder, 2021). If we want to understand how these categories are filled with meaning in a particular case, we need to turn to intensity and its *effectuation* in sense, which grounds and ungrounds a specific actuality. Intensity gives quality to both virtual and actual reality. A particular, determined actuality must thus not only be understood as derived from a virtual multiplicity but also as endowed with a specific quality or position, incorporated in a "state of affairs" (Deleuze, 1990, p. 63) that is the effectuation of a particular intensity (Roffe, 2017, pp. 280–281).

Building on these arguments, I suggest that *The Logic of Sense* situates and applies the abstract framework of ontogenesis developed in *Difference and Repetition*, making it possible to understand concrete instances of worldmaking in the interplay between intense nonsense and actual sense. In *Difference and Repetition*, Deleuze refers to pure difference in itself as an intensity that functions ontogenetic insofar as it is the source of extensity and quality (Deleuze, 1994, p. 144; Roffe, 2017, p. 281). Deleuze conceptualizes intensity against an account where the former is entirely reducible to quantifiable terms, as it can be found in the natural sciences or indeed Russell's analytic philosophy. Here, intensity is rendered explicable through the conversion into extensive qualities (Mader, 2014; 2017). A change in the intensity of heat, for example, becomes a particular, measurable, and generalizable increase or decrease in degrees of Celsius or Fahrenheit. Deleuze contrasts this with an understanding of intensity that is pure difference, heterogeneous in itself, and cannot be broken up into equal and stable extensities. As a consequence, "the fiction of a homogeneous quantity vanishes with intensity" (Deleuze, 1994, p. 237).

Deleuze acknowledges that it is difficult to think of intensity in a way that cannot be broken up into extensive quantities. We regard such an intensity "with epistemic suspicion" (2017, p. 271), Mader argues, because it can never be known in itself but only be "grasped once it is cancelled out in extensity and quality—that is, once it has "undergone" the sorts of conversions and reductions" (p. 271) that make it calculable and thereby intelligible. Intensity cannot be thought as such, and thus sparks thinking as the ontogenetically productive reduction of intensity. Differential intensity here becomes the constitutive outside of thought. In the famous passage on the encounter in *Difference and Repetition*, it is the experience of intensity that sparks thought, that forces us to think (Deleuze, 1994, pp. 139–140). The idea of the world that emerges is then at once the reduction of the intensity of pure difference and a production of a particular line of differentiation. Intensity gives form to actuality, but only insofar as the emergent actuality conceals its differential origin. As Deleuze puts it, "difference is the sufficient reason of change only to the extent that the change tends to negate the difference" (Deleuze, 1994, p. 223; see also: Roffe, 2017, p. 281).

Intensity drives sense-making. In *Difference and Repetition*, Deleuze describes intensity as "the form of difference in so far as this is the reason of the sensible" (Deleuze, 1994, p. 222). I argue that this passage should not be read as an account of how an exclusively material-physical intensity produces a particular sense-expression (different e.g. from Roffe, 2017).

Rather, *The Logic of Sense* reveals intense nonsense as composed of the chaotic mixture of material and metaphysical bodies—nonsense is the form in which creative incorporeality unfolds when sense is expressed. Intense, incorporeal nonsense is thus the quasi-cause that drives sense-making as the necessary reduction of intensity that makes nonsense intelligible, and thereby draws sense from nonsense (Deleuze, 1990, pp. 175–176). At the same time, it functions creatively only while being conditioned. Nonsense is not a creative potentiality existing prior to and located on the outside of sense. Rather, it is only opened up in the process of sense expression. Deleuze here refers to "surface nonsense" (pp. 156–157; p. 176) to distinguish his account of nonsense as located on the surface of sense from alternative, ontologically "deep" conceptions. The surface interplay of sense and nonsense conditions the ontogenetic event of sense that is both immanent to and transcendent of itself.

A final question that remains to be answered is whether Deleuze provides any insight into the location of this interplay between sense and nonsense, which can help us specify the kind of ontogenesis that takes place in sense. Here, at least two passages in *The Logic of Sense*, Deleuze's "psychoanalytic book" (Lecercle, 2008, p. vii), suggest that the domain of nonsense is the pre-personal field of drives and desires that make up the subject's psyche. These are, first, the discussion of Antonin Artaud's dramatic theory in the 13th "Series of the schizophrenic and the little girl," following immediately after Deleuze's exploration of the productive relationship between sense and nonsense (Deleuze, 1990, pp. 82–93), and series 25–34 at the very end of the book, where Deleuze explores sense-making through the lens of Lacanian psychoanalysis (pp. 177–250). Artaud, Deleuze shows, offers an alternative perspective of creative nonsense. Here, nonsense does not result from the mixture of corporeals on the surface of sense. Instead, it is the manifest reality of the schizophrenic consciousness where all distinctions and boundaries of ordered sense have collapsed (pp. 87–89). In Artaud, sense rises to the surface from an ontologically primary abyss of nonsense, "a monster even more awesome than the Jabberwocky" (p. 82), in a linear process of ontogenesis. Here, "everything happens, acts and is acted upon, beneath sense and far from the surface. Sub-sense, a-sense, *Untersinn*" (p. 90).

Deleuze shows great admiration for the radical way in which Artaud's schizophrenic nonsense ruptures the notion of stable, pre-ordered sense. He "would not give a page of Artaud for all of Carroll" (Deleuze, 1990, p. 93).

However, in the end, Deleuze concludes that Artaud can only tell us about the collapse of sense, and of the reality it grounds, which is continuously pulled into an abyssal nonsense in Artaud's schizophrenic vision. Carroll's relational surface interplay of sense and nonsense can, on the contrary, illuminate the operational mechanisms behind ontogenesis in sense—and it is for this reason that philosophy (of sense) must remain on the surface (pp. 91–93). Deleuze here seems to employ Carroll to argue for a structuralist "psychoanalysis of sense" (p. 93), which unpacks the "geometrical dimensions" (p. 93) that condition worldmaking in sense "before being concerned with historical anecdotes" (p. 93). He does not dismiss the idea that ontogenesis in sense is ultimately a psychological process taking place in the mind of the subject. This fits with Deleuze's return to psychoanalysis at the end of *The Logic of Sense*. Here, he locates the creative potentiality of nonsense in the figure of the pre-conscious phantasm that emerges from the interaction of desire and language. The phantasm embodies "the nonsense that generates sense, underpinning the identities of denoted bodies, signified concepts, and the self that manifests or expresses itself in language" (Widder, 2008, p. 140).

The phantasm situates the creativity of sense, which is "immanent only to itself: it recovers or incorporates everything by giving it a new form, even and especially its beginning in 'external' castration and all this implies" (Bowden, 2011, p. 244). Like Bowden and Widder, I believe that Deleuze's proximity to psychoanalysis does here not take away from the innovative quality of his thoroughly immanent logic of sense, but directs its theoretical grasp. At no point does Deleuze's creative sense rely on constitutive or ordering *a prioris* located in the depth of the unconscious. The creative moment of ontogenesis in sense remains the product of a surface nonsense that is productively intertwined with relations of actual sense and not an absolute outside charging sense-making externally. However, I do argue that Deleuze's turn to psychoanalytic thought limits the analytical purchase of his theory of sense. At this juncture, Luhmann's in many ways parallel, systems theoretic conceptualization of sense as paradoxically unfolding in the interplay between sense and nonsense without a discernible external cause broadens the scope beyond ontogenesis in the mind of the subject to the way social structures are produced by different social realms that try to grasp their social function and environment. Luhmann's insistence that social systems also "make sense" and thus produce the world they structure, and which subjects inhabit, lays the ground for using immanently creative sense as a perspective for critical political analysis.[5]

Luhmann's Sense: Medium and Form, Mind and Politics

To the reader less familiar with Luhmann's work, it might come as a surprise that many Luhmann scholars view sense—not the system, not autopoiesis—as the theoretical core and innovative contribution of his work (Schützeichel, 2013; Kirchmeier, 2012; Arnoldi, 2012; Stäheli, 2000). As Moeller concludes in the final section of *The Radical Luhmann*, "Luhmann's theory is about the contingent social constructions of sense that have no ultimate meaning, no transcendental or transcendent anchorage, and do not manifest or conform to a unified reason" (2012, p. 113). Luhmann's theory, in other words, is about open-ended creative production in sense. While Deleuze's theory of sense is confined to a single book, *The Logic of Sense*, none of Luhmann's many works are explicitly "about sense." Rather, Luhmann's theory of sense is scattered across his work, but especially underpins his later writings from *Social Systems* onward. Luhmann's theoretical prioritization of sense relations over the systems that this sense produces and upholds clearly distinguishes his work from Talcott Parsons's systems theory. Parsons's work not only motivated Luhmann's academic endeavors but also influenced their direction decisively. It is after a study visit to Harvard in 1961, where Parsons taught at the time, that Luhmann abandons his local civil service position in Lüneburg to embark on an academic career (Baecker, 2012). Luhmann repeatedly emphasizes his debt to Parsons's "completely un-Weberian" (Luhmann, 1990a, p. 255) structuralist and post-humanist sociology where action is not produced by a rational, autonomous actor but the functional effect of systemic relations (1988, pp. 127–128).[6]

However, in terms of the actual content of his systems theory, Luhmann abandons many of Parsons's main assumptions, or at least turns them on their head. A central point of divergence between Luhmann and Parsons is Luhmann's rejection of positivist structuralism (1980, pp. 7–9). While social systems are ontologically real in Parsons, Luhmann argues that such a systemic ontology is both impossible to substantiate with empirical evidence and theoretically inadequate as an "account of modern society" in its "irritating realities" (Luhmann, 1990a, p. 254). Luhmann's systems theory should thus not be understood as a theory that observes, describes, and maps social systems as independently existent, manifestly real structures of social life. Rather, his theoretical project aims to unpack how a radically contingent social reality made of functionally closed systems is produced, reproduced, and changes in sense "from moment to moment" (Luhmann, 2012a, p. 18). For this reason, Luhmann's theory is only a systems theory insofar as it is, first and foremost, a theory of sense as the productive medium that brings forth, and disrupts, any systemic order.

While Deleuze's theory of immanent ontogenesis in sense unfolds from an investigation of what lies beyond the rabbit hole of *common sense* and *good sense*, Luhmann explicitly identifies sense as the domain in which the world of systems is made. Like Deleuze, Luhmann uses Husserl's phenomenology as a stepping stone to unfold his theory of sense (Arnoldi, 2012). Luhmann draws from Husserl that the world known to us is never perceived directly but instead assembled by our consciousness out of a complex multiplicity of experiences in the domain of sense (Luhmann, 1995a, pp. 82–83; Moeller, 2012, pp. 46–47; Arnoldi, 2012, pp. 30–33). The thoroughly immanent production of a particular sense against the background of multiple alternative options introduces a fundamental element of contingency to the process of worldmaking in sense, understood as "the contemplation of the given from the perspective of other possibilities" (Luhmann, 1971a, p. 9). Like Deleuze, and contrary to Husserl, Luhmann does not resolve this contingency through the transcendental figure of an ordering *common sense* implanted in the consciousness of the subject to guide immanent sense-making toward the adequate representation of external reality, but rather embraces its radical consequences. Moeller argues that Luhmann turns to Deleuze, and away from Husserl, as a point of reference for his concept of sense to make it clear that reason cannot contain but rather relies on contingent grounding in sense, "making reason ironical" (2012, p. 112).

In a world composed of nothing but contingent relations of sense, their production against the background of a multiplicity of alternatives becomes, for Luhmann, the fundamental problem of any "sense-using [sinnverwen-dendes] system" (Luhmann, 1971a, p. 12)—and thus must be the focal point of a systems theory that seeks to understand worldmaking in sense. Importantly, for Luhmann, both the psychic system of human consciousness and social systems as different as politics, the economy, law, or love, operate in sense and thus function through the permanent reduction of complex information to a particular world they can grasp (Arnoldi, 2012, p. 31). Both subjects[7] and social systems produce and inhabit worlds of sense, and it is the domain of sense that allows them to interact. Luhmann thus proposes sense as the "key concept" for understanding and analyzing the "contingency of possible worlds," which, in his systems theory, replaces any analytical attempt to ascertain "the accuracy with which [concepts] reflect the given" (Luhmann 1971a, p. 26) in both thought and social life. Luhmann's systems theory does not seek to make sense of the world as accurately as possible, but rather aims at unpacking how the particular, contingent social world we find ourselves in is made in the medium of sense, which is "coextensive with the world" (Luhmann, 1995a, p. 41).

In analogy to Deleuze's turn away from the height of ideas and the depth of matter, Luhmann posits sense, rather than "world and truth" (Luhmann, 1995a, p. 41), as the medium of worldmaking. Compared to Deleuze, Luhmann is less explicit in setting up his theory of open-ended worldmaking in sense against the different strands of existing philosophies of sense. However, like Deleuze, he rejects an understanding of sense in which its productivity is contained or pre-directed by stable, logically discernible meaning relations or the ideas of the rational mind. For Luhmann, sense "cannot be understood as the result of obedience to the methodological instructions of the Viennese school of 'logical empiricism' . . . nor can it be understood in relation to the subjective aspiration of individuals and what seems meaningful to them and for them" (p. 41). "To avoid such limitations" (p. 41), Luhmann, like Deleuze, proposes a concept of sense that is necessarily excessive. Every possible use of sense, even if it takes the form of its denial, can only produce sense (Luhmann, 2012a, pp. 21–22).

We have seen that Deleuze turns to the Stoic concept of the incorporeal to explain the *sui generis* creativity of sense, which emerges from the mixture of bodily causes and is thus externally conditioned, but not determined. As shown above, the incorporeal is of the quality of intense difference-in-itself. It enacts the expression of a particular line of sense but is nonsensical insofar as it can never be made sense of as such, and thus must remain outside of sense. Luhmann takes a different route to reach the same conclusion. Following it allows us to add to the theory of immanent ontogenesis in sense established with the help of Deleuze in two distinct ways. First, while Deleuze shows how the creativity of sense emerges from the incorporeal mixture of physical and metaphysical bodies and therefore cannot be retraced to a solely material or epistemic cause, Luhmann highlights the distinction between matter and ideas as itself contingently produced in sense. Because the worldmaking interplay between sense-relations and their nonsensical outside is not exclusive to the psychic relations in the mind of the subject in Luhmann, his theory secondly opens up the possibility of a political theory of sense that can be used to understand the contingent structuration of the social world as it unfolds in sense.

Luhmann renders explicit what can be discerned only indirectly from Deleuze's theory of sense: sense can function immanently creative because it is both medium and form (2012a, p. 28). Sense is both the medium of worldmaking, as shown above, and produces the forms that make up the world that is being made. The reality of the (sense-based) system is composed of forms of sense. The relationship between medium and form in Luhmann can be better understood against the background of George Spencer Brown's *Laws of Form* (1969). Spencer-Brown's calculus theory is one of the more unusual sources amongst the wide range of philosophical and scientific references that inform Luhmann's thinking. Luhmann's use of Spencer Brown's theory reveals that he shares with Deleuze a desire to discover and make useful concepts and lines of thought in the works of mostly forgotten "minor" thinkers. Both, however, also have in common that they interpret their philosophical sources often with considerable liberty, and Spencer Brown's work is no exception here. Spencer Brown's laws of form provide Luhmann with an epistemological alternative to Aristotelian logic, which is not centered on the observing subject but rather on the continuous and contingent becoming of entities consistent of nothing but sense relations that are constantly made, unmade, and remade. Luhmann's metaphysics "is not the ontology of subjects trying to agree on how to look objectively at the world but that of an ontogenetics of issues trying to prove their value" (Baecker, 2012, p. 2).

Like Deleuze, Luhmann starts from the assumption that every sense-expression always produces new sense. From Spencer Brown, he adopts the idea that "we cannot make an indication without drawing a distinction" (1969, p. 1). As a consequence, "the form of distinction" (p. 1) becomes the form in which the indicated comes into being. What was once productive medium becomes form, and then grounds further acts of production in the medium conditioned by this form. Spencer Brown characterizes the distinction that gives form to the indication of sense with two laws: (I) the law of calling, according to which the infinite repetition of a distinction produces the same value as the first distinction, and (II) the law of crossing, which states that a first distinction can always be altered or cancelled out by a second distinction (Spencer Brown, 1969, pp. 1–2). What Luhmann draws from Spencer Brown's laws is, first, the idea that every supposedly stable essence or identity is contingently produced by drawing a distinction, and second, that this distinction is conditioned, but not determined, by previously produced distinctions, and remains genuinely open-ended at all times.

Primary in Luhmann is not the system, nor its environment, but the distinction that draws a contingent line between the two. The system emerges only once this distinction is drawn, and is upheld by it (Schützeichel, 2013, pp. 76–87). The medium in which this distinction is drawn, and the form it takes once drawn, is sense. Deleuze has shown that the mixture of material and metaphysical bodies provides the necessary ground for creative sense to unfold, yet this unfolding takes place in a completely independent way not determined or directed by either the material or the epistemic realm. In Luhmann, the creative distinction is grounded in a previous distinction, and so a previously produced form of sense. This means that any attempt at ontologically locating the driving force that charges creative sense-making can only take the form of yet another act of sense-making. It does, as in the case of the Cretan liar paradox, reflect only a contingent distinction in sense, but it does not reveal an originary truth about its referent object.

More explicitly than in Deleuze, Luhmann's work thus makes it clear that the distinction between the epistemic realm of thought and social relations, on the one hand, and materiality, on the other hand, is itself an example of sense-making as, and through, distinction in sense. The operative form of sense that performs sense-expression as a creative distinction is, following Luhmann, cognition for psychic systems and communication in social systems (Luhmann, 2008b, pp. 30–35; Arnoldi, 2012, pp. 30–31). At first glance, this seems to be at odds with the above suggestion, as both communication and cognition appear to belong firmly to the epistemic realm. A creative sense-expression identified in this manner thus seems to diverge from Deleuze's sense-making bodily mixtures by indicating the dominant role of language and thought. Luhmann is indeed partially read in this manner. Equating Luhmann's "Sinn" with purely linguistic meaning, rendering communication the transmission of the former, a number of works draw out the kinship between Luhmann's sense-making through distinction and the iterative productivity that unfolds in the space between signifier and signified in Derrida (Teubner, 2001; Stäheli, 2000).

Luhmann himself appears to uphold a strict distinction between the productivity of materiality and that unfolded in sense relations in some passages of his writings. In *Law as a Social System*, he argues for instance that "[i]n its physical features, writing belongs to the environment of the communication system" (Luhmann, 2004, p. 235), which "assimilates writing" (p. 235), but only in terms of the meaning it conveys, "not to its physics" (p. 235). However, it is important to remember that any such ontic demarcation in Luhmann is always the product of a contingent distinction in the medium of sense. Luhmann's insistence should thus not be understood as an ontological claim, but rather as a description of how the exclusive focus on epistemic productivity, which is a contingent product of modern

Western sense systems, operates and is reproduced in the path-dependencies of creative production in sense.[8] Luhmann defines communicative and cognitive sense-expression in a strictly functional manner: "communication means limitation" (Luhmann, 1995a, p. 39). Communication performs an act of distinction and thereby delineates a particular inside from a particular outside. This delineation is contingent, so the distinction could be drawn in a different way, and, following Spencer Brown's second law of crossing, remains open-ended. Necessary is only the distinction itself, which brings a particular identity into existence—as a limited form of sense (pp. 59–60; Luhmann, 1990a, pp. 25–27). A first consequence is that the operation of communication, which emerges from sense and then brings forth forms of sense that ground further communication, is profoundly non-anthropocentric (Bryant, 2014). As Luhmann famously states, humans "cannot communicate; only communication can communicate" (Luhmann, 1995a, p. 57).

While this still does not necessarily render Luhmann's sense all too different from Derrida's theory of language, Luhmann states explicitly that his account of communication is intended to "correct the widespread over-estimation of the role of language" (Luhmann, 1995a, p. 10). Linguistic signs are just one example of what communicates in sense (Luhmann, 2008b, pp. 114–116). The fact that we only make sense of human, and predominantly linguistic, sense-expression as such is in itself conditioned by the forms of sense that make up our social worlds. How societies exclude or "dissimulate" (Philippopoulos-Mihalopoulos, 2014, p. 395) the materiality that co-conditions their production in sense is most convincingly shown in Andreas Philippopoulos-Mihalopoulos's (2011; 2014) work on Luhmann and law. Materiality, he suggests, "is, at least impressionistically, absorbed" (2014, p. 395) in Luhmann's communication. Social systems rely on materiality to communicate—for the legal system, communication requires judges, lawyers, and ideas of justice, but equally "statutes, court decisions, fines, appeals, mediation, law school classes, lawyers, judges, research papers" (p. 396). Like in Deleuze, the constituents of sense-expressions are thoroughly mixed, composed of ideas, subject, and objects. Yet, at the same time, the constitutive role of materiality is concealed by the particular way we "make sense" of legal proceedings. In line with Philippopoulos-Mihalopoulos's argument that the presumed outside of materiality is inherently involved in communication and "wafts inside in ways in which the inside [of sense relations] cannot control" (2010, p. 178; see also: Bryant, 2014), Luhmann himself does suggest that materiality, from spaces to religious objects, does unfold "a coordinating function not dependent on language" (2012a, p. 20) within the process of communicative sense-expression—it is just not (usually) made sense of as communication.[9]

The same line of argumentation can be applied to cognitive sense-making in psychic systems. Luhmann has been criticized for distinguishing between the sense relations of the human consciousness and the material-organic system of the body in his account of cognition (Calise, 2015; Dziewas, 1992). This distinction is, however, merely another "dissimulation" of the material, which takes place as a necessary part of the way individuals, and societies, make sense of cognition. Materiality, from neuronal connections to bodily chemicals, vitally conditions cognitive sense-making. Yet, the rational subject only rarely, and comparatively recently, thinks of their thoughts and actions as conditioned by the particular state of their neuronal relations. Luhmann is clear that physical bodies contribute to the complexity that charges distinctions in sense and that becomes intelligible only through the former, as it is the case for Deleuze's incorporeality. Bodies "invite their possibilities of reduction . . . by presenting their own complexity" (Luhmann, 1995a, p. 246). For Luhmann, "[c]orporeality is and remains a general . . . premise of social life" (p. 246). For this reason, "one cannot display corporeality as relevant by opposing it to something else. One can only differentiate it as a specific condition, chance, or resource in the formation of social system (p. 247).

Materiality is located on the outside of Luhmann's sense systems, but this not an ontic fact—it rather is the contingent product of the very particular way these sense systems, comprised of the social systems of Western democratic societies and the subjects inhabiting them, have evolved together. The outside of materiality does not pre-exist systemic sense. It rather is co-produced with the inside of ideas, subjects, and social relations in the distinctions drawn through sense-expression. External materiality is thus the particular form of sense that sense-systems use to grasp their constitutive outside. Materiality comes into play at two points in the process of sense-making. Communicative and cognitive sense-expression, far from being purely epistemic, is first in fact driven by a synthetic mixture of material and epistemic constituents whose material part is however *ex post facto* concealed in the particular distinctions expressed in sense. Second, the selective distinction that functions creative in sense requires an outside that the form of sense to be produced is distinguished from. Within modern Western sense systems, materiality is the form given to this outside in the sense-relations that make up thought and social relations. In different ways,

Deleuze and Luhmann have both shown that the material and the epistemic inform sense-making only as always-already intertwined in synthetic sense.

At this point, it seems apt to draw the reader's attention to a very particular liberty that I have taken in the English translation of Luhmann's "Sinn." While the English editions of Luhmann's works translate the relatively ambiguous German *Sinn*, which spans a number of different connotations ranging from the more narrowly linguistic "meaning" and "signification" to the more open "mind," "appreciation," "use" and finally "sense," as *meaning*, this book instead uses *sense*. Beyond the obvious reason of facilitating the theoretical encounter between Deleuze and Luhmann unfolded here, I argue that translating *Sinn* as *sense* is helpful to ward off a reductionist reading of sense-making in Luhmann, which is overly focused on the role of language. The concept of sense makes it possible to draw out how Luhmann, like Deleuze, theorizes an immanent creativity of sense relations that lies precisely in their synthetic openness to both the epistemic and the material realm, but cannot be retraced to either. Luhmann himself notes in exactly this sense in the opening passage of *Die Realität der Massenmedien* that the English "sense making" conveys a more accurate understanding of the open productivity of sense than the German "Sinngebung" (Luhmann, 1996a, p. 19). This indicates not only that Luhmann himself did not object to equating *Sinn* with *sense*, but that he even viewed this translation as advantageous to carve out the unconditioned creativity of sense. As suggested by Moeller, " '[s]ense,' as a linguistic alternative to the term 'meaning,' is made, while something *has* a meaning" (Moeller, 2012, p. 76). For this reason, Moeller suggests that *sense* might in fact be the better translation for "Sinn" (p. 76).[10]

In Deleuze, the incorporeal multiplicity that emerges from sense-expression as the "something unconditioned" that allows sense to function immanently creative is nonsense. For Deleuze, nonsense is not the absence of sense but rather an intense field, which is prior to the effectuation of a particular line of sense, but conditions this emergence as its constitutive outside. We left Deleuze's nonsense on the insight that there is at least some ground to believe that its location is the psyche of the subject. This does not necessarily take away from the immanent functioning of creative sense, as the nonsensical multiplicity of the phantasm still opens up in sense rather than pre-existing it in an absolute sense. However, it does fix the analytical lens of Deleuze's theory of sense on a particular focal point, which is the open-ended process of ontogenesis in the mind of the subject freed from the theoretical shackles of *good sense* and *common sense*. At this juncture, I suggest that Luhmann's systems theoretic account of the outside of sense, which is noise or complexity, offers a theoretical route to under-stand immanent creativity in sense beyond the subjectivist bias of Deleuze's psychoanalytically inflected theory of sense. In Luhmann, not only psychic systems but also social systems exist as realms of sense delineated from an outside of complexity that would rupture their sense-relations upon direct contact. Luhmann's theory of immanently creative sense can thus not only provide insight to how the world the subject perceives is contingently made, unmade, and remade, in sense. It can also tell us something about how the structures, hierarchies, and lines of distinction that run through society are upheld in immanently creative sense.

In Luhmann, sense produces defined actuality by delineating what is made sense of from an outside. The outside excluded when a distinction is drawn in sense is the environment of the relational sense system actualized, which Luhmann defines by drawing on cybernetic theory. Spearheaded by Norbert Wiener, the cybernetic theory that gained prominence in the 1940s and 1950s owes its name to the ancient Greek term for steersman. Cybernetic theory seeks to understand how second-order systems function—how they steer and reproduce themselves. Systems, generally speaking, are machines that function by transforming a particular input to a particular output. For cybernetic information systems, which are "effectively coupled to the external world [. . .] by a flow of impressions, of incoming messages, and of the actions of outgoing messages" (Wiener, 1985, p. 42), the input received, and the output produced, are pieces of information.

For second-order machines, the functional obstacle here does not lie in being able to respond to an external stimulus, as is the case for first-order systems, but to maintain this reactivity. Second-order systems are self-aware. They observe themselves and their contingent decisions against the background of a set of alternative input-output pathways. The question that second-order systems face with every input received is then not *whether or not* a particular piece of information can be processed, but rather *how exactly* it is to be made sense of in order to continue a particular line of decision making within the system. Second-order systems include their own, path-dependent position of decision making amongst the factors taken into consideration when calculating a particular output. Because this position changes with every act of information processing, second-order systems are necessarily entropic—they are subject to a constantly increasing internal complexity (Wiener, 1985, pp. 42–44; Geoghegan, 2011).

Second-order machines make sense by drawing a distinction between the pathway they actualize and the alternatives they discard as outside noise.

This distinction not only continues information processing within the system but also, at the same time, wards off the encroaching informational entropy (Weinbaum, 2015; von Foerster, 2003). Luhmann adopts the cybernetic understanding of noise as the outside excluded in the distinction of sense-making. Noise is a chaotic multiplicity of information signals too complex to be understood and processed by the system (Luhmann, 1995a, p. 32; Arnoldi, 2012, pp. 31–33). In both its quality and its function, Luhmann's informational noise, which he, for the most part, simply refers to as complexity, is equivalent to Deleuze's nonsense. Like nonsense, complexity is not opposed to sense; it does not mark the absence of sense, but rather its excess. The system distinguishes its sense-relations from noisy complexity that thus, like nonsense in Deleuze, "enacts the donation of sense." The encounter with complexity forces the system to draw a distinction in sense—to think, one could say, borrowing from Deleuze's *Difference and Repetition*.

Like the schizophrenic depth of nonsense in Deleuze, which can be accessed only at the expense of collapsing all stable sense into madness, informational noise is existentially threatening to the system. Under conditions of high complexity, "it is no longer possible" for the system "to connect every element with every other element" (Luhmann, 1995a, p. 24). This renders the continuous processing of information, on which the functional integrity of the system relies, impossible. In both Deleuze and Luhmann, the only reality that is possible is located on the surface of sense that conceals and thereby keeps at bay the complexity of nonsense. Luhmann somewhat mystically refers to complexity as "the Midas touch of modernity" (1998, p. 45) in this sense. Complexity is the force that makes immanent creativity work for any sense system—but direct exposure to this complexity would ultimately prove fatal for the former.

Sense can function immanently creative because it "must be fashioned as basally unstable, restless, and with a built-in compulsion to self-alteration" (Luhmann, 1995a, p. 65). Luhmann uses the concept of "re-entry" to describe how complexity is both reduced and produced in every act of sense-making. In "Observing re-entries" (1993a), he argues that expression in the medium of sense always has the character of a distinction in the form of sense that re-enters itself. For example, in every discussion of the political in Aristotle, the distinction between *oikos* and *polis* resurfaces, to be either affirmed or undermined by the new line of argumentation developed (p. 5). Luhmann's re-entry adapts the cybernetic problem of informational entropy for sense systems for which complexity is both threat and necessary condition for immanent creative genesis. In a sense system, the multiplicity of past distinctions which re-enters every new instance of differentiation is composed of past system/environment distinctions (Schönwälder-Kuntze, 2009). Re-entry is then the continuous return of any past "distinction between high complexity and low complexity into low complexity" (Luhmann, 1993a, p. 13). The re-entry of complexity in sense allows sense-making to function truly immanently—it continuously opens sense-relations to the outside complexity previously excluded, which then conditions further sense-making. Sense-making both resolves and requires the re-entry of complexity for the sense system. It "achieves both the reduction and preservation of complexity by filling immediately given, evident experience with references to other possibilities and with a reflexive and generalizing negation potential, thus equipping it for . . . [further] selectivity" (Luhmann, 1990a, p. 29). While worldmaking in sense reflects "a preference for meaning over world, for order over perturbation, for information over noise," it yet "does not enable one to dispense with the contrary" (Luhmann, 1995a, p. 83). Creative production in sense can only function immanently insofar as it "lives off disturbances, is nourished by disorder, lets itself be carried by noise" (p. 83).

As is the case for Deleuze's nonsense, second-order systems do not encounter the constitutive outside of complexity as externally pre-existent. It is rather immanently co-produced together with sense. Every expression of sense produces not just a concrete form of sense but also an outside complexity. As shown above, modern societies produce materiality as the complex outside of the social system in order to avoid having to take into account its creative capacity. A particular actuality is produced in sense at the border of "order and perturbation, between information and noise" (Luhmann, 1995a, p. 83), and through their continuous interplay (Moeller, 2012, pp. 127–129). Immanently creative sense-making "presupposes the operationally functioning unity of what is differentiated" (Luhmann, 2012a, p. 25)—sense and nonsense—"comprehensible only as paradox, but not observable" (p. 25).

Different from Deleuze, Luhmann does not specify the location or quality of complexity beyond its entropic intensity. Environmental complexity is the unmarked outside of the constitutive sense-making process. It is thereby part and necessary condition not only of how psychic systems generate the world that is accessible to them. Sense-making at the unstable boundary between existing forms of sense and external complexity is also the mode of worldmaking through which social systems experience themselves and their environment (Luhmann, 2012a, pp. 3–4, 36). While Deleuze locates intense, nonsensical potentiality in the phantasm and thereby marks creative sense-making as taking place within the mind of the subject, the "unmarked space" (p. 21) of complexity not only requires, but allows for, no such situating act in Luhmann. As a consequence, immanent world-making through the interplay of sense and nonsense is here theoretically generalized as the mode of creative production in relational systems. This includes society as a whole, its different sub-systems and the subjects, or rather, psychic systems, inhabiting them. While sense is being made in the mind of the subject, it is also being made in the judicial processes of the legal system, in the decisions of the political system or indeed the affectionate expressions of love as a social system. These sense-making processes are non-anthropocentric insofar as the world being produced is here the world of the particular system, which is related to but distinct from how this world is then experienced by individual subjects in their very own, psychic sense-relations. Luhmann's society exists as and through multiple simultaneous and intersecting processes of continuous, selective structuration in sense. A theory of immanently creative sense can thus not only provide insight to how subjects make sense of the world by making a particular world in sense, but can also provide understanding for how the particular configurations of the social world made in sense emerge, are maintained, and change in the relations through which different social realms make sense of themselves and their respective social outside.

Luhmann's work lays the ground for employing immanently creative sense as the analytical lens of a political theory that seeks to understand how continuity and change are, in their manifest social reality and independent from the gaze of the individual subject, made in sense. When Luhmann speaks of social systems, he refers to the functionally differentiated systems of modern Western societies, which are a particular product of its historical evolution. It is not so much the case that in these societies social life is organized into functionally differentiated systems. Rather, social life itself is made in, and in the form of, these social systems (Arnoldi, 2012, pp. 34–36). Maybe best understood through the organizational studies in which his theory is rooted, Luhmann's social systems are functional entities. Just like bureaucratic departments, they exist to fulfill, and only as long as they do fulfill, a specific purpose (Luhmann, 1958, pp. 102–105). Luhmann suggests that the formation of social systems must be understood as the socioevolutionary response to a significant increase of social complexity at the dawn of modernity. The Enlightenment advancements of science and philosophy, and the subsequent, and profound, changes in politics, religion, the economy, and the making and enforcement of law, amongst others, meant that across the social sphere the processes and procedures of social life became more diverse and intricate, and the options and pathways for sense-making increased drastically. Adopting the lens of cybernetic theory, Luhmann identifies this drastic increase in complexity as a serious threat to the integrity of social reality in sense. It had to be managed through inside/outside distinctions in sense that reduced this social complexity in a profound and lasting fashion. This resolution happened, Luhmann argues, through society's functional differentiation into distinct social systems (2009a, pp. 9–19; Luhmann, 1995a, pp. 744–746). Social systems are focused on a specific functional role they fulfill for the society as a whole—the economic system ensures that the material needs of citizens are met, the political system produces collectively binding, steering decisions, the legal system enforces them, and so forth. Their particular responsibility renders social systems functionally closed off from the rest of society. Their respective functional logic means that they only register, process, and respond to information that is relevant to fulfilling their designated social function. The resulting, reduced complexity makes distinctions in sense possible, and allows a functionally differentiated societies to persist despite a high, and increasing, level of complexity (Luhmann, 1998, p. 56; 2013, pp. 84–85).

As a consequence of their functional closure, social systems rely on communicative connections to other systems. Not only subjects, but also social systems are linked through sense-relations in Luhmann. Internal sense-making does not advance but rather replaces a genuine understanding of how the other person, or the other social system, operates in their own logic of sense. Other systems form part of the environment for the sense-based system. Systems must communicate to gain information about the respective other precisely because they cannot actually understand what lies outside of them. The requirement of maintaining themselves as a realm of limited complexity against a complex outside means that the existence, function, and communication of other systems can be understood only as forms of sense produced on the inside of a system's own sense-relations, and so in a way that is distinct from the sense relations of the system that is communicating. A parliamentary committee that forms part of the political system can make sense of the economic system's financial markets but does so within a political logic. Two people discussing their experience of participating in a protest can make sense of what the respective other is saying but will do so against the background of their own experience, impressions, and ideas.

The systems on both sides of the communicative process are aware of their lack of genuine understanding, and thus build expectational structures to order, classify, and predict the behavior of the respective other (Luhmann, 1995a, p. 103). Here, the particular way in which existing forms of sense are configured establishes "schemata that guide new sense making" (Arnoldi, 2012, p. 34). What emerges is a "complicated structure of opaque systems oriented to an environment containing systems oriented to an environment" (Luhmann, 1995a, p. 113) that all function through, and thereby structure the social world into, particular lines of distinction in sense. They contingently exclude certain outsides with the help of complex schemata operating through forms of sense and their communicative expression. In Luhmann, it is in sense that society is structured into specific domains, communicative links, hierarchies, power relations, and exclusions (Luhmann, 2013, pp. 223–225). Understanding how worldmaking in sense functions can thus not only provide insight into stability and change on the level of ontology, and the "images of thought" that orient it, as is the case in Deleuze. Thought with Luhmann, immanent creativity in sense unlocks the very practical production and reproduction of social order.

Chapter 2

Nomadic Monads at the Autopoietic Fold

The last chapter explored worldmaking with Deleuze and Luhmann as a continuous process of distinguishing sense from nonsense. The building material that gives reality to a particular world produced is an always-already synthetic sense. It was shown that this constituent sense can be broken down to its material and epistemic components only in a further act of worldmaking in sense, which produces rather than reveals any original source or quality of this creative sense. But so far, this world in sense is unpopulated; we have barely touched on the subjects and social realms that exist and orient themselves in a reality that unfolds in sense. This chapter adds a third dimension to the Deleuzian-Luhmannian account of ontogenesis: worldmaking in sense is always, at the same time, self-making. The existent self is a product of sense but also endows sense-making with a point of view that grounds and directs it. In under to understand the co-production of world and self in sense, this chapter links Luhmann's systems theory to Deleuze's reading of Leibniz's two-tier monadic existence in *The Fold*. The arguments developed here are indebted to Philippopoulos-Mihalopoulos's chapter "The Autopoietic Fold: Critical Autopoiesis between Luhmann and Deleuze" (2013), which performs the speculative exercise of enfolding Luhmann's and Deleuze's theories predominantly through the latter's reading of Leibniz. In particular, the account of autopoiesis developed here aligns with what Philippopoulos-Mihalopoulos terms "critical autopoiesis" (2013, p. 61) and which presumes an ontologically ungrounded, freely oscillating system that unfolds and refolds at the border between matter and sense. In the following, I will conceptualize Luhmann's systems as monadic nomads.

Like Leibniz's monads, they are "without windows" and unfold the entire world on the inside of their souls. All productivity takes place at the fold between soul and matter, system and environmental complexity, where both the systemic self and the world it perceives are constantly made. However, Luhmann's system is also nomadic. Instead of unfolding self and world along a straight line compossible with the worlds unfolded by others, existence is here fundamentally contingent and self-grounding and can change its direction with every new fold.

Being for the World that Is Inside

In *The Fold*, Deleuze characterizes the mode of existence set out by Leibniz's monadology in the following way. Famously, Leibniz's monads are without windows to the world "through which anything may come in or go out" (Leibniz, 1990, p. 456). The perceptions and experiences of individual monads are radically closed off from any contact with the outside world in which they exist. Monads exist for the world instead of in the world (Deleuze, 2006a, p. 26). Because the monad cannot receive any information from its outside, it exists by producing the world that surrounds it on its inside. Windowless existence requires that the "world must be placed in the subject in order that the subject can be for the world" (p. 26). Existence is conditional on a continuous process of worldmaking that takes place entirely on the inside of the monadic subject. The mode of existence that Deleuze draws from Leibniz's philosophy folds neatly into Luhmann's systems theory. This enfolding makes it possible to explore what the worldmaking in sense that was drawn out in the abstract in the last chapter means for the subjects populating this world in sense who perform this worldmaking.

Monads are "incorporeal Automatons" (Leibniz, 1990, p. 458). They are machines of perception that exist only because, and as long as, they make sense. For Leibniz, everything there is—objects, animal souls, human minds—is composed of monads that are completely closed off from their environment. Even where monads enter into compounds and form more complex bodies, their existence remains inward-oriented and driven by their particular substance. The monad's substance is the constantly changing aggregate of its perceptions. For Leibniz, "there is nothing besides perceptions and their changes to be found in the simple substance" (p. 457). Because the existence of the monad is windowless, its perceptions cannot be understood as the direct effect of an external reality imprinting itself on the monad.

Leibniz's incorporeal automaton does not function according to the logic of mechanism but is driven by a continuous, creative process of sense-making. The monad's logic of existence is "the autonomy of the inside" (Deleuze, 2006a, p. 28). Monadic perceptions must thus be understood as the sense of the world that the monad creates independently and autologically in the absence of any way to access its environment (Strickland, 2014, p. 68; Bredekamp, 2008, pp. 106–112). Monadic worldmaking, as Deleuze puts it, is an "intrinsic psychic causality which goes from each monad on its account to effects of perceptions of the universe that it produces spontaneously, independently of all influx from one monad or the other" (2006a, p. 97).

Not only does the monad therefore create the world it perceives, but all changes it is subject to as a consequence of what is being perceived are also the effects of its own, internal, creative force. The "natural changes of monads come from an internal principle [that may be called active force], since an external cause would not be able to influence a monad's interior" (Strickland, 2014, p. 16). For this reason, Leibniz's monads have a constant "appetite" (Leibniz, 1960, p. 457) for new perceptions that allow them to evolve and change course in a process of constant becoming. The monad's substance is composed of the perceptions of the world it generates, and its existence unfolds in this process of creative sense-making. Word and self are co-produced effects of the monadic striving for perceptive becoming. The monad makes itself a world to exist in order to exist, but this existence is based on the monadic capacity to orient itself in the world it creatively perceives (Brandom, 1981). Everything that exists, and everything that will ever exist, is here a product of the creative relations on the inside of the monad, whose "present is pregnant with the future" (Leibniz, 1990, p. 458). Monadic creativity "must be incapable of limits and therefore must contain fully as much reality as is possible" (p. 6). When Caesar crosses the Rubicon, "everything that happens to Caesar is encompassed in the individual notion of Caesar" (Deleuze, 1980b). If we assume that "the entire world is encompassed in the universal notion of Caesar, then Caesar crossing the Rubicon only acts to unroll [. . .] something that was encompassed for all times in the notion of Caesar" (Deleuze, 1980a).

The self-referential existence of Luhmann's systems aligns closely with Leibniz's self-sufficient automata of sense-making. In his very first publication, "Der Funktionsbegriff in der Verwaltungswissenschaft" (1958), Luhmann explores self-referential existence through the lens of organizational sociology as the operational mode of administrative units. It is quite likely that Luhmann's own experience in the public administration of Lüneburg, a small city in northern Germany, where Luhmann was still working at the time, strongly inspired his idea of self-reference. For Luhmann, systemic units, for example a particular branch of administration, lead a purpose-directed existence. They exist to fulfill, and exist for only as long as they do fulfill, a specific function (Luhmann, 1958, pp. 102–105). The important innovation that Luhmann's concept of self-reference introduces here is that this purpose or function is not externally determined but produced entirely on the inside of the system, where it becomes the system's *raison d'être*.

An administrative unit, Luhmann argues, might have been set up to fulfill a particular purpose within a larger organization. But once it has come into existence, this administration takes on a life of its own. It functions according to a self-produced purpose, and with the sole aim of sustaining itself through this purpose-directed functioning, in complete independence from any externally ascribed aim or usefulness. Self-reference "designates the unity that an element, a process, or a system is for itself. 'For itself' means independent of the cut of [sic] observation by others" (Luhmann, 1995a, p. 33). In a certain way, Luhmann suggests (pp. 98–99), systemic self-reference is a teleological mode of existence, but with a *telos* that is flexibly and independently defined by the system itself. Self-referential systems direct purposeful operation toward the goals they set themselves and that do not pre-exist them as foundational essence or external force (Luhmann, 2009c, pp. 16–20). Deleuze detects a similar "phenomenology of motives" (2006a, p. 69) in Leibniz. Because the creative striving of the monad that unfolds a world is entirely closed off from any external influence, the purpose that guides this creative unfolding is here also the autonomous product of the sense-relations on the inside of the monad. Like Luhmann's system, the monadic "soul is what invents its own motives. and these are always subjective" (p. 69).

Luhmann's teleology of purposiveness unfolds a circular process of self-referential production. Self-reference is the system's mode of existence—it directs its functioning in the present as well as its course of future development. The concept of autopoiesis radicalizes the idea of self-reference, which had occupied Luhmann since the beginning of his career. While autopoiesis might be the concept that Luhmann's theory is known best for, it entered his work comparatively late, in *Social Systems*, published in 1984 (Klymenko, 2012). Luhmann encounters the concept of autopoiesis in biological and neurophysiological scholarship in the early 1980s, more specifically in the writings of the biological systems theorists Humberto

Maturana and Francisco Varela (Klymenko, 2012, pp. 69–72).[1] Exemplified by the early essay "What the Frog's Eye Tells the Frog's Brain" (Lettvin et al., 1959), the constructivist neuroscience of Maturana and Varela suggests that nervous systems function self-referentially. A neuronal response, they argue, should not be understood as the direct effect of an external stimulus that a sensory organ, such as the frog's eye, simply passes on to the brain. On the contrary, Lettvin et al. argue that the image produced in the brain is in fact the result of a complex process of neuronal self-stimulation that originates in the sensory organ itself. Neuronal networks, Maturana and Varela (1980, pp. 81–82) conclude, do not process external influences. They react first and foremost to themselves, according to internal and self-produced rules—neuronal networks are *autopoietic* systems.[2] Maturana and Varela's autopoietic neuronal system is "homeostatic (or rather relations-static)" (Maturana and Varela, 1980, p. 79) insofar as keeping its own relations constant is its dominant functional principle and operational aim. In contrast to an allopoietic, externally produced, and static machine, an autopoietic system "continuously generates and specifies its own organization through its operation as a system of production of its own components, and does this in an endless turnover of its components" (p. 79). Autopoietic systems function autologically in every respect, and reproduce themselves through this self-directed functioning.

Luhmann does not think that all aspects of Maturana and Varela's research can be applied to his systems theory, as there is an important qualitative difference between their biological systems, which reproduce life, and his psychic and social systems, which perform their autopoiesis in the medium of sense (Luhmann, 1995a, p. 119). He nevertheless adopts the concept of autopoiesis to theoretically improve on his earlier concept of self-reference to argue that sense-based systems do not only autonomously produce the purpose that directs and maintains their existence. They are autopoietic, meaning that they produce all elements that constitute this existence, and are necessary for its reproduction, on the inside of the system reproduced (Luhmann, 1990a, pp. 2–35).[3] Luhmann's system is an "autopoietic monad" (Philippopoulos-Mihalopoulos, 2013, p. 64) insofar as it is truly windowless. Borrowing the words of Deleuze, it is "a cell," resembling "a sacristy more than an atom: a room with neither doors nor windows, where all activity takes place on the inside" (2006, p. 28).

However, beyond Deleuze's Leibniz, Luhmann's concept of autopoiesis makes it possible to specify how such a windowless existence can be maintained as both co-produced with the world that situates it and completely closed off from this world. Importantly, autopoiesis does not equate to isolation. Luhmann's sense-based systems do not exist in complete detachment from each other, and from the world they populate—and indeed cannot do so (Luhmann, 2010, pp. 53–54; 1995a, pp. 29–37). In order to function self-referentially, systems must "be able to use the difference between system and environment within themselves" (Luhmann, 1990a, p. 9). Autopoietic existence "is possible only in an environment, only under ecological conditions" (p. 9). What Luhmann draws attention to here is that, in order to constantly reproduce themselves autopoietically, systems must have available "building material" that allow for this reproduction. As in the case of the frog's eye, the creative response is internally incited, but the image produced is nevertheless the image of something externally seen to which the internal creative stimulus can be linked. The system's autopoietic reproduction thus relies on new information, a singularity not yet made sense of, to reproduce itself. Luhmann's systemic autopoiesis thus subverts the distinction between open and closed systems. Systems must be informationally open to be able to operate as functionally closed (Luhmann, 1990a, p. 9). They require new, external information in order to continuously reproduce their self-directed existence.

However, this openness to external stimuli is, importantly, itself a creation of the autopoietic system. Windowless systems have no way of accessing information that is genuinely external to them—like the frog's neurons, they can only affect themselves. Consequently, the externality of the world is not really the origin of the information that autopoietic systems perceive and make use of to reproduce themselves (Maturana and Varela, 1980, pp. 6, 53–55). The external environment is only the source to which the system attributes immanently created information. Luhmann's windowless systems are open to external information insofar as this information can be processed within the system and reproduce its inside/environment distinction. However, the relationship between external information and systemic effect is not that of stimulus and response but rather a selective, creative process of self- and worldmaking: in order to respond to any external information, the system must produce this information on the inside of its sense-relations. The symbiotic relationship between sense and nonsense unpacked in the last chapter reappears here as the principle of motion of Luhmann's autopoiesis. Autopoietic existence requires the constant presence of nonsense, of something not-yet-made-sense-of, attributed to a co-produced world but produced on the inside of the system.

The Fold of Individuation

The relationship between inside and outside, self and world, is central for understanding windowless, self-reproductive existence. In Deleuze's reading of Leibniz, existence is reproduced at the creative fold between the inside of the monadic soul and the outside of matter. Here, windowless existence requires a folded surface. Following Deleuze, Leibniz's Baroque philosophy sets up "a world with only two floors" (2006a, p. 29): matter and soul. The two floors of Leibniz's world are clearly distinct—as we saw above, sense-making in the monadic soul takes place in the absence of any possibility to access and thus represent rather than create its material outside. The situation is no different for physical-bodily monads—they function according to a logic internal to them in complete independence from the aims and intentions of the soul. The two-floor structure of the Baroque world, however, indicates a clear hierarchy between the monads of the soul and those of material bodies. The soul is the driving force that reproduces subjective existence through its continuous creative striving. And yet, its material outside plays a vital role in the process of sense-making that continues the soul's monadic existence.

Deleuze's Leibnizian discussion of creative production from obscurity to clarity at the folded surface of the monad fits smoothly with Luhmann's autopoiesis. Taken together, they reveal what happens at the border between system and outside in a creative instance that produces both systemic existence and the world that surrounds it. For Leibniz, the philosophical turn to the depth of objects or the height of metaphysics is erroneous. Philosophers in search for the origin of creative expression are "ordinarily like boys who are persuaded that a golden pot is to be found at the very end of the rainbow where it touches the earth" (Leibniz, 1890, p. 58). Leibniz's world is produced and "exists only in the folds of the soul which convey it, the soul implementing inner pleats through which it endows itself with a representation of the enclosed world" (2006a, p. 22). For Leibniz, the soul can function immanently creatively because it "has folds and is full of folds" (p. 22). But what is enfolded here? The relationship between internal sense and its outside at the folded surface, or "façade" (p. 28), of Leibniz's monadic soul echoes the influx of internally produced, externally attributed information at the border of Luhmann's autopoietic system. The façade of the soul is permeable; it "can have doors and windows—it is riddled with holes" (p. 28). The creative fold at the monadic surface can enfold material singularities to charge self- and worldmaking. However, any attribution of the singularities enfolded to either a material outside or a representational inside is secondary to the worldmaking process that is being charged (Leibniz, 1890, pp. 356–358). The monad's creative folds are, at the same time, "pleats of matter" and "folds in the soul" (Deleuze, 2006a, p. 4).

This is exactly the lack of a foundational source that was demonstrated for the self-productive medium of sense in the previous chapter. The self-referential existence of Leibniz's monadic subject, which is always co-produced with the world that situates it, thus endows creative sense-making with a particular location—and point of application. Not only worlds but also the subjects that populate them are produced in one and the same process of creative sense-making. What takes place at the creative fold is a process of individuation from a complex virtuality, whose singularities have not been attributed a particular quality yet, to a clearly defined, monadic subject. Deleuze credits Leibniz as the first philosopher who rejected the rationalist orthodoxy of the clear and distinct, which produces "knowledge of effects only" (Deleuze, 1992b, pp. 133–134), and explored the generative principle behind distinct existent entities—the principle of creative folding (Deleuze, 1994, pp. 213–215). Deleuze draws on Leibniz's example of "the confused murmur that people hear when nearing the sea shore" (Leibniz, 1989, p. 325) to suggest two alternative couplings that can help us understand creative production in the fold: clear–confused and obscure–distinct. The creative folds at the monadic surface are "distinct because they grasp differential relations and singularities" (Deleuze, 1994, p. 213)—they are filled with pleats of matter and folds of the soul. Yet, at the same time, they are obscure because "they are not yet 'distinguished,' not yet 'differenciated'" (p. 213). In the fold, "the whole world is only a virtuality" (Deleuze, 2006a, p. 23), but it yet lacks the specificity that allows a particular subject to orient itself in it. Creative production in the fold moves from a distinct-obscure potentiality to a specific "apperception which in turn is only clear and confused" (Deleuze, 2004, p. 213). The sense that is produced in the fold, and which forms the building material for both existent self and situating world, is, like the murmur of the sea, clearly delineated in its quality and attributable to a source. However, like Leibniz's murmur of the sea, it is also confused because the particular singularities that constitute it—the formation of the waves, the wind that whips up the water—are hidden from view.

However, creative folding does not end there, with the clear and confused, because its unfolding has changed the configuration of the fold, creating the conditions for another unfolding. Deleuze approaches this creative production at the folded surface through Leibniz's mathematical calculus. While Leibniz himself stresses that the calculus does not provide a model for psychological or social individuation (Deleuze, 1980b), Deleuze engages with the calculus not in a directly mathematic sense, but rather using it as a model to understand creative production as an immanent movement from the complex obscurity of the fold to the clarity of the individuated subject (Duffy, 2006, 2010). Leibniz (1890, pp. 34–37) situates his differential geometry in opposition to the static functioning of dialectical mathematics. His differential calculus dy/dx describes a dynamic duration with infinitely small changes. It captures the becoming of a curve whose differentials are independent from an original (formal) starting point, and defined by nothing but the differential relation itself, to which the contingent and ever-changing forms it expresses are always secondary (Duffy, 2006, pp. 50–74). The calculus expresses the infinite creative primacy of the fold's curve. The particular, finite figures of dy and dx, enfolded materiality and unfolded subject, are secondary to the creative fold and change in response to it (Duffy, 2010, p. 134). Leibniz replaces the idea of creation *ex nihilo* with a creative expression that functions as an "art of combinations" (1989, p. 73) where clear subjects unfold from an immanently dynamic, complex fold. Following Deleuze, "Leibniz does not believe in the void. For him it always seems to be filled with a folded matter . . . that both the decimal system—and Nature itself—conceal in apparent voids" (2006a, p. 41).

In *The Fold*, Deleuze repeatedly refers to the soul's creative becoming as a process of individuation (2006a, pp. 8, 25, 64). The concept of individuation is central to the techno-biological theory of Gilbert Simondon. In his short review of Simondon's *Individuation and Its Physical-Biological Genesis*, Deleuze emphasizes the "wealth and originality" (Deleuze, 2004, p. 89) of Simondon's philosophical concepts. Deleuze's particular interest lies in Simondon's theory of individuation, where existence is produced through the same relations that also bring forth the world that an individual is individuated from (pp. 86–87). Simondon's theory, and particularly its relationship to Deleuze's thought, has received much attention over the past few years (D'Amato, 2019; Voss, 2018; Hui, 2017; Alloa and Michalet, 2017). It is not my aim to enter into competition with these readings of Deleuze's thought to argue that Deleuze is in fact more "Luhmannian" than he is "Simondonian." On the contrary, Simondon's individuation offers a useful theoretical interlude for the enfolding of Deleuze and Luhmann performed here. It reduces the distance between Deleuze's philosophy and Luhmann's systems theory on the subject of individual existence and its genesis, but also helps to clarify the particular benefit of thinking self- and worldmaking through Luhmann rather than through Simondon.

Like Luhmann, Simondon draws on cybernetic theory to understand the existence and functioning of relational, technical objects as input-output machines. Simondon sets up his cybernetic theory of individuation against a humanist science that uses the subject as hinge and starting point to understand existence. For Simondon, existence cannot be conceptualized other than as continuously unfolding individuation. Individuation is "not a mere isolated consequence arising as a by-product of becoming, but this very process itself as it unfolds" (1992, p. 301); it brings "about the emergence of both individual and milieu" (p. 301). Simondon's individuation is essentially relational. Both the existent individual and the pre-individual milieu of intense matter are produced in the reciprocal process of transformation that is individuation (Bardin, 2015, pp. 51–55). In this sense, individuation is always the production of a particular self that is co-produced with the environment it inhabits (Combes, 2013, pp. 13–15).

Simondon's individuation of technical objects shares a number of similarities with Luhmann's systemic autopoiesis, namely the self-referentiality of the existent individuals produced, the primacy of the self/outside relation, and the post-humanist scope of the theory. In Simondon's take on cybernetic theory, systemic unity is not pre-given but produced in a process of individuation. Any existent self is secondary to a particular and contingent process of individuation, which "does not admit of an already constituted observer" (Combes, 2013, p. 7). For Simondon, cybernetics "frees man from the unconditional prestige of the idea of finality" (2017, p. 120). Against what he perceives as the narrow-mindedness of a scientific humanism that remains bound to the telos of human advancement and emancipation, Simondon views the output of any process of subjective or social individuation as completely contingent in theory but self-reproductive in practice (Bardin, 2015, pp. 22–28). While individuation is primary to both the existent entity produced and the pre-individual milieu the existent individual is distinguished from, the continuous individuation of a particular existent entity establishes a certain path-dependency. Like a crystal growing continuously from previously crystallized material, individuation follows a self-created structure along which it unfolds. Simondon refers to the path-dependent unfolding of individuating existence as transduction (Simondon, 2017, p. 33; Voss, 2018, p. 97).

The principle of transduction implies that information from the pre-individual field is continuously integrated in such a way that an existent individual unfolds smoothly. The problem faced by the continuously individuating entity is, as for Luhmann's systems, entropy. Intense complexity keeps seeping into the unfolding individual from its permeable boundary to an intense pre-individual field. While this entropic outside keeps individuation in motion, it also renders necessary a technical mechanism of selection and allocation at the border of the individuated entity to prevent encroaching entropy from endangering the continuous becoming of the former (Simondon, 2017, pp. 79–83). Simondon's individuating entities, like Luhmann's systems, organize the relationship between informational input and individuated output in a self-referential fashion. What counts as information is dependent on the processes of individuation that separate an existent entity from the world it is individuated from. The external world of the pre-individual milieu unfolds relative to whatever entity is being individuated contingently but smoothly (Simondon, 2017, pp. 147–149; Bardin, 2015, pp. 25–27).

Not only subjects, but also social entities, specifically labor, belief, and language, come into being through individuation and thus hold a status comparable to Luhmann's social systems in Simondon (2017, pp. 185–190). Paralleling Luhmann's account of functional differentiation, Simondon suggests that in the course of social evolution the structures and processes of these social fields have become increasingly independent from the rest of society (Bardin, 2015, pp. 98–99). With reference to Gabriel Tarde, Simondon, like Luhmann, argues for understanding the evolution of language, labor, and belief from a functional perspective. Even morality is a functional, or techno-aesthetic, as Simondon (2012, pp. 3–5) specifies in a letter to Derrida—a system-internal product developed in the course of the individuation of different social realms. Morality or labor constitute technical extensions that link the individuations of several psychic and social units and thereby condition the gradual enfolding of culture (Simondon, 2005, pp. 101–109).

These parallels between Simondon and Luhmann are useful to show that the autopoiesis of Luhmann's systems theory, with its technical language and cybernetic underpinnings, is not completely foreign to Deleuze's philosophical world, which was developed in explicit reference to Simondon. However, I suggest that Luhmann's autopoiesis in fact provides a more radical, and in a way more "Deleuzian," account of relational self- and worldmaking at the border of existent individual and material outside. The basis for this claim is that Simondon does not completely divorce his theory of relational individuation from a notion of external primacy. Individuation is located in the intense potentialities existing in the pre-individual field as a "technical essence" (Simondon, 2017, p. 45) from which it unfolds as a process of clarification and perfection. Simondon's individuation does not begin in the sense-relations of the individuated entity but is driven by a creative intensity pre-existing the individual in its milieu of individuation. While this intensity is transformed in every instance of individuation, it is not itself a product of this individuation (Simondon, 2002, pp. 205–211). Individuation is double-sided but "nonrelational" (Simondon, 1992, p. 310) and unfolds in a nonteleological but yet one-directional manner through "phases or steps through which the genesis of the individual being passes" (p. 310). The "true principle of individuation is mediation" (Simondon, 1992, p. 104), and not a thoroughly relational production where world and self emerge from nothing but the previously produced relations that separate both.

Simondon objects to the idea of linear, objectively measurable progress for both subjects and social fields (2010, pp. 230–234). Yet, his theory seems to retain a certain notion of teleological, pre-directed unfolding—closer to the becoming of the *élan vital* in Bergson, whom Simondon read with interest (Chabot, 2013, pp. 149–153), than to the self- and worldmaking of Leibniz's windowless monad. As Bardin (2015, pp. 46–57) notes, a certain notion of Kantian rationalism also persists in Simondon's thought, and prevents his individuation from unfolding a radical perspectivism. Simondon's work aims to bridge the gap between the positivist sciences and the phenomenological humanities of his time by grounding social philosophy in its own axiomatic truths. While he reveals epistemic and normative frameworks as functional products of social evolution, Simondon thus at the same time insists on a positivist truth value for his theory of individuation as the most accurate approximation of how being and thought emerge (Bardin, 2015, pp. 55–57). The relational folding between individual and milieu replace neither the need for absolute ontological primacy nor do they undo the analytical possibility to access the former for Simondon.

Self, World, Autopoiesis

In his short review of Simondon's theory of individuation, Deleuze interestingly praises the concept precisely for its radically reciprocal nature. For Deleuze, Simondon's individuation is a process of creative production that takes place between "two disparate levels of reality" (2004, p. 87) without absolute ground or original starting point. Deleuze credits Simondon with overcoming the doxa of both ontological and epistemological origin by revealing that both are secondary to a continuous process of individuation (1994, pp. 131–132). Individuation, as read by Deleuze, is "problematic" insofar as its relations unfold a creative potentiality that always exceeds and outlives any particular individual "solution" produced, and thus begets further creative production. The process of individuation functions as a self-reproductive system that produces individuals as responses to its unfolding problematic, which always outlives any individuated response. Individuation is thus "the organization of a solution . . . for a system that is objectively problematic" (Deleuze, 2004, p. 88), and reproduces itself by perpetually producing responses to its self-produced problems. Every fold individuates, but every fold also produces the field against which this individuation takes place through enfolding.

While especially some earlier interpretations suggest that there is onto-logical primacy in Deleuze in an absolute sense, regardless of whether it is attributed to virtual difference (Smith, 2012; DeLanda, 2006), the event (Badiou, 2005; Bowden, 2011), or a becoming understood as Bergsonian force of life (Bryant, 2008; Beistegui, 2004), more recently the emphasis has shifted toward a more radically relational, processual understanding of Deleuzian ontology (Widder, 2012; Somers-Hall, 2011; Clisby, 2015). As Clisby suggests in "Deleuze's secret dualism?," neither individuating inten-sity nor individuated actuality "are of particular importance in-themselves" (2015, p. 133) for Deleuze. What is important "is the role that each plays within a system that is 'always-already' involved in the reciprocal process of creation" (p. 133). In this sense, Deleuze's interest in Simondon is driven by the desire to think self- and worldmaking as the reciprocal ends of one and the same process of creative production. No side is ontologically pri-mary or singularly charges this creative unfolding, which, as in the case of Simondon's crystal, is conditioned only by what it has previously produced.

François Zourabichvili, whose provocative remark that there is no "ontology of Deleuze" (Zourabichvili in: Aaarons, 2012, p. 20) constitutes the most explicit rejection of any kind of Deleuzian foundationalism, sug-gests that Deleuze's postfoundational commitment to ungrounded creation that unfolds at the border between inside and outside, emergent self and world, is hinged on the concept of sense. In his review of Hyppolite's *Logic and Existence*, Deleuze programmatically declares that philosophy "must be ontology, it cannot be anything else" (1997). However, the Being that this philosophy is to explore "is sense . . . not the knowledge of an Other, nor of some other thing" (1997). Thus, "philosophy, if it means anything, can only be . . . an ontology of sense" (1997). Deleuze's alternative to the

Hegelian dialectic between the One and the negative is a dualist ontology of sense where self and world are continuously co-produced in relations of sense that are ungrounded but filled with what they have previously produced (Zourabichvili, 2012, pp. 80–85).

Sense-relations form the boundary between the emergent order of the existent self and the outside world that this self inhabits. In order to achieve and maintain this separation, they must exclude its actual complexity, and produce a particular, graspable outside world in sense. But because this sense-making at the border of self and world continuously recombines the singularities of both, it can always radically alter the selves and the worlds co-produced. As Widder puts it, sense "is immanent to our world, but it resides within it as something different from the world's immediate appearance. For this reason, sense must present itself in the internal passage from one side of the divide to the other, in the movement from the empirical to the conceptual and back" (2008, p. 37).

It is against this background that Deleuze reads Simondon, and pushes his concept of individuation in the direction of Luhmann's autopoiesis. Ontologically, Luhmann's autopoietic unfolding means a radical turn to the inside. Both self and environment are the perspectivist products of the continuous self-reproduction of their boundary in sense. In Deleuze's ontological turn to relations of sense, and in Luhmann's autopoietic systems, it is the distinction between inside and outside, existent self and environment, that co-produces both of the latter. As Spencer Brown, the calculus theorist who inspired Luhmann's primacy of the inside/outside distinction, suggests: "[I]f certain facts about our common experience of perception, of what we might call the inside world, can be revealed by an extended study of what we call, in contrast, the outside world, then an equally extended study of this inside world will reveal, in turn, the facts first met within the world outside: for what we approach in either case is the common boundary between them" (Spencer Brown, 1969, p. xvii). Self makes world, and world makes self—because both are made in sense. Luhmann makes the postfoundational perspectivism of autopoietic existence unfolding at the border between self and world explicit. Continuous differential production at the fold of sense, which takes place in a distinct and completely autonomous way on the inside of every subject and social system, removes the need for ontological grounding, but also erases the very possibility of any investigation that goes deeper than the surface of sense (Luhmann, 1990a, pp. 127–130). Without an Archimedean point that removes the observer from her systemically situated position, sense, and the knowledge it conditions, cannot be anything but radically perspectivist on the existent self unfolding in sense (Rasch, 2000; Stäheli, 2000). Objectivity and trans-systemic generalization "in which knowledge could find an ultimate foothold and secure correspondence with its object" (Luhmann, 1995a, p. 35) are rendered impossible. The immanent position of observation always remains a "blind spot" to the sense-making system. It can be observed from the outside, by other systems, but only from the perspective of their respective logics of sense (Luhmann, 2012a, pp. 198–199; 1995a, pp. 109, 265). Rasch uses the example of the "unseeable" eye to illustrate Luhmann's ontological perspectivism: "I see right now the room before me, the computer which I use to produce this text, the desk on which it sits, the hands that do the typing, but I cannot see the object that does all this seeing, namely my own eye. In the act of describing what I see, my eye remains hidden to me; I cannot see it seeing, therefore it slides into nothingness" (2013, p. 42). Luhmann's perspectivist ontology captures the mode of being Deleuze sets up for the monadic soul perfectly: "Inclusion of the world in the monad is surely unilateral, but cannot be localized. It cannot be localized at the limit since the limit is outside of the monad" (2006a, p. 51). At the beginning of *Social Systems*, Luhmann famously insists that the "following considerations assume that there are systems. Thus, they do not begin with epistemological doubt (Luhmann, 1995a, p. 1). For Rasch, Luhmann's insistence on the existence of systems illustrates his tendency to theorize "with a distinctively Kantian and perhaps especially neo-Kantian flavour" (2013, p. 38). Indeed, Luhmann's work offers examples of such Kantian statements. In an essay on constructivism, "Das Erkenntnisprogramm des Konstruktivismus und die unbekannt bleibende Realität," he suggests that "there is an external reality, which is already evident in the fact that the self-produced operation of knowledge [Erkenntnis] can be executed at all" (2009e, p. 32), even if this external reality always "remains unknown" (p. 32) to the philosophical observer. Rasch deducts from this that Luhmann theorizes "on the cusp of a reality that remains unknowable to all of us" (2013, p. 56), but of which, "perhaps, out of the "corner of our eye" we occasionally catch a glimpse of" (p. 56). Even though ultimately unknowable, we can yet indirectly discern such reality because it is what "makes our well-ordered world possible" (p. 56), just like the spark of divine creation in Leibniz.[4]

Different from Rasch, I believe that such speculation about an ontological origin, be it a creative force or a foundational ordering grid, is ultimately foreign to Luhmann's theoretical project. Everything a system perceives is the immanent product of the sense-relations that the system is comprised of—including Luhmann's systems theory. This precludes any original insight to either the existent self or the world made sense of—both become observable only as they are produced in sense. Creation and observation are one and the same act. Rather than taking a strong antifoundational stance, Luhmann's theory turns the theoretical gaze inward—for him, everything important happens on the level of sense, where world and self are produced and reproduced in their particular configurations—and it is here that change in these configurations is rooted and plays out. In this sense, Luhmann's thought performs a "de-ontologisation of reality" (Luhmann, 2009e, p. 35; my translation). It merges the recognition that reality is real *because we can make sense of it* with the insight that it is only real to the knowing subject *because the subject makes sense*, because they immanently produce their self and the world they inhabit in sense in the absence of any possibility to access an external reality (pp. 34–39).

Akin to the way Deleuze discusses Artaud's dive into the depth of subconscious nonsense where nobody can follow in *The Logic of Sense*, Luhmann emphasizes the unproductive character not just of ontological speculation but of any attempt to classify the origin of world and self beyond the sense relations that bring forth both. Rather than trying to escape "the circle of self-grounding knowledge [Erkenntnis]" (Luhmann, 2009e, p. 34; my translation), Luhmann renders self-grounding existence and radical perspectivism the condition of his theoretical investigation. Here, "knowledge is what knowledge considers to be knowledge" (p. 32; my translation) within the context of particular sense relations that reproduce themselves in their distinction from a complex environment. When Luhmann states that "[t]here is no doubt that an external reality exists, and equally no doubt that contact to it is possible as the condition which gives reality to the operations of the system" (p. 39; own translation), he draws attention to the fact that autopoietic existence requires the production of a world from which the existent self is differentiated. It can only continue in its self-produced distinctness from the external world if, and as long as, this world functions delineating, which means that it *must be real* within the perspectivist order of sense germane to the existent self.

Perspectivism is a Pluralism

If we take what has so far been established about windowless monadic existence with the help of Deleuze's reading of Leibniz and Luhmann's thought, the monadic subject firstly creates itself vis-à-vis a world that is co-produced in this process of self-making in complete autonomy from any actual environment that the self-referential monad might inhabit. This process of self- and world-making that takes place at the permeable border of the monadic soul and moves from obscure complexity to clear actuality is, secondly, not grounded in anything but a monadic body that is itself the product of this creative folding, and can always change in the course of it. The consequence is not only a world populated by autonomously functioning subjects, but a multiverse. Multiple windowless selves inhabit multiple worlds with no ground to ensure their cohesion and semblance. "Perspectivism is clearly a pluralism" (Deleuze, 2006, p. 20), Deleuze notes.

This perspectivism as pluralism is the radical consequence of Leibniz's theory—but not the consequence he draws himself. On the contrary, Leibniz's monads unfold in "well-ordered dreams" (Leibniz, 1890, p. 77). The harmony of their self- and worldmaking is *a priory* ensured by the ordering impetus of divine creation. For Leibniz, "God created the soul, or every other real unity, in the first place in such a way that everything with it comes into existence from its own substance through perfect spontaneity as regards itself and in perfect harmony with objects outside itself" (1890, p. 77). In theory, as Leibniz illustrates with this famous example, a world in which Adam would not have sinned in the Garden of Eden is possible. But contrary to what one might assume, it could not be a better world, as otherwise it would be this other world without Adam the sinner for which divine creation would have laid the seed in every monad. Because it was established as a path-dependent result of divine creation, this world is necessarily the best of all possible worlds, and thus must be the world creatively produced by all windowless souls. Adam's sin is theoretically avoidable, but its absence is incompossible with the divine choice of the best possible world (Bowden, 2011, pp. 58–71; Deleuze, 1980b).

If we remove the hinge of divine choice from Leibniz's philosophical universe, his harmoniously ordered worlds collapse into a chaotic pluriverse composed of a multiplicity of alternative parallel words that are all possible outcomes for monadic self- and worldmaking processes. Not only might each monad produce a different world to inhabit, but the worlds and selves co-produced might radically change shape in every path-dependent but fundamentally open-ended instance of creative unfolding. The idea of possible worlds, even if they form a chaosmos, might seem difficult to reconcile with Deleuze's philosophy. Deleuze famously develops his concept of the virtual as a theoretical alternative to the Kantian idea of the possible that is a derivative of the real. Deleuze objects to the idea that reality is only the actuality we perceive, and that what is possible is merely a variation drawn from this actuality. For Deleuze, reality is always more than what we make of it. His virtual is thus a real but inaccessible multiplicity that inspires thought and action from the outside of what is currently actualized (Deleuze, 1994, pp. 254–258). I suggest that Leibniz's possible worlds, however, fold neatly into Deleuze's philosophy because they do not follow the Kantian possible/real dichotomy. Leibniz's possible worlds do not set up an *a priori* transcendental limitation on what can become real. Like Deleuze's virtual, they mark the excess of reality that accompanies every particular actuality distinguished, and to which this actuality remains open. Any self and world produced could always be different from the "realized possible" (p. 213) of a particular monadic existence.

In "May 68 did not take place," Deleuze and Guattari do indeed discuss a "field of the possible" (2006, p. 233) that aligns with Leibniz's (secularized) possible worlds in this sense. Zourabichvili (2017) draws on this essay to argue that there is indeed such a thing as a Deleuzian concept of the possible. Zourabichvili acknowledges that Deleuze seeks to overcome the idea of the possible as a transcendentally pre-ordered potentiality secondary to actual reality. However, for Zourabichvili, Deleuze replaces the Kantian idea of realization from a pre-existent possible not with one but with "two words: to actualize [actualiser] and to accomplish/fulfill [accomplir]. To actualize the virtual, or to accomplish the possible" (2017, p. 161). The significance of the possible is that it allows us to complement Deleuzian ontogenesis with a political task. Because actualization is not limited or directed by a pre-existent realm of the possible, the task for political resistance is to transgress a particular world by interrupting "the expressible of a situation" (p. 157) and make sense of it in a different way, so that different pathways for thought and action are opened up. In close proximity to Leibniz's possible worlds, Zourabichvili's possible is based on a change of direction in the creative production of sense, which changes both the sense-making self and the world in which it can act.

The chaosmos of multiple intersecting and overlapping worlds that Deleuze extracts from the divine machinery that produces Leibniz's well-ordered dreams folds smoothly into Luhmann's thought, where the radical perspectivism of autopoietically closed systems produces a multiverse. Every existent system must create its own world in sense. But the unfolding world co-exists not only with the worlds produced by countless other subjects but also with the environments unfolding from the autopoiesis of social systems and interaction systems. The consequence is an in-itself inaccessible, chaotic externality composed of multiple worlds through various contingent and intersecting lines of relational self-production—a post-human multiverse. For Luhmann, even life on Earth is amongst the contingent outcomes of multifaceted relational self-production. Without foundational grounding or ontological necessity, it can disappear through a shift in the dynamics of intersecting self-production, albeit that, as he observes laconically, the "evolutionary one-off invention of life has proved remarkably stable" (Luhmann, 2004, p. 466). But how open can the possible worlds of autopoietic systems really be? Is a world structured into autopoietic subjects and social systems not always one of well-ordered dreams, a nightmare in this case, where openness and the possibility for change are limited by the parameters of autopoietic existence?

This is an important question, as the deterministic appearance of Luhmann's systems theory, specifically if used to describe a current state of society, as attempted in this book, is a central obstacle to its enfolding with Deleuze's philosophy. I suggest that Luhmann's systemic order—as a mode of social organization—is indeed not incompossible with radical change that leads to the unfolding of a very different possible world. Luhmann's social history is focused on the internal differentiation of society, and its development in the course of social evolution. Society has not always been differentiated into autopoietically closed, functionally differentiated social systems. However, Luhmann does suggest that primitive societies were already structured into certain subsystems, even if these were comparatively simple segments, such as families or territorial units (Luhmann, 2013, pp. 11–40). Bound to an external, collectively shared scheme of social organization, such as kinship or political authority (p. 50), these horizontally segmented or vertically stratified systems were not closed off from their social environment and able to exist autonomously. For this reason, the concept of autopoiesis is notably absent from Luhmann's analysis of prefunctional social differentiation. However, Luhmann does conceptualize the households, territorial entities and hierarchically stratified units of his prefunctional societies as "systems" in the sense of his general systems theory. While they are not autopoietically closed, they exist and function as relational entities that reproduce their sense relations with a focus on their organizing principles selectively against a social environment of comparatively higher complexity (pp. 16, 44–54).

As a mode of social organization, relational self-production in sense is thus not necessarily coupled with functional differentiation but rather precedes it. In addition, all sense-based societies analyzed by Luhmann are populated by subjects that operate as sense-based psychic systems (Fuchs, 2012). This theoretical uncoupling of self-referential existence in sense and functional differentiation as a mode of social organization has important consequences for the way Luhmann's theory can be used. Societies structured into self-referentially operating sense relations have undergone—and are thus able to accommodate—vast changes in the way subjects interact and live within them. This signals that, at least in principle, a reorganization of society away from autopoietically closed social systems is possible. Functional differentiation is the path-dependent product of social evolution—but it is also a contingent, non-necessary mode of social organization. As Luhmann states clearly, a "social system is not, like an organism, fixed in its type. A donkey cannot become a snake, even if such a development was necessary for survival" (2009a, p. 18).

Why then does Luhmann never acknowledge the contingency of systemic autopoiesis as a mode of social organization, and speculate beyond it? A simple answer would be that Luhmann, thoroughly skeptical toward any kind of politically loaded commentary, is simply not interested in social change. But another answer seems to fit the thinker Luhmann, who was keenly interested in contingency, better. As pointed out in the opening passages of this book, Luhmann prefaces his *Theory of Society* with the following Spinozist axiom: "That which cannot be conceived through anything else must be conceived through itself." Luhmann accepts the perspectivism of his theory. Radical perspectivism becomes a foundational principle in a world composed of autopoietically existent entities. Co-produced selves and worlds become ontological reality—rendering the contingency of the particular path-dependency that directs their unfolding the blind spot of the existent self. As Eva Knodt observes in her foreword to *Social Systems*, "[w]hatever distinction is selected" as the basis of self- and worldmaking, each "cut highlights certain aspects of reality and obscures others" (1995, p. xxiv). However, the contingency of this cut, "the unity of the observing system and its environment, . . . remains inaccessible; it is what "one does not perceive when one perceives it," the "blind spot" that enables the system to observe but escapes observation" (p. xxiv). The unfolding of a radically different world at the border of the autopoietic self and its outside is possible, but it only becomes conceivable once it has been produced here, as both ontological reality and epistemological observation are grounded in one and the same process of creative sense-making. As long as an alternative has not come into being in sense, the world of functionally differentiated systems and their autopoietic reproduction is the only world which Luhmann's systems theory can see. However, this world is here "not the best of all possible worlds, up to the basic elements of its socio-cultural and natural constitution it is always problematic, possible in a different form" (Obermeier, 1988, p. 155; my translation).

While the unfolding of world and existent self from the pleated surface of the monadic soul is pre-directed by the divine selection of the best possible world in Leibniz, it is open-ended, and open to the radical reconfiguration of world and self in every new instance of creation in Deleuze and Luhmann. Monadic souls have become autopoietic nomads "astraddle over several worlds" (Deleuze, 2006a, p. 137). However, as Deleuze concludes at the end of *The Fold*, even if we realize the full theoretical potential of a secularized Leibniz who "considers absolute necessity the enemy" (Deleuze, 1992b, p. 79), monads remain only ever "half open" (Deleuze, 2006a, p. 137) in practice. Devoid of an absolute, pre-given ground, the "folding, unfolding, refolding" (p. 137) of self and world is conditioned by the self-produced path-dependency that keeps a particular self, and a particular world perceived, variable but stable. This path-dependency of monadic unfolding becomes the self-produced ground of creative production at the monadic surface and delineates a particular world actualized in sense from other possible worlds. In both Luhmann and Deleuze, open-ended self- and worldmaking needs to function self-grounding in this sense. The immanently creative monad needs to give itself a ground to continue its, in principle, completely open-ended creative production.

In his engagement with Leibniz, in *The Fold* but also in the early lecture series *What is Grounding?* delivered at the Lycée Louis-le-Grand in Paris, Deleuze is clearly occupied with the question of whether and how immanent and free creative production requires a ground. Deleuze here posits the body as the solution to the question of grounding. Very different from Deleuze's exploration of creative materiality, of "what a body can do" (Deleuze, 1992b, p. 218),[5] in other parts of his work, to have a body here means simply to have a ground. In both works, Deleuze argues that it is *necessary* to have a grounding body in this sense. We "must have a body . . . because our mind possesses a favored—clear and distinct—zone of expression" (2006a, p. 85; see also 2015, p. 152). Deleuze's interest in Leibniz's monadic body lies not in its creative capacity, but on the contrary in its limiting, *passive force*. Contrary to the creative folds of the monadic soul, the body "asserts nothing, expresses nothing but the imperfection of the finite" (Deleuze, 1992b, p. 223). Its distinct role within the process of monadic self- and worldmaking lies precisely in the "limitation of active force" (p. 224). The body that occupies Deleuze in his reading of Leibniz is not a material, physical entity—or at least not necessarily. It is rather the existent self, made in previous instances of creative production, which limits and directs new creative expression toward the continuous unfolding of this self. Here, the "empirical body . . . is nothing but the expression of the monad's point of view" (Deleuze, 2006a, p. 104; see also: Jorgensen, 2015, p. 74).

The monadic body fulfills a functionally necessary role within the windowless existence of the monad. It provides the hinge that limits and grounds creative expression in a particular monadic self and directs the continuous creative folding at its surface toward the reproduction of this self. The monadic soul must have a body because only this body gives the "obscure object that lives in it" (Deleuze, 2006, p. 85) its immanent, open, and unfocused creativity, something specific to produce and reproduce. Leibniz's Baroque fold is an "infinite work or process. The problem is not how to finish a fold, but how to continue it" (p. 34). The grounding body orients expressive unfolding and allows it to continue in a particular direction. The monad's windowless existence can function only as long as the monad provides itself with a limiting body to ground its continuous self- and worldmaking. The co-production of self and world in sense is ungrounded, and open-ended in principle, but always self-grounding, which renders it path-dependent or "half-open" in practice.

In Luhmann, the same necessity for a limiting zone of expression produced in previous instances of autopoietic self- and worldmaking underpins the primacy of the inside/outside distinction. Playing, like Deleuze, at the secularizing implications of his iteration of windowless creative unfolding, Luhmann suggests that "creation is nothing but the injunction: "Draw a distinction!" Heaven and earth are thereby distinguished, then man, and finally Eve" (2006, p. 43). But the creative inside/outside distinction that maintains autopoietic existence requires something to orient itself on—it requires a previous distinction to either reproduce identically or diverge from. If "a distinction is supposed to become operational as a unity, it always already presupposes a distinction within the distinction" (p. 44). In place of an ontological ground, Luhmann's autopoietic distinction requires a previous distinction to always-already be present. The "hidden paradox" (p. 44) of autopoietic self- and worldmaking in sense is that it is only supported by the contingent ground of a distinction previously produced, which does not pre-exist autopoietic sense-making in any absolute sense. As Jaap de Hollander (2010) argues in his discussion of Leibniz and Luhmann, both achieve the *Aufhebung* of historicism. The immanent creative freedom they theorize is perspectivist and contingent, but absolute. The creative becoming of monad and system is not structured by any historical lineages outside of them. Rather, monad and system immanently produce the path-dependencies that structure self and world, which can thus be completely undone and remade in every act of sense-making.

The path-dependency of previous distinctions function grounding only if it is real to Luhmann's self-observing autopoietic systems. As shown in the previous chapter, Luhmann's windowless selves are second-order machines. They observe not only the world they inhabit but also their own existence and actions. Sense-making at the border between windowless self and external world thus creates not only the first-order observation that renders both sides ontologically real through this grounding distinction but also generates a second-order observation of existence in the world, and the relationship between both. In Luhmann, self- and worldmaking in sense blurs the distinction between ontogenesis and epistemogenesis. It "not only explains how cognition works but is also an ontology: it explains how reality is produced" (Moeller, 2012, p. 8). A second-order system must cope with the entropy that results from the contingency of its position in the world—that fact that it can always imagine self and world as otherwise. Sense-based second-order machines must develop ordering frameworks that provide orientation and allow for the selective reduction of complexity in the face of these multiple selves and worlds.

Here, Leibniz's divine order resurfaces as one such ordering framework. Religion, if adopted by subjects and social systems, keeps the entropy resulting from self-observation at bay and allows for continuous autopoietic self- and worldmaking, just like ethics or Enlightenment rationalism (Rasch, 2000, pp. 70–83). These ordering frameworks are necessary because the autopoietic self cannot be exposed to the entropic abyss of its fundamentally groundless and contingent existence, which would undo the grounding functioning of any autopoietic distinction. They must *deparadoxify* the paradox of their ungrounded, self-grounding existence (Luhmann, 1988). The question that emerges from Luhmann's insight that subjective and social selves not only produce their existence but also observe this process of production is how epistemological ordering frameworks can deparadoxify self-grounding existence by rendering its outcomes real, and its pathways of unfolding necessary. The tentative answer that Luhmann provides here is—in time (Luhmann, 1988, 2009e).

Chapter 3

The Circle of Time
Must Be Decentered

The idea that time is an ordering framework that we turn to for orientation and structure seems hardly remarkable. The division of time into hours and minutes tells us when we need to get up, take our kids to school, show up for an exercise class or a rendezvous. The order of days, weeks, months, and years locates aims, achievements, and cesurae. Ordering time is neither universal nor apolitical. E. P. Thomson's (1967) work on time and work-discipline in industrial capitalism has shown not only how the enforcement of temporal structuration was utilized in the exploitation of factory workers but also how these workers mobilized temporal measurement to resist precisely this exploitation. The particular way we understand time is a product of Enlightenment modernity whose universalization, for example in the context of imperial rule, is intrinsically linked to the exercise of power (Barak 2013). The insight that time is a contextually particular ordering framework with political potentiality situates the exploration of time that will be undertaken with Luhmann and Deleuze in this chapter. Their theories provide insight into the making and functioning of ordering time. With Luhmann and Deleuze, it will be shown that ordering time is always at the same time necessary, contingent, and self-subversive.

Time is necessary to orient the open productivity of sense and to allow for the creation of stable selves inhabiting a changing but continuous world. The temporalization of sense transforms its open-ended creativity into the reproduction of path-dependencies of its own making, while at the same time ensuring that the open potentiality of sense remains available for every new instance of creation. For both Deleuze and Luhmann, time is the orienting framework that allows sense-making to produce *something*, but in practice always facilitates the self-reproduction of particular relations. The functional necessity of time is the product of the self-productive sense relations that require orientation, and as such are contingent on the relations whose reproduction it facilitates. This radicalizes the political potentiality of time. Not only is the expression and use of time contextually specific and thus politically loaded, but the making of time itself is intertwined with a particular way a society functions and is structured. The reproduction of a particular status quo in time is however never deterministic. Time only functions ordering insofar as it is passing—it is a self-subversive or self-deconstructive framework of orientation. Where Luhmann focuses on the necessary continuity of orienting time, Deleuze directs our theoretical gaze to the continuous collapse of ordering time. Time can provide orientation for sense-making only as long as it is continuously decentered—as long as it is continuously exposed to a rupturing potentiality that can change the order of time itself and actualize a different past that opens new future possibilities.

The Necessary Irreversibility of Luhmann's Time

Luhmann starts his analysis of time with the observation that time does not really exist—at least not in any ontological sense. As Petra Gehring (2007, p. 423) observes, it is therefore somewhat difficult to ascribe Luhmann with a theory of time at all. While time features prominently in *Social Systems* and is the topic of a few dedicated papers (2009b, 2009c, 1976), it is mostly absent from *Theory of Society*. However, Armin Nassehi's *Die Zeit der Gesellschaft. Auf dem Weg zu einer soziologischen Theorie der Zeit* (2008) demonstrates powerfully how Luhmann's discussion of time can be employed to contrast analytical and phenomenological philosophies of time with a theory of time that is thoroughly postfoundational. For Luhmann, the origin of time is not ontological but operative (Luhmann, 2009c; Tang, 2013; Nassehi, 2008, p. 48). Autopoietic systems make their own time. In place of an absolute origin, time, like sense, unfolds from the inside/outside distinction that grounds autopoietic existence. Luhmann's starting point for his discussion of time is the, as he puts it, "both trivial and exciting thesis" that "everything that happens, happens at the same time" (2009c, p. 94).

The alternative, a world of multiple co-existent temporalities that have to be understood and processed by those subjects and systems acting in it would be infinitely more complex. We thus have to assume, Luhmann suggests, that biological and social evolution has produced entities that observe self and world within the same time, even if part of this sense-making involves attributing a different temporality to parts of the world—for example, in order to exclude them from certain operations. Everything happens at the same time because self and environment emerge from one and the same process of distinction in the present. The order of time, with a fixed past and a future yet to come, are, just like ascription of a qualitative difference to the inside and outside of this distinction, mechanisms to manage the fundamental contingency of this distinction (Luhmann, 2009c, pp. 93–97). By closing itself off from its environment, the autopoietic system endows itself with its own timeline, which it progressively unfolds in every new act of sense-making. Our temporality is a product of the systemic organization of cognitive and communicative sense relations. We cannot presume that what we call time has always existed, or the universality of what we presently call time. The idea of time is certainly present in societies much older than Luhmann's functionally differentiated, modern social systems, and Luhmann does not deny this. For him, it is rather that the role and relevance of time changes at the dawn of modernity. Now, not only subjects but functionally differentiated systems operate according to their own time—and they need time to continue to exist (Nassehi, 2008, pp. 161–163).

As an ordering framework, the functioning of time is always particular to a certain system of sense relations—a consciousness, an interaction, or a social system. As Opitz and Tellmann suggest, the particular temporal order of each system is the product of its distinct " 'temporal atoms' . . . The economic system, for example, is a highly dynamic sequence of monetary events. Likewise, the legal system is a sequence of determinations about lawfulness and unlawfulness" (2014, p. 109). While the existence of time is thus contingent on a particular mode of social life, it must evolve with the relations it directs to sustain self-reproductive sense. When "systems close themselves off from their environment through differentiation" they are automatically "confronted with the problem of time" (Luhmann, 1971a, p. 9). Luhmann's choice of words here is telling: time constitutes a solution as much as a "problem" for the autopoietic system. On the one hand, as we will see, time offers a framework of orientation that resolves the problem of absolute contingency for creative sense-making by rendering its products irreversible. On the other hand, because systems thus need to be temporalized, they must ensure that the ordering framework of time is always available. Time orients sense-making by making its products *irreversible* (Luhmann,

2009c; Wolff, 2021; Gehring, 2007). It provides self-reproductive sense with a history that has passed, and thereby with historical timelines to continue—in identical or altered fashion.

Orientation in time requires an orienting history that functions as the "drama of the presence of the past, the simultaneity of the nonsimultaneous" (Luhmann, 2012a, p. 164). Because it is present, but as something distinct from the present—ancient wisdom, historical events, archival sources—history can orient the present. Memory, operationalized as history for social systems, guides orientation toward the future through a complexity-reducing structuration of the past (Nassehi, 2008, pp. 197–203). Memory functions as a mechanism of selections that streamlines past complexity into an ordered timeline to continue toward the future. The primary function of memory is here, however, not remembering but forgetting. Memory selects content to be remembered and thereby orients the reproduction of systemic sense relations toward the future. In this sense, "every memory [works] with a reconstructed, if not fictional past" (Luhmann, 2002, p. 172; my translation). As Luhmann suggests in *Die Wissenschaft der Gesellschaft*, "it is not necessary to know how the world really is. What is necessary is only the possibility to record experiences and (as always selectively and forgetfully) to remember them" (1990b, p. 136; my translation).[1]

The production of irreversible time creates not only an orienting past but also a momentous present. Only a limited amount of time is Retrieved from any given moment. The passing of momentous time is also a condition of its ordering function. Time provides orientation as a selective mechanism for the external complexity that a system can attend to in a limited present. Because there is simply not enough time to process all environmental complexity, the system is effectively immunized from the former. It responds to what it perceives as external stimuli "partly not at all, partly belated, partly anticipatory—and only to a small extent immediately" (Luhmann, 1971a, p. 9). Temporal irreversibility generates path-dependencies and offers a selective mechanism to orient sense-making. Orientation in time is the basis on which other ordering frameworks, such as causality, are generated—in order to locate cause and effect it is necessary to be able to distinguish a before from an after (Luhmann, 2009c, p. 110).

Time grounds sense-making but also passes in relations of sense. Luhmann offers a split conception of time modeled on Husserl's phenomenological time. In both Luhmann and Husserl, time is the functional product of a closed-off entity produced as the domain in which relations of sense can be established, but only because time constantly disappears as sense is being made. Both are possible at the same time because of the co-existence of two presents: a "punctual present in which future continuously and inexorably becomes past, and a specious present which distances future and past more effectively, in which one can remain and possibly mediate what is about to happen" (Luhmann, 2009b, p. 151; my translation). While Luhmann theorizes this two-dimensional order of time for "action systems" (p. 151), recent secondary literature has demonstrated the possibility—and fruitfulness—of a more general philosophical discussion and sociopolitical application of Luhmann's split time (Wolff, 2021; Gehring, 2007; Opitz and Tellmann, 2012).

How Luhmann's two presents work together to make orienting time can be understood better against the background of a closer look at Husserl's time, which serves as Luhmann's source of inspiration here. Against theories that assume an externally given linearity of time, Husserl's phenomenology posits time as a product internal to consciousness. Time is produced by an "intuition of an extent of time [which] occurs in a now, in one time-point" (Husserl, 1991, p. 20). This is the first, "specious" present, which makes time in Luhmann by creating an orienting history and a future that unfolds from the historical lineage created. In Husserl, a previously perceived object can be retained as "primal impression" (Husserl, 1991, p. 31) here, providing points of contact for perceptive sense-making before it fades into the past. This *retention* allows the present time-consciousness to situate itself in the context of a succession of past events it retrieves. At the same time, it constitutes itself as durational unity toward the future through a *protention* that generates expectations on the basis of the past brought to life within the productive present (Finlayson, 1975). Retention and protention are not identical with the multiplicity of perceptions in the living present but are rather selective representations of the former. Importantly, however, this does not mean that Husserl considers them to be of secondary importance. Correcting what he identifies as a mistake in Hume, Husserl insists that neither retention nor protention is merely "a poor imitation of a perception or a mere weak echo of it" (2001, p. 613). Rather, together they institute "a new fundamental type of consciousness" (p. 613) that makes subjective understanding possible in the first place.

While the order of time is secondary to subjective consciousness, its orienting function is nevertheless necessary to allow consciousness to operate. In order to make sense, consciousness in the present must be situated between a past and a future (Murphy, 1980, pp. 110–111). Husserl illustrates this with the example of what happens when we hear a melody:

Let us take the example of a melody or of a cohesive part of a melody. The matter seems very simple at first: we hear the melody, that is, we perceive it, for hearing is indeed perceiving. However, the first tone sounds, then comes the second tone, then the third, and so on. Must we not say: When the second tone sounds, I hear it, but I no longer hear the first tone, etc.? In truth, then, I do not hear the melody but only the single present tone. That the elapsed part of the melody is something objective for me, I owe—or so one will be inclined to say—to memory; and that I do not presuppose, with the appearance of the currently intended tone, that this is all, I owe to anticipatory expectation. (Husserl, 1991, pp. 24–25)

Without orientation in time, we can hear a sound, but not make sense of it—we cannot discern whether it is a warning sound or a song, and neither can we identify it as part of a melody being played. In order to do so, we need both retention and protention. Sense-making in the creative present functions through employing a retained past to produce an envisioned future. In Husserl's phenomenological time, memory and expectation are immanent to a living present of perception that immanently creates past and future, and thereby conditions thought. Within the living present, both past and future are created as relations within time, detached from any external grounding, as the necessary condition to make sense of the world (Husserl, 1991, pp. 56–58; Nassehi, 2008, pp. 69–70).

Luhmann's time is clearly inspired by the immanent temporality that unfolds between retention and protention from a creative present in Husserl. The present distinction between system and environment sets up the temporality of the autopoietic system. As in Husserl, both future and past are secondary to this ordering distinction—with every new distinction, the system writes its own history and creates its future horizon. The unfolding of temporality is path-dependent on the system's self-produced order of time—but it is also fundamentally open because the present produces future and past, and can continuously rewrite both, changing the timeline of the autopoietic entity. But different from Husserl, the psychic system of individual consciousness also holds no monopoly for the immanent production of ordering time through memorized past and future. Because time, in Luhmann, functions to provide orientation for sense-making, it works across and is shared by all sense-based systems, even though their distinct orders of time are still products of the autopoietic functioning of individual systems

(Nassehi, 2008, pp. 191–195). Rather than being a form of interiority, as is the case for Husserl, time is a form of exteriority in Luhmann—it allows subjects and social systems to orient themselves in the world.

Time connects subjects and social systems to the world they exist in while at the same time unfolding the functional closure of the time-making system. It is the condition for a mode of engagement with the world that Luhmann terms *structural coupling*. Like autopoiesis, the concept of structural coupling is borrowed from the work of Maturana and Varela (1980), and enters Luhmann's systems theory comparatively late. Partially in response to critics, Luhmann uses the idea of structural coupling to emphasize that his autopoietic systems are solipsist in their mode of sense-making, but do obviously interact with the world from which their mode of existence is functionally closed off—they simply do so in their own way. Structural couplings allow the autopoietic system to engage with the systems that form their environment as they observe the latter (Baraldi, 2021a, pp. 116–120; Luhmann, 2009c, pp. 99–100). This engagement can take the form of direct interaction but can also simply mean that others are allocated a specific role in how a subject or system makes sense of the world. Structural couplings "bundle and intensify certain causalities" between system and environment that "affect the coupled system, irritating it and thus stimulating it to self-determination" (Luhmann, 2012a, p. 56).

John Donne's famous dictum that no man is an island goes for Luhmann's systems as well—and Luhmann is acutely aware of this. Autopoietic social and consciousness systems all need to sustain multiple and complex relationships with their environment to perform their own function—the legal system requires politics to provide it with legislation, and art as a social system could not function without relationships between artists, critics, galleries, norms, and tastes established in the social system as well as relationships to the economic system. The consciousness systems of individual subjects exist in society through complex couplings with the sense relations of various social systems including education, politics, the economy, or love (Luhmann, 2012a, pp. 57–60; Baraldi, 2021a, pp. 115–116). Structural coupling is the underside of autopoietic closure. It allows autopoietic systems to observe environmental complexity by simultaneously excluding it as the functional responsibility of others. A subject does not worry about the continuation of their bodily functions, about what happens with the money stored in their bank account or about how their children best learn structured writing and calculation because other systems take care of these functions. Time, as temporal order shared by all sense-based systems, even if their systemic times can vary greatly, is the basis on which systems observe the world through structural coupling in sense (Nassehi, 2008, pp. 170–175).

The creative present that Luhmann borrows from Husserl brings forth the ordering temporality that underpins all sense-making that takes place within the social system, but links it to the world. However, as in Husserl, there is a second present in Luhmann, which is equally necessary to making orientation in time function. This second, specious, momentous present is the present that passes into the past and is replaced by the future to come. The creative present is itself atemporal because it is here that both past and future can always be altered, changing the temporal order of sense in time. The creative present, in Luhmann's words, "endures and thereby symbolizes the reversibility that can be realized within all systems" (1995a, p. 78). The second present "appears as punctual" (p. 78). Its position vis-à-vis future and past is thus not one of creative primacy. On the contrary, the position and functioning of this specious present is dependent on past and future, and thus secondary to their linear order. The specious present must pass for the movement of time to continue (Luhmann, 2009c, pp. 106–108). Luhmann's temporal order produces orientation in time—but only for the momentous duration of the present, as the present must constantly pass for orientation in time to be possible at all.

Time can produce order only in time—the creative present produces the sequence of past, specious present, and future to orient sense-making. Luhmann's orientation in time seems to present us with the dead end of another paradox—orienting time is self-grounding and ultimately ground-less. It does not precede the sense relations it orients in any absolute way but rather is itself a functional product of their autopoietic organization (Luhmann, 2009c, pp. 103–104). The order of time that co-emerges with the sense relations it orients is self-undermining. It functions orienting only as long as it constantly disappears, as oriented time constantly passes and must be made anew, but there is no original source from which time can constantly return. In Husserl, the paradox of a temporal order that presumes what it constantly has to make does not present itself because the consciousness of the subject anchors temporal intuition. But Luhmann, whose theory of self-grounding relation allows for no such anchoring *a prioris*, is confronted with the full force of the paradox of self-implicating time. Luhmann, with an uncharacteristically philosophical air, here quotes Marquis de Vauvenargues to suggest that the intersubjective time of modernity both needs the momentous present to continuously pass, and the creative present to continuously return in order for orientation in time to continue.

Vauvenargues's present is restless and limited. It is the time where action takes place as a movement that allows for connecting present to present, resisting the annihilation of social life within transient time.[2] The creative present of actions and events thus functions as "counter flow principle" (Luhmann, 2009c, p. 127; my translation) that, at the same time as the present moment passes into the past, endows time with a new, momentous happening to order, and thereby ensures that the flow of time continues. "If you understand time, with Vauvenargues as the self-annihilation of reality," Luhmann suggests, "temporal binding is exalted to the saviour of reality" (p. 134; my translation)—but only insofar as it also functions self-annihilating.

What we are left with is a Luhmannian temporal order that is self-subversive. It must continuously crumble to reveal the complexity in sense that it orders so that time can be made again. "The theory of temporalization's most impressive consequence" is thus, for Luhmann, "the *interdependence of the disintegration and reproduction* [. . .]. Systems with temporalized complexity *depend on constant disintegration*" (1995a, p. 48; original emphasis). Luhmann concludes that this renders autopoietic systems "immanently restless, exposed to an endogenously generated dynamic" (p. 47). To understand how self-implication in time creates an ordering function that is self-subversive, it is useful to turn to a thinker for whom the paradox of self-implication is essential, and omnipresent—Nietzsche. In *Orientierung im Nihilismus—Luhmann meets Nietzsche* (2016), Werner Stegmaier draws out the intellectual kinship of both thinkers, which is centered on the combination of groundlessness and creativity that marks the works of both.[3] Following Stegmaier, both Nietzsche and Luhmann seek to understand how processual relations—communication, thought, life—can continue without a stable ground. For both, the answer lies in emergent and meta-stable orientation. Nietzsche's affirmative nihilism and Luhmann's theory of functionally closed but creatively open systems are both hinged on the postfoundational insight that historical order in sense and creation in the present condition each other. Both thinkers conceptualize order in sense as perspectivist, self-referential, and always in flux (Stegmaier, 2016, pp. 70–87). As Nietzsche observes, the "form is fluid, the 'sense' even more so" (2006, 61).[4]

Problems of self-grounding and self-implication have a prominent place in Nietzsche's work. He confronts them in typical Nietzschean fashion with a blend of philosophical analysis, sociocultural critique, and subversive irony. On the topic of sensation, Nietzsche (2002, p. 29) notes in *The Birth of the Tragedy* that sensory organs can indeed be identified as the real causes of sense perceptions, but only insofar as both these organs, and the environment sensed, are at the same time conditioned by sensory perceptions (Landgraf, 2013, p. 480). On the subject of rationalist philosophy, Nietzsche suggests that the analytical optimism of the Socratic paradigm must end with the realization that all logical insight "bites its own tale" (Nietzsche, 2002, p. 56). For Nietzsche, the paradoxical self-implication of sensation and thought, of all sense, cannot be resolved. He thus turns to time not as a universal ground that can offer such resolution, but to understand how directed creative production and action can take place in the absence of any grounding that is not paradoxically self-produced. Nietzsche replaces ontological foundations with an orientation in time that operates through his idea of the eternal return. The eternal return captures the constant becoming of the ungrounded creative force that is Nietzsche's will to power (Nietzsche, 2002, pp. 35–36). Beyond a general affirmation of life, the eternal return plays a vital functional role within Nietzsche's philosophy. After the death of God, it is the eternal return that makes it possible to draw meaning from the finitude of things. The directed movement of the eternal return on the one hand temporally grounds ontological order, but on the other hand perpetually displaces this order through its continuous, open-ended movement. In *Nietzsche's Life Sentence: Coming to Terms with Eternal Recurrence*, Lawrence Hatab observes that the concepts of self-justification and necessity are vital to understanding Nietzsche's eternal return (2002, pp. 128–129). The eternal return sets up a temporal order that is self-justifying. Like Luhmann's time, it is grounded in nothing but its own self-productive relations. In the absence of any grounding deeper than these relations of time, order in time is necessary. But because time must constantly move, must constantly become-other in order to renew the grounding effect of temporal order, the eternal return that marks the continuous self-subversion of time is just as necessary. Temporal order must constantly collapse in the event that is the eternal return. As Nietzsche states in *The Will to Power*, "event and necessary event is a tautology" (1967, p. 639).

Nietzsche's conceptualization of time points to the impossibility of a stable temporal order that grounds social life from the outside. Temporality is the effect of an *ad hoc* ordering that requires recurrent moments of creative rupture to fulfill its function, and orients social life only insofar as it is also relative to its workings. As Stegmaier puts it, Nietzsche's eternal return is "a strategic concept" that also reveals the "failure of all conceptions" (1987, p. 226; my translation) that provide orientation. In the eternal return, the "conception takes itself down and gives way to the alternative time of times"

(p. 226; my translation). What Luhmann draws from Nietzsche is the idea of a self-constituting time that does not need a creator or origin because it is made in the very moment a problem of orientation becomes apparent—and always already fulfills the necessity for orientation by ordering whatever has emerged in time. With Nietzsche and Luhmann, existence in sense means not only to "live with time and its nothingness, but also through time and its nothingness. Orientation is the most primary and deepest art of life: to find stability within instability" (Stegmaier, 2016, p. 59).

Luhmann's Nietzschean time unfolds the paradox of ungrounded self-reference in sense by rendering the products of creative sense-making irreversible. But the order of time does not resolve the paradox of self-grounding that haunts Luhmann's ontology. It rather is merely *displaced* to relations of time. Relations of time also operate self-referentially, as creative present and produced future-past condition each other. The self-reference of temporality is necessary because Luhmann's time, like Nietzsche's, can function ordering only insofar as it perpetually subverts the order it establishes, upon which ordering time can return again (Stegmaier, 2016, pp. 105–106). In Luhmann, the continuous collapse of temporal order allows the self-production of time, and thereby the self-production of sense in time, to function as a *perpetuum mobile* by ensuring that there is always order in time to be made. But at the same time, it conceals the fact that the momentous novelty of the present is itself a product of self-referential time (Tang, 2013, pp. 43–44). Sense-based systems are thus "temporalized systems which can gain stability only in the form of dynamic stability, only through the continuous replacement of transient elements by other, new elements" (Luhmann, 2012a, p. 23).

Two points can be taken forward from the above discussion of orienting time in Luhmann—one that directly reflects the arguments made, and one concerning its wider context—namely, its political implications. The first point consists in the fact that Luhmann's ordering time, because it, like sense itself, ultimately unfolds self-referentially, must involve the production of rupture as the underside of the temporal ordering it generates. As a necessary condition for the continuous autopoietic making of sense in time, Luhmann's systems not only produce time's irreversible movement from past to future on the inside of systemic sense-relations, but passing time also continuously subverts its own ordering function to allow the present moment that directs sense-making to return again (Luhmann, 2009c, p. 145). Temporal autopoiesis ensures the connective continuation of sense relations in time. It does so through the constant oscillation between a time that functions ordering, and where the passing present is situated on a linear timeline between past and future, and a return of "temporally unordered" complexity from which the present can be made again.

The second point unfolds from what Leon Wolff, in a recent reading of climate change politics through Luhmann's temporality, referred to as the "latent political dimension" (2021, p. 83) of Luhmann's self-productive temporal order. As Petra Gehring argues similarly, a theoretical investigation into Luhmann's time, where irreversibility is always also reversible because it is produced and could be produced differently, leading to a new future unfolding from a different past, must necessarily uncover "the problem of power" (2007, p. 428; my translation). By determining the conditions under which "actuality becomes irreversible, power governs not only the use of time, but is production itself" (p. 428). Luhmann himself does at no point explicitly discuss a politics of time, or a theory of time that is sensitive to issues of power, as demanded by Wolff (2021) and Gehring (2007). However, he is acutely aware that the way in which the ordering function of time plays out in his social systems in practice affects their structuration and evolution significantly. It is not by accident that Luhmann, in the opening passages of "Gleichzeitigkeit und Synchronisation" (simultaneity and synchronization), refers to the "power of time" (2009c, p. 92; my translation). Time appears fixed, primary, and immune to the contingency of sense, and yet "is joint to the former hidden from view" (p. 92; my translation).

In "The Future Cannot Begin," Luhmann suggests that the orientation of social life in time "led . . . to a series of relief measures: to the concept of system, to increasing interest in mechanisms and in security, and, during the eighteenth century, to the interpretation of existence as sentiment" (1976, p. 133).[5] However, the systemic self-production of a temporal order that supports and stabilizes the functioning of a particular system was only fully achieved with "the economic and political breakthrough of the bourgeois society [that] provided the background for solving time problems by temporal means: by extending the time horizons of past and future and by orienting the present toward their difference" (p. 1976). What happens at the dawn of modernity, as a result of political, scientific, and economic changes, is a futurization of time—a refocusing of its orienting function toward a future now perceived as open (Luhmann, 1976, pp. 131–133). What can be analyzed with Luhmann, although such investigations are absent from his own work, is how this futurization opened up new spaces for economic exploitation and political control. Opitz and Tellman (2014) unpack how a Luhmannian futurization conditions and legitimizes present governmental strategies aimed at securing the future before the fact through pre-emptive military action or mass surveillance. When sense relations are politically and economically stratified, it is not just the case, as E. P. Thomson has shown, that the order and measurement of time is being utilized for the purpose of control. Rather, a self-referential temporal order *makes time* in a way that orients the social life toward the reproduction of the economic and political status quo. If sense reproduces itself through orientation in time, the order of temporality becomes the foundation of political power and social hierarchies.

Autopoietic Orientation as a Politics of Time

Even though Luhmann's interest in temporality is focused on its simultaneous contingency and necessity, not its political quality, almost by accident he sketches out the contours of a political theory of time. Autopoiesis in sense requires an ordering temporality to function—time is necessary—but how and where temporal irreversibility is produced and applied depends on the particular relational system in question, and is productively intertwined with its functioning. Ordering time aids in the reproduction of a particular status quo. But, because of the self-displacing nature of Luhmann's time, it must also leave open the possibility for change. Luhmann is not alone in sensing a political quality of time that demands exploration. At this point it is useful to situate the political implications of Luhmann's ordering temporality in the context of other prominent political theories of time to clearly carve out what specifically Luhmann's perspective offers. Paul Virilio's work provides one such alternative account of the political quality of time. Virilio argues that the technological innovations of the twentieth century, specifically the development of audiovisual mass media, give rise to a general acceleration that spans all areas of sociocultural life (Virilio, 2007, 2012). Within the realm of the economy, value becomes increasingly detached from the materiality of labor and goods, conditioning an economy of accelerated stock market trade where nanoseconds determine gain or loss (Virilio, 2012, pp. 11–19). In *Speed and Politics* (1986), Virilio draws out how both military and social conflicts in the late twentieth century are no longer primarily matters of space—of spatial distribution, territorial conquest, and geostrategic positions. Under conditions of general social acceleration, they are rather increasingly decided by the speed of action and reaction in time.

The new technology outpaces the slower movement of subjective experience and reflection. Audiovisual transmissions set up a new social temporality that is diachronous with subjective time, and places the subject in a permanent state of temporal insecurity. The subjects of contemporary accelerated Western democracies feel permanently out of sync with the pace of events (Virilio, 2007, p. 110). The subjective experience of "daily life" is now "deprived of the intervals of time needed for reflection and responsible action" (Virilio, 2012, p. 29). The new, accelerated time blurs the tripartite division of time into past, present and future and replaces it with the nano-chronology of an infinitely extended "time now passing" (Virilio, 2012, p. 22). This accelerated, eternally extended present does not mean the end of history, but rather "the end of [linear] time" (p. 80) where the present orients itself on a past history and is directed toward a future yet to come. The perpetual instantaneousness of the time now passing reduces "to little or nothing the time for human decision to intervene in the system" (Virilio, 2006, p. 156). The consequence is a radically reduced scope for political action. At the end of time, politics can merely act "choreographic" (Virilio, 2012, p. 56). Governmental regulation can ensure that the bodies and minds of citizens move in tune with accelerated economic transactions and cultural communication. But it has no power, or rather, *no time*, to resist and change the accelerated flow of social life—or even to develop a game plan for such political action. Virilio, only half-jokingly, suggests that "a Ministry of the Times" (p. 22) would be necessary to analyze and understand accelerated time sufficiently for it to be politically seized and transformed to once again allow for meaningful human agency.

Giorgio Agamben offers a different but not unrelated account of time as politically productive. Like Virilio, Agamben views the time of contemporary social life as a constantly displaced present diachronous with genuine subjective experience. Here, this displaced present further feeds into and maintains the biopolitical mechanism of sovereign governance. Time plays a vital role in Agamben's account of sovereign governance in the state of exception (Agamben, 2003, pp. 33–59). The exception that allows the political-legal apparatus of sovereign governance to transcend and thereby reproduce itself from a constitutive outside position unfolds in a present marked as unprecedent. Because the present emergency is without example and thus lies outside of historical time, it marks a "case in which the vis and ratio of the law find no application" (p. 23). Contemporary politics, where governance through a continuously recurrent exception has become the norm, unfolds in a sequence of exceptional presents. Instances of ad hoc crisis management replace long-term planning and steering. The unfolding series of present crises institutes a political mechanism through which the future of regular, safe democratic governance is perpetually displaced by the next threat, renewing the legitimacy for exceptional political means. As long as the future democracy is still to come, the political sovereign must still do whatever it takes to ensure that it *will* come.

The sovereign exception can unfold its eschatological functioning because it is situated within an order of time that is itself diachronous and displaced. Agamben suggests that the event of language has separated the experience of time from the possibility of its discursive representation. What unfolds as a consequence is a chronology indefinitely extended toward a future of re-unification and stability that yet never arrives. In *The Time That Remains* (2005), Agamben develops a theory of messianic time as the time that can both reproduce this eschatological displacement and overcome it. Messianic time is the space between the experience about to become past and its representational preservation for the future. Drawing on the linguistic theory of Gustave Guillaume, Agamben argues that messianic time measures the "being out of sync and in noncoincidence with regard to [the] representation of time" (p. 67).

When messianic time is "caught up" (Agamben, 2005, p. 68) in structures of representation, it feeds into the displacement between experienced and represented present, creating the conditions for its political use. The displaced instance of messianic time is however, in itself, external to this epistemically and politically stratified time. For this reason, it can function as a Kairos, a right time, for "taking hold of" (p. 67) time and undoing its displacement (Doussan, 2013, pp. 187–193; Agamben, 1993, pp. 102–105). The role of messianic time for the temporal order of social life here somewhat parallels Agamben's discussion of the *form-of-life* in his later work (Agamben, 2013; 2016). Both open up a liminal space that escapes dialectic divisions and thus avoids feeding into the relationally self-reproductive mechanism of sovereign governance. Messianic time does not rupture the displaced chronology of social time but escapes it as a representational void where this displacement has not yet been completed, and where a genuine experience of being in time is thus possible (Sharpe 2009, pp. 7–8, 40; Britt, 2012, pp. 283–287).

In both Virilio and Agamben, time is out of joint. As in Shakespeare's *Hamlet*, this diachronicity is the sign of a more profound human malaise with the potential to unfold severe and dark consequences. The time of genuine experience has been dislocated, sped up, contracted, and extended to generate a social time that renders the human condition permanently alienated and insecure. Time is here not genuinely political but *rendered political* through this displacement. In Virilio, diachronous social time makes genuine political action impossible while, in Agamben, it provides the conditions for the self-reproductive mechanism of sovereign governance to unfold. This politicization of time then also renders political the moment that interrupts displaced time to reinstate a genuine temporal experience, which here becomes a moment of resistance.

The Luhmannian politics of time drawn out here sharply contrast with both Virilio's and Agamben's accounts. Both of the latter are haunted by a Heideggerian ghost in the machine. In both Virilio and Agamben, the starting point is a social time that is linguistically or technologically displaced and opposed to a genuine state of human experience. This renders the quality of temporal political productivity automatically negative—social time annihilates political action or facilitates governmental subjection (as well as governmental subjectivization). The political aim of both accounts of time, formulated more or less explicitly, is to escape the displacement of social temporality and re-unite the order of time with the subject's true ontic experience. This genuine, nondisplaced time remains an unmarked space in both theories, and one that sits somewhat uncomfortable with their postfoundational set-up. Virilio and Agamben presume an original order of time appropriate to subjective experience and social life that has been lost in the course of social evolution, but that can and must be politically recovered. Only this second, socially produced, false temporality functions productive here.

Luhmann's politics of time, on the contrary, starts from the assumption that all time is produced as well as productive. In place of a genuine time of human experience there is only ever a particular temporal order created by an autopoietic system that relies on its ordering function. Temporalization provides order by instituting irreversibility, selecting sense to retain as history or memory and guiding the production of a certain future on this basis. Sense-based systems are self-referential in their particular order of time, but they share temporal frameworks that provide orientation, reduce complexity, and facilitate self-reproduction. Whatever is made irreversible in time thus has implications for the functioning of society, its subsystems and the subjects that inhabit it, and grounds permanence and change. For political theory, this Luhmannian time provides the basis for a genealogical analysis that not only examines how the history written from the perspective of a particular, present society is intertwined with its power structures, but of how the functioning of time itself is productively intertwined with the structures that stratify a particular society. Different from Virilio's and Agamben's time, Luhmann's stratifying temporality does not need to be politically ruptured, as it can function only as long as it perpetually undermines itself. If a task for critical political thought and action was to be drawn from such an analysis, it would be to examine more closely this moment of rupture to understand how it can be used to make time differently, and thereby offer a different framework to guide worldmaking in sense. Such a critical pursuit is of course absent from the work of Luhmann. It is not at all alien, however, to the philosophy of Gilles Deleuze.

Deleuzian Time as Circle and Labyrinth

Deleuze's philosophy of time folds smoothly into the framework of Luhmann's autopoietic temporality. Like Luhmann, Deleuze borrows from Husserl and Nietzsche to conceptualize time as the orienting supplement that makes self-grounding sense-making work. Yet, Deleuze's time, like Luhmann's, is also a relational order that unfolds in a self-productive but always open-ended way in its own right. Time in Deleuze is always both produced and productive. The three syntheses of time that Deleuze sets up in *Difference & Repetition* create a three-dimensional temporality that is always composed of a compressed time that passes, a creative time that charges the former, and a moment of rupturing displacement that resolves the paradox of mutual grounding between the first two.

Whereas Luhmann lays the theoretical foundation for exploring the political implications of a temporal order that is contingent, produced, and productively intertwined with the social context of its production, Deleuze's account of time remains firmly within the realm of ontology, and detached from any discussion of practical consequences or political applications. Beyond Luhmann, Deleuze's theoretical attention and his political interest are directed toward the moment when an existing order of time collapses and reveals the multiplicity it had concealed. While Luhmann discusses the return of openness to the order of time mainly as a functional necessity that allows orientation in time, and thereby social life, to continue, Deleuze thinks the return of openness as a rupture with political significance. From the eternal return, the orienting framework of time can be made differently.[6]

Unlike Virilio and Agamben, Deleuze grounds his philosophy of time in the presumption that time has always been out of joint. He credits Kant with the discovery of an autonomously functioning time that "has shaken off its dependency on all extensive movement" (Deleuze, 1996, pp. xii). Such a temporality is "no longer the determination of objects" and equally does "not depend on the intensive movement of the soul" (p. xii). Deleuze takes the combination of autonomy and grounding quality that Kant attributes to time forward. Deleuze's time is not determined by space or subjective thought but rather "prior to thought and existence" as the "milieu on which their relation depends" (Coluciello Barber, 2014, p. 65). As in Luhmann, time is here the condition for sense-making. And, as in Luhmann, the order of time is not grounded in matter or thought but unfolds as an in-itself productive "pure form of interiority" (Coluciello Barber, 2014, p. 65; see also: Moulard, 2003). Different from Kant, Deleuze does not stratify the productivity of time by identifying it as a transcendentally fixed *a priori* intuition available to the sense-making subject (Voss, 2013b, p. 195; Somers-Hall, 2011, pp. 58–63). On the contrary, productive time is synthetic—it always has to be made.

Deleuze unfolds the making of time through three syntheses. The first synthesis is the synthesis of the contracted present and equates to the formation of a temporal habit. For Deleuze, time is, first and foremost, a habit of the mind. Produced "through contemplating" (Deleuze, 1994, p. 73), it generates time as the condition for thought. The making of time as a habit can be understood only against the background of the theoretical doubling of the present that Deleuze performs here—analogous to Luhmann. The first synthesis contracts a living, creative present that is infinitely complex to a second, derived present that can be placed within a historical sequence and thereby automatically simplified. "[A]scribing an arrow to time" (Williams, 2011, p. 28), the first synthesis establishes a linear temporal order that spans from past to present and future. This order of time provides orientation for the mind; the serialization of perceptions in time functions as the condition for sense-making. For example, Deleuze suggests, it allows the mind to recognize the distinct elements of the sequence AB AB AB as serial repetition, to project their connection into the future—and thus to think in terms of sameness and difference, change and continuity (Deleuze, 1994, p. 72).

The contraction of the present produces both future and past. Past, contracted present, and future are all secondary to the relations of the living present that performs this contraction. The contraction of the present is a Humean habit insofar as its relations—the relations of time it produces—are external to their terms. In *Empiricism and Subjectivity*, Deleuze suggests that a habit marks relations that, even if they are grounded in sensation and experience, "act 'on their own' on ideas" (2001, p. 66). The contraction of the present acts autonomously creative insofar as it produces as secondary both the past that came before it and the future that will follow it. The first synthesis of the contracted present "draws something new" from the order of consecutively unfolding presents, "namely, difference (in the first instance understood as generality)" (Deleuze, 1994, p. 73). It institutes a linear temporality flowing from past to present and future that can then function as a general ordering framework for thought. Deleuze understands the contraction of the present as a passive synthesis because the order of time derived from it is produced. Yet, the contracted present at the same time functions as creative insofar as it makes the order of time. Deleuze's time is thus underpinned by the Husserlian notion of the doubled both creative and produced present that sets up a temporal order that orients sense-making (Shores, 2014). However, like Luhmann, Deleuze radicalizes the immanent functionality of Husserlian time by removing it from the stabilizing *a priori* of subjective consciousness.

Deleuze's synthesis of the present makes time (not a particular time; this is the role of the active synthesis of memory) as an ordering framework in a way that is neither controlled by, nor readily accessible for, the mind subject to it. The mind rather requires time to make sense of the thinking self and the world it perceives, rendering this perception as secondary to the orienting framework of time. But this means that Deleuzian time faces the same paradox that we already encountered in Luhmann's temporal order. If self-productive time causes itself to constantly pass, which it must do to be able to guide sense-making, it must also supply itself with an indefinite source of moments to be ordered in time to keep the former in motion. For Deleuze, this is precisely the "paradox of the present" (Deleuze, 1994, p. 79): it makes "time while passing in the time constituted. We cannot avoid the necessary conclusion—that there must be another time in which the first synthesis of time can occur" (p. 79).

The paradox of the present has implications for how we understand the past, which is the subject of Deleuze's second synthesis. Like the present, the past is split. It is composed of the derivative past produced in the first synthesis, which orients the present by providing particular pathways toward the future, and another past, from which the creative present can draw to make time (Deleuze, 1994, pp. 80–83; Lampert, 2006, pp. 20–22; Widder, 2008, pp. 89–90). This second past is, as Widder puts it, the "Bergsonian moment" (2008, p. 89) of Deleuze's theory of time. With reference to Bergson, Deleuze describes this other past as a "pure past" (Deleuze, 1994, p. 81) that functions as the ground or form of interiority to which all present contractions are immanent. Bergson's pure memory, which Deleuze borrows from here, is a-psychological, intersubjective and anti-anthropocentric. Bergson develops it to "correct [. . .] the element of exaggeration in our conclusion" (1991, p. 65) that phenomenology falls victim to when instituting subjective perception as the sole source of time. Pure memory, as the unity of all pasts, is fundamentally nonrepresentational. As Bergson states clearly, "any attempt to derive pure memory from an operation of the brain should reveal on analysis a radical illusion" (p. 73). This is the case not because pure memory does not contain representations or precedes them in any absolute sense but rather because the complex multiplicity of connections between bodies, matter and signs it contains can never in itself be represented—only a particular past drawn from it can be (pp. 50–61).

In Deleuze, the pure past exists because each present produced through the contraction of the first synthesis is always generated as about to pass, but does not perish once a new present moment has been compressed, and has created with it a new corresponding past. The pure past "is the form by which a former present remains visible" (Lampert, 2006, p. 39). It is a creative multiplicity comprised of all pasts unfolded by former presents, by far exceeding whatever past is actualized in any given moment. In the second *Cinema* volume, Deleuze likens time to a crystal growing from the inside (Deleuze, 1989, pp. 69–72). The crystal of time does not project a particular future. Instead, its sheets, lines, and edges hold available multiple points of contact for becoming toward the future (Al-Saji, 2004). The pure past supplies the contraction of the present in the first synthesis with the flows of sensations, perceptions, and signs from which it then draws a linear order of time. It contains a multiplicity of alternative historical lineages that can be actualized in the making of time (Widder, 2008, pp. 90–91). This renders the pure past a creative resource without which the first synthesis of compressed time could not function, because it would have nothing to synthesize. As Jay Lampert pointedly puts it, for Deleuze's pure past "[t]he metaphor of the past as a storehouse is no longer adequate (except for the tale of the department store whose mannequins come alive at night)" (2006, p. 50).

While Deleuze initially refers to pure past as the "ground" (1994, p. 79) of time when introducing his three syntheses, he later specifies that it is simply "a substantial temporal element [. . .] playing the role of ground" (p. 82). The pure past is only "playing the role of ground" because the first synthesis of habit is "truly the foundation of time" (p. 79).[7] While the pure past conditions the synthesis of habit, the past can become actual only through the first synthesis of the present. As in Luhmann, the relationship between past and present set up in Deleuze's philosophy of time reveals a paradox of self-implication. Both syntheses ground each other, requiring the respective other as a necessary condition for making time. But neither synthesis functions as the impulse to make time. What causes a particular timeline from the pure past to be actualized in the synthesis of the present? And how can the synthesis of the present perpetually return to make time yet again once a present moment has faded into the pure past? Deleuze suggests that the second synthesis of the past "points beyond itself in the direction of a third which denounces the illusion of the in-itself" (p. 88). This third synthesis allows time to be made continuously without requiring an ontologically primary source or ground. Like Luhmann, Deleuze turns to Nietzsche to resolve the paradox of self-implication in his third synthesis of the future.

Deleuze conceptualizes this third synthesis by drawing on the eternal return as the continuous recurrence of rupturing openness. The eternal return is not a mechanism of identical repetition in which the same actuality returns perpetually, but rather a continuous temporal rupture, a cut, that reintroduces action and movement to time (Deleuze, 2006b, pp. 25–28; Widder, 2008, pp. 92–93). The eternal return is the "divine game" (Deleuze, 2004, p. 116) of a "child-player" (p. 116). Following no pre-established logic or pattern, it emerges as a moment of temporal rupture that reproduces "diversity at the heart of synthesis" (Deleuze, 2006, p. 52). The rupturing difference re-introduced to the order of time in the eternal return displaces the otherwise "too well centred natural or physical circle" (Deleuze, 1994, p. 115) of time. This "displacement" (p. 124) requires a new present to be contracted from the pure past, allowing time to continue. The eternal return thus provokes a leap in time toward a new contracted present. While the new present can reconstruct exactly the same past from the creative memory of the pure past, every leap in time incited by the eternal return contains at least the possibility that past and future will be made differently in the contraction of the present (Williams, 2011, pp. 22–25; 2008, pp. 125–129). The third synthesis of the eternal return "unites all the dimensions of time, past, present and future" and plays out "their reorganisation" (Deleuze, 1994, p. 115). It produces the conditions for both the reproduction of the same and the actualization of difference *in time*.

In Deleuze, the rupture that the eternal return brings about is both a logical necessity to make his theory of time function and a political opportunity to actualize change. While Luhmann's theory of time provides a framework to analyze how a particular social status quo is reproduced in the making and remaking of time itself, Deleuze's critical philosophy zooms in on the eternal return as the moment where order can be changed in time—where a different contracted present can orient sense-making, based on a different past, toward a new future. What returns is the "disequilibrium of forces relating through an internal quantitative difference that includes both power and resistance" (Widder, 2003, p. 265). In *Thus Spoke Zarathustra*, Nietzsche pairs the eternal return with a second concept of time in order to express the link between the eternal return and actual change: *Kairos*, the right time, the time of the transformative event. In Nietzsche, Kairos marks a critical moment in the present where "the access [to] an untimely creative force" (Leston, 2013, p. 42) allows it to change the direction in which the future unfolds. Deleuze himself uses the concept of timing in jazz music to illustrate the creative capacity of Kairos as the "favorable occasion, the opportunity, the spot . . . the moment when the trumpet can take things over there" (1981, p. 8). Kairos is not the outside of time but the moment where a particular timeline is opened up to multiple alternatives from which a different past-future lineage can be drawn. Kairos marks Zarathustra's rupture of time, after which the world is forever changed (Nietzsche, 2002, pp. 167–169). It is important to note that Nietzsche's Kairos is thoroughly contextual, and unfolds from the particular relations it is to disrupt. The productive moment of the right time is only "right" for a particular philosophical, political, or social order (Nietzsche, 1999, pp. 18–34, 93–110; 2002, p. 168).

Within Deleuzian secondary literature, the open potentiality and manifest opportunity for change that the eternal return's third synthesis of the future marks is usually understood as ethical and personal (Ansell Pearson, 1997; Widder, 2003, 2008; Böhler, 2010). Keith Ansell Pearson (1997) suggests that the eternal return allows the subject to let go of the illusion that identity, will, and action are the result of a rational choices. It prompts us to accept the produced, contingent and open-ended quality of subjectivity to recognize ourselves "as the fortuitous case, as just like everyone else (perhaps as all the names in history)" (Ansell Pearson, 1997, p. 81). Similarly, Widder, in *Reflections on Time and Politics*, reads the perpetual displacement performed by the self-reproductive order of time as a displacement and opening-up of subjective identity. The subject is "caught up . . . in diverse lines of time referring to different subjectivities. 'I' am a multiplicity of subjects living different temporalities within the same, not so unified being" (2008, p. 95; see also: pp. 175–176). For Widder, the "ethical transmutation of the eternal return" is thus "not meant to secure an 'I' who wills" but rather reveals that "the ego, must be taken far less seriously" (2008, p. 99).

Deleuze's discussion of the making, functioning, and rupture of temporal orientation in *Difference & Repetition, Nietzsche and Philosophy* but also *The Logic of Sense* certainly provides plenty of ground to understand time as the ordering framework that allows for coherent selves and subjective thought to be made and remade differently. It is thus not my aim to suggest that temporal orientation for sense-making is not about the subject. Rather, provoked by the link to Luhmann, and supported by Nietzsche's discussion of the eternal return as a Kairos for a not personal but social rupture, I want to encourage a reading of Deleuze's orientation in time as being about *more than the subject*. The productive sense-relations that are ordered in time are not the tools of sense-making subjects deployed at their will. Rather, subjects and the worlds they inhabit are co-produced in relations of sense that are partially located within the minds of subjects but always also exceed the former as the ground of intersubjective interaction and cultural production. Understood in this sense, the potentiality of the eternal return allows for the reproduction of a particular social order—as we have seen in Luhmann. But what can be rendered explicit with Deleuze is that it can at the same time function as a Kairos for social change.

The eternal return does not feature in the theory of time that Deleuze develops in *The Logic of Sense*—at least not explicitly. However, another time appears here which Deleuze, in *Nietzsche and Philosophy*, describes in terms uncannily similar to his account of the eternal return detailed above: it is the Aion, "a child who plays, plays at draughts" (Deleuze, 2006b, p. 24). The equivalence of eternal return and Aion makes it possible to shed light on the moment where, as Luhmann puts it, time is "joint" to sense "hidden from view"—where the order of time, sense, and the psychic and social structures built from the relations of the former are made and unmade. Deleuze's discussion of time in *The Logic of Sense* takes, like Deleuze's account of incorporeal sense itself, inspiration from the Stoics. Deleuze suggests that sense is oriented in time through the interaction of two distinct temporalities: *Chronos* and *Aion*. Chronos "measures the action of bodies as causes" (Deleuze, 1990, p. 61). It is the chaotic present of social life that constantly passes as the state of the corporals it captures changes. Instantaneous Chronos knows no past and no future and is thus, on its own, insufficient to create sense in time, and thus history. To do so, Chronos must interact with the "unlimited past and future" (p. 61) of the Aion. The Aion is the time of the incorporeal. It does not in itself exist as an actual timeline but rather contains a multiplicity of past-future timelines that Chronos can render actual (Lundborg, 2009; Deleuze, 1990, pp. 60–63). While "the living present" (Deleuze, 1990, p. 63) of Chronos is the cause that makes time unfold, its interaction with "the line of the Aion" (p. 63) divided "eternally into a proximate past and an imminent future" (p. 63) decides which particular timeline is produced when a new present is given sense in time.

The Aion causes open potentiality to return to an existing order of time. Its incorporeal nature reveals that the Aion's potentiality is nothing other than the excessive creativity of sense. Ordering time, which orients sense-making, is folded back onto sense in the moment when the order of time is remade. Deleuze describes the Aion in this sense as "the Event for all events" (p. 64) insofar as it encompasses the creative potentiality of all instances of sense-making that are ordered and re-ordered when a new Chronos is given its place, and thereby its meaning, in time. When Chronos is exposed to the "straight line of the Aion there is . . . an eternal return which is no longer that of individuals, persons, and worlds, but only of pure events" (p. 176). While Luhmann shows how a self-reproductive temporal order requires perpetual rupture to continue to function, Deleuze renders explicit what Luhmann had at best hinted at: that orientation in time can never exclusively be a mechanism of sociopolitical reproduction but always also produces the opportunity to make time differently. Change, as the actualization of an otherwise in sense, is drawn from the Aion's "event for all events" in the moment when it is reopened by Chronos. As Deleuze states in *Nietzsche an Philosophy*, the right time does not create transformative events—it rather "interprets" (2006b, p. 55) time itself to draw a different past-future from the Aion. When and how the "right time" becomes an actual moment of rupture that allows for transformative interpretation, and which actualized lines of sense can function as transformative, depends on the order of sense the Aion draws from.

Chapter 4

Bifurcating the Political Event

Having followed Deleuze and Luhmann through the rabbit hole of self-grounding sense, where the continuity of selves and worlds is hinged on ordering time and its eternally returning rupture, we now find ourselves directly facing this rupture itself: the event. There is hardly another concept that has driven and shaped twentieth-century Continental philosophy in the same way as the event has. Whether experienced as the spontaneous revelation of being à la Heidegger or incited by the force of revolutionary action, the event is here imagined as a moment of potentiality that opens a portal to the otherwise. Because the event makes real change possible, critical theory must decipher the event—it must understand the conditions of its emergence, map the event so that it can be recognized, and provide insight to how it can be seized.

In many ways, Deleuze's event fits well within this programmatic outline. Deleuze conceptualizes an event with open-ended, creative potentiality and seeks to understand how this potentiality can be accessed and politically employed to create actual change. However, this chapter will show that there is more to Deleuze's event than meets the eye. The event of Deleuze's philosophy is not intrinsically and necessarily rupturing. Rupture and change must rather be drawn from an event that could always also reproduce a philosophical dogma, political oppression, or economic exploitation through counter-effectuation. The fundamental indeterminacy of evental creativity can be understood better if we retrace the Whiteheadian roots of Deleuze's event. In Whitehead, the event of the actual occasion results from the connective interaction between a material singularity emitted by an object and received by a sensory organ, and the nexus of conceptual abstractions

99

and previous perceptions in which the new evental singularity is situated.

The contingent link between singularity and the nexus of sense gives reality to the event—and determines whether it actualizes change or continuity. Like Deleuze, Whitehead advocates for utilizing the event to resist the "tyrannical ossification" (Toscano, 2008, p. 65) of philosophical concepts and sustain their contextually sensitive potentiality to think the world differently. But, as in Deleuze, such resistant actualization through the event requires investment—here, in the form of a "leap of the imagination" (Whitehead, 1978, p. 13). Luhmann's event is equally built on Whiteheadian foundations. In the place of any absolute distinction between event and systemic structure, we find sense-based systems that produce themselves as continuously disrupted by the events of new information. Evental ruptures are functionally necessary and allow systems to adapt their structures to changing conditions, but their complexity always also constitutes a genuine threat to the integrity of the system. While Deleuze explores how genuine change can be actualized from the connective moment where a new singularity becomes event in the nexus of sense, Luhmann's interest is dedicated to how this connective moment, which conditions any outcome between identical reproduction and radical change, is possible in the first place.

Luhmann reveals how any contingent connection established in the event is arduous and remarkable insofar as it requires a leap that bridges evental complexity and actualizes a particular line of sense. Here, not only revolutionary change but equally unchanged reproduction requires investment, and must be supported by structural apparatuses that facilitate the connective decision on the complexity event. What Luhmann's event unfolds is his very own take on the decision on the exception. While Schmitt, Benjamin, and Agamben employ a decisionist view on politics to understand the functioning of sovereign power, Luhmann's decision on sense in the complexity event is farther reaching. Luhmann outlines how sense-making against complexity, which requires socially developed structures of expectation to perform their reproductive decisional leap, is the mode in which all sense-based entities, including but not limited to modern politics, exist.

Whitehead in the Chaosmos of the Deleuzian Event

No other concept in Deleuze's philosophy, maybe with the exception of virtual difference, has received more attention in the secondary literature than the event (Badiou, 2007; Massumi, 2011; Zourabichvili, 2012;

Bowden, 2011; Lundy, 2013). Whether embraced or criticized, Deleuze's event is taken as the culmination of his philosophical and political efforts, a "Copernican revolution of its own in philosophy" (Smith, 2012, p. 255) that makes rupture, change, and "the problem of the new (difference) not simply a question to be addressed in a remote region of metaphysics, but rather the primary determination of Being itself" (p. 255). Deleuze's philosophy replaces stable being with an evental becoming that can be stalled by economic and political forces but in which opportunities for actual change continuously return to any social order because the omnipresence of evental potentiality is the ontological condition of all (social) life. The incorporeal creativity that expressed sense unfolds in *The Logic of Sense* is evental. Sense is the "event" that "subsists in the proposition which expresses it and also happens to things at the surface and outside of being" (Deleuze, 1990, p. 34). For this reason, sense must always be understood as "sense-event" (p. 22; p. 31; p. 167).

Deleuze's concept of the event has generated a vast amount of interpretations, political applications, and critiques (Badiou, 2005, 1999; Crockett, 2013; Williams, 2009a; MacKenzie and Porter, 2011). For this reason, any reading of Deleuze's event offered is situated in a rich scholarship on Deleuze's philosophy of the event. A first theoretical perspective that can be found in Deleuze scholarship identifies the event as an ontological force of creative becoming. In Daniel Smith's ontological reading of Deleuzian philosophy, evental becoming constantly acts upon actuality. It "extract[s] singularities from the thought flow and make[s] them function consistently as variabilities on a new plane of creation" (Smith, 2012, p. 145). Here, Deleuze's event can function creatively because it is emitted and charged by a force of being that is difference, and that constantly returns to the order of sense in time. All creative expression in Deleuze is, following Smith, anchored in "a virtual object or event (an "object = x")" (p. 22) that has no fixed identity but that perpetually opens order to pure difference, from which it can be actualized otherwise (see also: Smith, 2009). Bowden's *The Priority of Events* (2011) similarly identifies the event as the self-iterative motor of ontogenesis that itself holds an ontological status. For Bowden, the event is the "objective ontological ideality" (Bowden, 2011, p. 46) that sets in motion a process of reciprocal determination that draws sense from the chaotic depth of bodies and materiality and the static series of linguistic signs. The immanent and relational quality of sense-events drawn out in chapter 1 does, for Bowden, not take away from "Deleuze's affirmation of the ontological priority of events" (p. 275; see also: Bowden, 2010). Bowden retraces evental creativity from the bodily quasi-causes of Stoic philosophy to the iterative excess of linguistic expression and finally the phantasm expressed on the psychic surface zones of Lacanian thought. The phantasm-event that emerges here is charged by a preconscious, prelinguistic multiplicity that functions as the underside of sense and allows it to generate linguistic expression (Bowden, 2011, pp. 228–234). Importantly, this process of evental emergence unidirectionally moves "from noise to the Voice, from the Voice to speech, and from speech to language or the verb" (p. 243). While every particular expression of the sense-event is dependent on pathways of actualization that involve subjects, the bodies, and ordered series of linguistic signifiers, these do not condition the possibility of creative emergence as such, which is located in a chaotic, preconscious subsense.

Rather than anchoring Deleuze's philosophy of the event in the depth of ontology, François Zourabichvili (2012) and Patton (1997, 2000) develop a genealogical-discursive reading of the creative event. Here, the event operates in and on structures of expression. It constitutes a theoretical tool that can recover an underlying differential multiplicity from structurally fixed representations to open up discursive space for the counter-effectuation of different expressions. In the introduction to his *Deleuze: Philosophy of the Event* (2012), Zourabichvili explicitly rejects an ontological interpretation of Deleuze's philosophy and instead argues that Deleuze's approach is in fact genealogical: "[T]here is no ontology of Deleuze. [. . .] It is not the univocity of being in itself that interests Deleuze, . . . it is the moment of history where the thesis of univocity arises" (2012, pp. 36–38). Zourabichvili develops Deleuze's philosophy of the event as a methodology to recover conceptual creativity from the notions of causality, teleology, and the dogmatic dualism of true/false.

As "the complex theme of the proposition" (Deleuze, 1994, p. 156), the event reveals the problematic difference that underpins every propositional expression. Evental singularities burst forth from every instance of sense-expression, which the method of dramatization can utilize to reveal an otherwise to the way in which evental series are actualized as sociopolitical forms. What is ultimately at stake in evental becoming is a becoming-different that philosophy must counter-effectuate once the potentiality of the event has disrupted existing representations (Zourabichvili, 2012, pp. 172–174; Debaise, 2016). Patton conceptualizes Deleuzian events in close theoretical proximity to Zourabichvili as "ideal forms abstracted from the specific features of any one occasion, or even as open-ended and indeterminate idealities characterized by their 'iterability' in Derrida's sense of the term"

(1997). For Patton, Deleuze's event is also a theoretical tool to uncover the creative multiplicity behind discursively fixed representations and to express new pathways for thought and action.

Finally, the new materialist-affective perspective on Deleuze's event begins with its relational situatedness. Brian Massumi employs Simondon's relational understanding of ontogenesis to show how Deleuze's event emerges from a field spanned and stratified by existing sociopolitical relations rather than being external or ontologically prior to them (Massumi, 2011; 1995). Massumi's aesthetic event, which can emerge from particular sequence of images on a television screen or an artwork, is therefore not the effect of a free ontological or epistemic productivity but always embedded in a particular sociopolitical context. The embedded event can nevertheless function rupturing because it incites a spontaneous, affective response in the body of the subject, prompting them to view, and act in, the world differently (Grosz, 2017, pp. 38–40). "The autonomy of affect," which allows it to exceed the relations that situate the affective event is grounded in "its participation in the virtual. . . . Affect is autonomous to the degree to which it escapes confinement in the particular body whose vitality, or potential for interaction, it is" (Massumi, 1995, p. 96).

Claire Colebrook also thinks Deleuze's event as an affective break with history. Following an immediate encounter with the world that forces us to think, the affective event unfolds from the relational interaction of singularities as a force external to its relational terms. For this reason, the event is able to escape state overcoding and the axiomatized flows of capital towards a new mode of political or economic production (Colebrook, 2002; see also: Massumi, 2011, pp. 6–15). In part, the political potentiality of the affective event lies in its capacity to create, coordinate, and mobilize groups from isolated subjects. As Colebrook suggests, a "group of Catholic churchgoers on Good Friday gathered around a procession of the crucifix" (2002, p. 46) sensing the "crown of thorns, the wood of the cross, the suffering body, the subdued lighting and the recording of Bach's cantata in the background" (p. 46) is a political event because it "produces a group through an organisation and coding of intensities" (p. 46). The 1968 protests and the Arab Spring uprisings can be understood as examples for such affective events that produced their own revolutionary subjects (Massumi, 2011, 2014; Williams, 2009a).

The reading of Deleuze's event developed here via the detour to Whitehead and the encounter with Luhmann links to various aspects of the above approaches. With the ontological perspective, sense-events are assumed to function ontogenetically. Like the genealogical-discursive reading of Deleuze's event, the sense-event is here not understood as a merely or primarily bodily-physical phenomenon. It not only affects the production of, but is also constituted by, relations of signs. And finally, as importantly drawn out by the new materialist-affective approach, creative sense-events are always relationally situated. However, the event conceptualized here also departs from and thus adds to the extensive scholarship on Deleuze's event in two distinct ways. First, the event drawn out in the following is creative, but not necessarily—and not in itself—transgressive or revolutionary. The existing literature on Deleuze's event, implicitly or explicitly, follows Deleuze's own interest the evental rupture, in how and under what conditions the event can lead to a change of tracks away from the status quo of rationalist philosophy, capitalist economics, and sovereign politics. While not all of the accounts summarized above suggest that Deleuze's event can exclusively tell us something about the making and quality of evental ruptures (see for instance Colebrook, 2002, pp. 45–48), the events they explore and use for illustrative purposes are revolutionary ruptures, or at least the failed attempts at such. The Deleuzian event that is conceptualized here with Whitehead, and against the background of Luhmann's interest in relational continuity through the event, is an event of open-ended creative potentiality that can produce anything between identical continuity and radical change. Deleuze comes closest to explicitly defining his concept of the event in *The Fold*, his book on Leibniz—but the definition he provides here is a puzzling one. Deleuze paraphrases Whitehead to suggest that the "Great Pyramid is an event, and its duration for the period of one hour, thirty minutes, five minutes" (2006a, p. 44). This durational Whiteheadian event looks nothing like the evental rupture that dominates Deleuze scholarship. If it produces anything then its product is continuity, not change. How the Deleuzian event of *The Fold* plays out within a continuum marked on the one hand by identical repetition and on the other hand by radical change depends on the interaction between evental singularity and the relational nexus that situates it. Because the event is enfolded in already existing relations that include truth and power structures, the default position is here that the event will reproduce rather than change the status quo. The rare, rupturing event emerges from a particular relational connectivity of the evental singularity rather than being the mere actualization of an inherently rupturing event.

Second, Whitehead's philosophy allows for conceptualizing the event in a way that complements—and completes—the turn to immanence performed by Deleuze's theory of sense. While the existing readings of Deleuze's event all, at least latently, locate evental creativity in a source external to the relations that the event impacts on, Whiteheads event is radically relational. In the ontological perspective, evental creativity is possible only insofar as the event is charged by an ontologically situated, differential force primary and external to the relations it actualizes. It is not the event itself, but rather this creative force of differential becoming, that causes something new to be conceived, experienced, or enacted. While this seems fairly straightforward for the ontological reding of Deleuze's event, where its ontological status forms an explicit theoretical premise, at first glance, the genealogical-discursive reading of Deleuze's event does not appear to be hinged on an external force. Here, evental creativity explicitly emerges from the excessive quality of expression and is thus effect rather than primary cause. However, on a closer look, the event here comes into being through an act of dramatization that requires the diagnostic agency of a critical-rational subject who "does not simply take the actualized event at face value" but refuses "the common sense view of events as standing outside and apart from the means of representation" (Patton, 1997).

As the agent of revolutionary change, the critical subject brings forth a novel expression that exceeds existing structures of representation and thus functions as the creative externality that drives evental genesis. While this account of the event is closely related to what will be discussed as counter-effectuation of Deleuze's event below, I suggest it is vital not to conflate both. The rupturing event is brought forth through counter-effectuation—it is not the event's "natural" form. Resistant interpretation does not bring forth creative events at will. It can hope to achieve rupture, but with no certainty that the interpretive context is indeed the "right time" for a transformative event. While the new materialist-affective event is conceptualized as inherently relationally situated, it still functions through the theoretical figure of a creative externality, albeit more latently. Here, embodied affect becomes a second, physically essentialized quasi-event "within life, producing the sense of the world, allowing life to change and become" (Colebrook, 2002, p. 51). This second, affective event retains an essentially rupturing quality that is retraced to an original, bodily or material, creative potentiality; it is here that, "the vital energy that is *bios/zoe* gets expressed in all its ruthless splendour" (Braidotti, 2006, pp. 173).[1] The detour to Whitehead undertaken below will reveal a different kind of Deleuzian event: a twofold sense-event where creativity emerges from the contingent link between a material singularity sensed and the perceptions and abstractions used to give actuality to it on the level of sense. It can produce duration just as it can produce an otherwise depending on the particular connective link that creates the event.

Whitehead's Twofold Sense-Event

Whitehead's philosophy has recently received much interest from theorists who draw a nonessentialist vitalism focused on relational becoming rather than an essential force of life from his thought (Robinson, 2009; Shaviro, 2009; Stengers, 2011; Cloots, 2008).[2] Indeed, Whitehead programmatically sets up his *Process and Reality* (1978) against what he terms the "fallacy of misplaced concreteness" (1978, p. 7)—the naïve belief that scientific and philosophical concepts readily correspond to the complex phenomena they are abstracted from. As Isabelle Stengers suggests, for Whitehead, "abstraction explains nothing" (2011, p. 417) but the constructed perspective through which we see the world. What we must understand, for Whitehead, is how these abstractions come to give meaning to a certain reality. But this does yet not render Whitehead a materialist in any established sense of the term. Whitehead situates his thought in explicit opposition to "[t]he evil produced by the Aristotelian 'primary substance'" (1978, p. 30) as the philosophical belief that ideas can be unambiguously deduced from a material actuality that therefore must be the focal point of philosophical investigation. Whitehead's speculative empiricism avoids attributing constitutive primacy to either ideas or materiality and instead locates creativity in the relations between both, which are established in the event (Faber, 2011; Halewood, 2009; Cloots, 2008).

For Whitehead, the world consists of actual occasions (1978, p. 18). Actual occasions are not stable objects but singular events. Events are the composites of the permanent flux of reality, which Whitehead, in *The Concept of Nature* (1920), describes as passage of nature. The passage of nature is a constantly flowing, creative potentiality filled with the singularities emitted by material objects and the natural world. Whitehead could be misunderstood as making an ontological argument about the creative, evental materiality of being here—which would come close to both the ontological and the materialist reading of Deleuze's event. However, Whitehead's passage of nature is not an original force of matter or substance of nature. The occasions that make up the passage of nature are not identical to the signals emitted by objects, but rather must be understood as the actuality drawn from them on the level of perception. The passage of nature unfolds in the process

of "becoming of actual entities" that "are also termed 'actual occasions'"
(Whitehead, 1978, p. 22). The becoming of the passage of nature is "[o]ur
knowledge of nature [which] is an experience of activity or passage" (Whitehead, 1920, p. 185) and thus not independent from but always interrelated
with the subject perceiving it. For Whitehead, events are the singularities
we receive from the material-natural world we inhabit as they are enfolded
and situated in the experience of the percipient subject. Nature, in Whitehead, is nature as it is experienced. Actual occasions attain their actuality
only as part of a connective nexus that links them not only to previously
perceived material occasions, but also to the realm of abstractions, ideas,
and knowledge that give meaning to the material singularities received by
sensory organs (Whitehead, 1978, p. 22). Relationally connected in this
sense, every actual occasion is "a mode of the process of 'feeling' the world"
(p. 80) or "a throb of experience including the actual world in its scope"
(p. 190). The actual occasion unfolds on the level of perceptive experience
when material-physical causes come into contact with a perceptive nexus
that forms the second cause of the event.

If we conceive of the materiality that brings forth the event as one
end of the perceptive nexus of sense, the other end is formed by eternal
objects. As Whitehead's version of Platonic forms, eternal objects are ideational abstractions with an immobile core. Like their material counterpart,
the passage of nature, eternal objects are potentialities that feed the process
of eventual becoming. While the singularities emitted by material objects
incite events, eternal objects guide the direction in which they unfold.
Eternal objects give conceptual form to whatever experience draws from the
material world (Whitehead, 1978, pp. 29–30; Shaviro, 2011, pp. 78–80).
Different from Plato's forms, eternal objects, however, do not exist as fixed
and autonomous but only become actual when given a specific form. This
specific form is experientially developed, and thus also shaped by the nexus
of sense that enfolds material singularities to generate the event of the actual
occasion. Only rendered particular in relation to a material singularity that
demands conceptualization can the eternal object "provide definiteness to
the experience of becoming" (Halewood, 2009, p. 50). Only if an eternal
object exists in the nexus of experience, once it has come into being in
sense as something that can be conceptualized, can it aid in grasping the
passage of nature (Faber, 2011, pp. 11–12). But at the same time, it is
only because eternal objects provide conceptual orientation that a material
singularity received by a subject can be linked to the nexus of sense and
can here become a materially real event (Cloots, 2008, pp. 64–65). For

Whitehead, "the object is located in the abstractive element" (1920, p. 160)—"objectification is abstraction" (1978, p. 110).

It is only in the context of our experience, which involves not only past sensation but also historical knowledge, that the unchanging continuity of the ancient Great Pyramid is rendered an event—as would be its sudden collapse. It is against the experience of structural racism within the UK society and the news images of erupting U.S. uprisings that the immobile presence of the statue of slave trader Edward Colston in the Bristol harbor became evental during the 2021 Black Lives Matter protests—and incited action that led to its evental toppling into the harbor water. The multiplicity that drives the becoming of the evental actual occasion, and endows the former with its open-ended creativity, is the multiplicity of connective possibilities among material singularities and abstractive relations in the perceptive nexus of sense (Cloots, pp. 67–69; Faber, 2011, pp. 15–16). The creative event of the actual occasion in which Whitehead's relational ontology culminates has no stable foundation but takes place as a double causality in the moment of connection that creates Whitehead's sense-event.

Whitehead's actual occasion is a twofold event that has one face turned toward the complex materiality from which the passage of nature is drawn and one face turned toward the realm of abstractions, knowledge, and the eternal objects it expresses. The nexus of sense, which renders the event actual, does not pre-exist the former in any absolute sense but only temporally. It is composed of nothing but past actualities and abstractions (Faber, 2011). Whitehead's bifurcated event thus succeeds in avoiding the "twofold danger" (Stengers, 2011, p. 66) of a materially-affectively conditioned event that is only passively received by the subject and an event that relies on the rationally acting subject for its creative actualization. Whitehead "has taken away from the mind its responsibility for the 'here' and the 'now' of all experience without . . . subjecting the concrete fact of passage to specialized knowledge. What seems to extend from nature to the mind has been referred to the register that no one can claim to appropriate: the event" (p. 66).

While Deleuze makes no mention of Whitehead in his discussion of the sense-event in *The Logic of Sense*, it seems apt to recall here that the sense-event also always has two causes: the corporeal causes that make it happen, and the incorporeal quasi-causes that render it creative (Deleuze, 1990, p. 94). Deleuze refers to the event that happens on the side of bodies and materiality as a singular point or singularity. On the contrary, the event that takes place on the level of sense is a set of singularity-events or "singularities which communicate in one and the same Event" (p. 50).

This "Event," "pure event" (p. 19; p. 63) or "Eventum tantum" (p. 207), is the Aion filled with multiple lines of sense to be actualized. The Aion is the relational context that enfolds and locates the evental singularity to constitute an actual event. While a creative event cannot happen without a change, movement, or signal on the level of bodies, the event is here, as in Whitehead, not equivalent to this change. Deleuze's twofold event is an effect on the level of sense. It comes into being only when sense receives the singular point of material intensity or bodily movement and enfolds it, rendering it actual according to the particular state of its relational connections.

Counter-Effectuation as a Leap of Imagination

In the most general sense, Whitehead's actual occasion is a continuation event—it continues the passage of nature as experienced by the subject; and it does so by connecting a new, sensed material singularity to the nexus that contains past experience as well as conceptual abstractions. As Stengers notes, creation in Whitehead must thus be understood as the relational, and fundamentally nonsubjective, "effect of a world that is [. . .] saturated with cultural artefacts that orient us, giving rise to due attention without our even having to be aware of it" (2011, p. 272). This continuation in the actual occasion, however, as yet tells us nothing about how the evental creativity it generates unfolds, and whether this unfolding reinforces or ruptures existing ideational, political, or economic relations. Continuation is, in Whitehead, the basis for both evental duration and change. Understood with Whitehead, the event of identical continuation, the duration of the Great Pyramid, and the event of change, the toppling of Colston's statue, have the same status. But how does the decision between them take place?

To grasp the relationship between duration and change in the continuous relations of the perceptive nexus, it is necessary to return to Whitehead's eternal object. As "potentials for the process of becoming" (Whitehead, 1978, p. 29), eternal objects charge the actualization of the actual occasion in the nexus of sense. As Steve Shaviro observes, their eternal quality must here be understood in the sense of Deleuze's ideas. Eternal objects "work regulatively, or problematically" (Shaviro, 2011, p. 87) insofar as their excessive potentiality always outlives any specific actualization or "solution" drawn from them. The eternal object binds materiality to a certain idea, but at the same time functions as a reminder that the link between matter and ideational abstraction could always be established differently to produce a different actuality. The actual location and political affect of an eternal object are radically indeterminate. The number two, which Whitehead offers as an example for an eternal object (Shaviro, 2007), can be part of a mathematical equation taught to a class of primary school children—or it can help ignite a protest movement that responds to the twenty-seven times George Floyd repeated "I can't breathe" to the police officer kneeling on his neck. In the words of Whitehead, eternal objects "involve their own nature's indecision" (1978, p. 29). They contain a creative potentiality but never "in themselves disclose in what actual entities this potentiality of ingression is realized" (p. 29). Whitehead conceptualizes his philosophy as an "experimental adventure" (1920, p. 9) in this sense: he experiments with the conditions of and pathways for the expression of divergent actualities. The hinge for Whitehead's speculative philosophizing is here the event of the actual occasion, in which these alternative pathways are opened up. Whitehead's event aims to be a "resource for telling our stories in another way, in a way that situates us otherwise—not as defined by the past, but as able, perhaps, to inherit from it in another way" (Stengers, 2011, p. 14).

Deleuze is of course equally interested in using philosophical lines of flight to think differently, but even more so in the political implications that can be drawn from conceptualizing the otherwise—in actual rupture. While Stengers views the Deleuzian focus on the rupture of the revolutionary event as one of the things that sets him apart from Whitehead (Stengers, 2011, p. 272), I suggest that Whitehead can in fact help us to understand how the connective sense-event in the nexus can become a revolutionary happening. The decisive moment is here the point at which a new eventual singularity is enfolded by the nexus relations of sense and linked to the abstractions it contains and conditions—to lines of meaning, orders of knowledge, and structures of power. This is the moment of the "decision" (Whitehead, 1978, p. 43) over which particular actuality is produced in sense through the connection between singularity and nexus. In the opening pages of *Process and Reality* that outline the book's philosophical project, Whitehead repeatedly speaks of the need for an "imaginative leap" (1978, p. 4) or "leap of the imagination (p. 13) that would allow philosophy to understand phenomena beyond the limits of existing trajectories of meaning. It seems that Whitehead shares with Deleuze a distinct dislike, and mistrust, of common sense. Whitehead uses a negative turn of phrase to describe this imaginative leap in the event as negation. A leap of imagination requires the thinker to negate rather than accept the connective opportunities most obvious and most readily available in the sphere of abstractions. The transformative event that follows this imaginative leap is not the simple actualization of a pre-given evental potentiality just waiting to unfold its rupturing force. It rather requires an imaginative-conceptual move against the grain to draw something genuinely different from the event.

Negation, going against the grain, is difficult and laborious. In White-head, the likely effect of the evental occasion is thus the smooth continu-ation of existing abstractions. In the moment of the connective decision, the default operation in the mind of the perceiving subject is to apply the existing frameworks of knowledge and understanding to the new singularity encountered, meaning that this encounter reproduces rather than challenges their explanatory potential. Against this default reproduction, imaginative resistance and interpretative leaps are required so that an event can actually make us think and act differently. While such an account of the event as predominantly reproductive, with the revolutionary event being "the unlikely case," at first appears alien to Deleuze's philosophy, I suggest that Deleuze actually develops a very similar account of the revolutionary event in *The Logic of Sense*. Here, too, do we encounter an event whose productive force, which lies in the creative potentiality of sense, is in theory open-ended. In practice, however, upon entering the conditioned nexus of the sense-event, with its links to existing structures of meaning, social production, and power, any singularity is always "in danger of being snapped up by its cause" (Deleuze, 1990, p. 95)—in danger of simply renewing existing lines of sense rather than making use of the creative potentiality it offers. In order to actually instigate a change of tracks in the way world and self are produced in sense and actualize something new, the event must be counter-effectuated.[3]

As Deleuze writes with Guattari in *What is Philosophy?*, the event is "counter-effectuated whenever it is abstracted from states of affairs so as to isolate its concept" (1994, p. 159). Deleuze and Guattari liken the act of counter-effectuation to the performance of a mime who "side-steps the state of affairs and "confines itself to perpetual allusion without breaking the ice." Such a mime neither reproduces the state of affairs nor imitates the lived; it does not give an image but constructs the concept" (pp. 159–160). Counter-effectuating the event, for Deleuze and Guattari, does not mean "willing what happens, with that false will that complains, defends itself, and loses itself in gesticulations, but taking the complaint and rage to the point that they are turned against what happens so as to set up the event, to isolate it, to extract it in the living concept" (p. 160). In the secondary literature, counter-effectuation is often linked closely to the Nietzschean task of willing the event or becoming "worthy of the event" (p. 160) understood as an ethical challenge for the revolutionary subject. Different from this line of interpretation, Deleuze's counter-effectuation will here be read with reference to Whitehead as a task of resistant interpretation that, importantly, unfolds through the subject rather than being controlled by it.

In *The Logic of Sense*, Deleuze describes the counter-effectuation that draws change from the event in uncanny similarity to Whitehead's imaginative leap as "the replacement of physic ingression by speculative investment" (1990, p. 238) through the "leap from one surface [of sense] to another" (p. 238). Like Whitehead's negation, counter-effectuation is a negative turn of phrase—it requires active investment and the resistance to established lines of sense in order to draw something new from the potentiality opened up in the event. While Stengers suggests that Deleuze's counter-effectuation amounts to a celebration of the heroic resistant actor (Stengers, 2011, p. 272), I suggest that counter-effectuation should rather be understood as something achieved through the combination of resistant action, social context, and time. In *Nietzsche and Philosophy*, Deleuze alludes to such a nonsubjective understanding of the actualization of change from the rupture of the event. Here, it is not the resistant actor but rather the right time that "interprets" (Deleuze, 2006b, p. 55) the event to create change. Deleuze, like Nietzsche, "has no faith in great resounding events" (p. 152). An event instead "needs silence and time to discover finally the forces which give it an essence" (p. 152). Only over time and through the combination of action in context and analytical engagement after the fact is the event given a significance "that it did not contain in itself" (p. 152). Resistant individual action is vital for counter-effectuation to take place—but not sufficient; it cannot on its own create a transformative event. Rather, whether such resistant action has been successful in drawing "the magnificent gift of exteriority" (p. 152) from the event that allows it to actualize something new can be established only retrospectively. For Deleuze, subjects must resist—but they can only do so in the hope of contributing to the creation of events rather than comforted by the knowledge that they are participating in a historical moment that is already, or will necessarily become, an eventual rupture.

Speculating about what such a counter-effectuation could look like, I will turn to a contemporary event that, like no other in recent history, has produced hopeful speculations about whether or not it will lead to the actualization of different social conditions on the part of political philosophers—the COVID-19 pandemic.[4] The lens of Deleuze's counter-effectuation offers a more cautionary view of the post-pandemic world than these optimistic accounts. At the same time, it is yet distinct from the deterministic, at times even dystopian, readings of other thinkers who suggest that existing mechanisms of political control and economic extraction continue uninterrupted, if not reinforced throughout and after the pandemic (Badiou, 2020; Agamben, 2020). Deleuze's counter-effectuation suggests that a social otherwise can be actualized from the pandemic event—but that it requires genuine interpretive resistance under the right social conditions. In his essay "Present Tense 2020: An Iconology of the Epoch," W. J. T. Mitchell asks on the topic of the murder of George Floyd: "Why did it make such an impression? Why did it go viral? I hope it does not seem cold-blooded to ask this question. His murder was cruel and indifferent, but we also know that it was not exceptional. [. . .] This is not the first video of a police murder: [. . .] What made the images of Floyd's murder exceptional?" (Mitchell, 2020). Mitchell's answer focuses on the affective quality of the video footage, the eight minutes and forty-eight seconds during which Floyd continuously repeats "I can't breathe." The lens of Deleuze's counter-effectuated sense-event instead prompts us to turn to the interpretive context in which the video footage was watched and shared. In May 2020, at the height of the pandemic's first wave, many citizens of Western industrialized nations found themselves confined to their homes under lockdown restrictions. Counter-effectuating the pandemic event might mean locating its meaning and political significance in the peculiar combination of spatial confinement and stillness and heightened digital attention it created when computer and phone screens became the main vehicles for labor, leisure, and news consumption. Maybe this combination rendered the pandemic the "right time" for the killing of Floyd to spark a wave of protests, drawing far-reaching, politicized public attention to issues of structural racism, negating established interpretations of colonial history and social inequality, and aiming at a radical rupture toward a social otherwise.

Expectation and Evental Continuity in Luhmann

Explicit references to Whitehead are sparing in Luhmann's work. However, the passages where Whitehead does feature reveal that the central building blocks of his theory of the event have indeed made their way into Luhmann's systems theory (Hernes, 2014, p. 263). The first important building block is the twofold manner in which the event is conceptualized. Luhmann uses the terms "event," "element," and, especially in his later writings, "operation" interchangeably to label his version of an evental singularity (Greshoff, 1999; Baraldi, 2021b, pp. 87–89). One would be mistaken to conclude from this conceptual slippage that the event is of little interest to Luhmann. Rather, it indicates that the event remained at the center of Luhmann's continuously evolving theory. Events are the basic constituents of Luhmann's autopoietic systems. The very definition of autopoiesis that Luhmann offers his readers suggests that autopoietic systems not only build their own structures in complete independence from an external environment but also "produce their ultimate elements as events that arise at a point in time only immediately to disintegrate" (Luhmann, 2012a, p. 23; see also: Luhmann, 1995a, p. 8; 2009d, pp. 40–41).

Autopoiesis in sense takes place through the continuous emergence of events that stipulate new sense-making and thus allow world and systemic self to continue in its sense relations. "In the philosophy of Alfred North Whitehead," Luhmann writes, "the concept of 'actual occasion' [. . .] was also endowed with the possibility of self-reference (it 'has significance for itself'). Self-reference became the criterion of reality pure and simple, and this occurred on the level of elements that could not be dissolved any further" (1995a, p. 290). Sense-relations expressed in "communication and thoughts occur only as events" (Baraldi, 2021b, p. 88). As in Deleuze, Luhmann's events are sense-events—they make up, and make, autopoietic sense relations. The central characteristic of Luhmann's event is its productivity—events keep autopoiesis in motion. They can do so because the system to be autopoietically renewed experiences the event as a transient moment of novelty external to its relations. In Whitehead, evental singularities have an external core insofar as they are emitted by a material object before they can be sensed, and made sense of, by the perceiving subject. However, the actuality of the event is the effect of a second cause, which is the enfolding of the singularity in the nexus relations of sense. Luhmann's event also has two causes—but their roles are reversed. Events are consistent of environmental complexity external to the system perceiving them. But the impulse that leads to the event being cut out from this constituent complexity and perceived by the system at all is the functional need for autopoiesis internal to its relations.

The event, in Luhmann, is a functionally necessary product immanent to sense rather than a Laruelleian Other-as-One. In order to exist autopoietically, as shown in the previous chapter, Luhmann's sense-based systems must continuously disrupt themselves. This disruption takes place in form of a continuously returning event that exposes the system to environmental complexity and thereby incites the relational continuation of sense. Cut out from environmental complexity, the event is actualized in sense. It becomes manifest to the system it impacts on as information (Luhmann, 1996a). New information is continuously enfolded in existing relations of sense and thereby continues them. As Luhmann puts it, information lends "itself to the crystallisation of sense. Americans would use the neologism 'sensemaking'" (Luhmann, 1996a). In Luhmann, Whitehead's distinction between evental singularity and percipient event in the nexus of sense takes the form of the distinction between information-event and structure, which Luhmann later more fittingly replaces with process (Luhmann, 1995a, p. 48; 2012a, p. 119). Like Whitehead and Deleuze, Luhmann radically relativizes the difference between both. Processual relations are nothing but temporalized events (Luhmann, 1995a, p. 58; 2012a, p. 362). "As soon as it has informed" (Luhmann, 1996a), information loses its informational character and becomes sense. There is thus no "'difference in character' or 'difference in quality' between operation and structure" (Luhmann, 1993a, p. 49) or process—between event and sense.

Where Deleuze reads Whitehead to understand the "special case" of evental change, Luhmann, arguably closer to Whitehead himself, is interested in continuity in the event (Hernes, 2014, p. 263). But in Luhmann, this continuity is more precarious than it is in Whitehead. The continuous return of the evental rupture, which renders the event a philosophical opportunity in Whitehead, constitutes a genuine threat to the integrity of the autopoietic system at the same time as it lays the ground for its reproduction (Baraldi et al., 2021b, p. 89). The return of evental complexity is a "factor of anxiety," "uncertainty or risk," and source of "problems of planning and decision" (Luhmann, 1995a, p. 28) that places the autopoietic system oriented toward the reproduction of its sense-relations in a state of functional emergency. For Luhmann, "the pre-eminent question" (1995a, p. 36) that follows the system's threatening encounter with new information is then: "How does one get from one elemental event to the next?" (p. 36). How is it possible to connect new informational singularities to existing relations of sense?

In Whitehead, eternal objects, despite a degree of context-dependent variation, always pre-exist the nexus enfolding of new singularities and can thus guide the making of actual occasions. Luhmann's sense-based systems have an equivalent means of orientation available: historically evolved structures of expectation. Structures of expectation evolve contingently in particular sense-systems for the sole purpose of offering guidance in the face of evental complexity. They transform "unstructured complexity into structured complexity" (Luhmann, 1995a, p. 282), replacing the open potentiality of the information-event with a finite number of different pathways available to continue sense. The threat of unprocessable complexity is thereby transformed into the task of continuing sense through the decision between different pathways for sense-making. In the presence of structuring expectations, the event does not lose its threatening ambiguity and openness altogether—but the former becomes manageable for the system (Luhmann, 2012a, pp. 138–140; Greshoff, 1999, pp. 22–23). For Luhmann, religion or morality should be understood as generalized social structures of expectation in this sense (Luhmann, 2012a, pp. 138–150). They offer frameworks for how new information is positioned and processed, allowing for it to be made sense of—and thus integrated in existing systemic relations that are thereby reproduced. Through the expectational lens of religion, evental occurrences, from natural disasters to a sudden illness, can be understood as the will of God, and the subject is confronted with the choices of repenting for their sins, praying for relief, or scorning the divine force.

Whitehead's "decision" over how to actualize the evental occasion with the help of abstractions resurfaces in Luhmann—as the decision between the pathways for reproductive sense-making made available through expectational structuring. In Whitehead, this decision does not just reflect the will of the perceiving subject—for example, the intent to negate established patterns of thought—but is also shaped by the interplay between the materiality actualized in the actual occasion and the abstractions available to render the former an object of thought and knowledge. Every decision on the abstraction "expresses the relation of the actual thing, for which a decision is made, to an actual thing by which that decision is made" (Whitehead, 1978, p. 43). While the agency of the resistant activist is emphasized in Deleuze's call for counter-effectuation, Luhmann instead fully embraces the nonsubjective quality of the decision on how to continue sense in the event (Wirtz, 1999, pp. 190–192; Luhmann, 1996a). "One can speak of a decision," Luhmann suggests, "if and insofar as the slant of [sense] an action has is in reaction to an expectation directed to that action" (1995a, p. 294)—if sense is produced in response to a structure of expectation. The line of sense continued through the connective decision in the event can mean that this decision is retroactively made sense of as the rational, intentional act of a subject—but it can equally conceal the evental decision behind divine will, natural order, or simply the experience of continuity.

As in Whitehead, the sense drawn from the event need not be the perception of an "event" in the established meaning of the term—it can equally be one of stasis and unchanged continuity. While Deleuze uses

Whitehead's event to show how we can draw from it the political potential to change the way things are, Luhmann reminds us, with Whitehead, that a world in which nothing changes requires the same evental creativity for its continuous reproduction. Standstill is not the absence of activity but rather the outcome of a continuously returning evental decision between different alternatives. As in Deleuze, the connectivity of Luhmann's sense-event always opens up the chance of change as well as that of identical continuity, because expectational structures never fully exclude evental complexity. The decision in the event remains a moment of uncertainty whose outcome is never guaranteed. Deleuze, like Whitehead, calls for utilizing this uncertainty in a "leap of faith" that makes it possible to think and act differently. Luhmann's theory of the event is not driven by such political aspirations. Luhmann's interest rather lies in understanding and mapping how sense relations reproduce themselves through the interplay of evental openness and structuring expectations, which always involves both continuity and change. Luhmann's focus on the systemic achievement of continuity is thus not opposed to Deleuze's interest in change but rather can accommodate it. Change, understood with Luhmann, is merely continuity in sense via a different path, and thus one particular form that autopoietic continuity in the event can take.

Exceptional Sense-Event and Sovereign Decision

In Luhmann, the decision that resolves evental complexity in the actualization of a particular line of sense is constitutive for worldmaking. The evental decision in sense must return in order for selves and worlds to continuously exist in sense. But which worlds, and which selves, these are is the contingent product of this decision. Aided by Deleuze's call for counter-effectuating the event, the latent political quality underpinning Luhmann's order in time comes to the fore, heightened, in the decisional continuation of sense. In Deleuze, the event must be counter-effectuated to be rendered political as a tool for revolutionary politics. In Luhmann, the event's latent political quality is on the contrary attached to the decision in sense itself, regardless of its outcome. The actualization of sense it performs is political insofar as the particular way in which evental complexity is resolved here gives continuous reality to a radically contingent formation of ideas, knowledge, and social relations within the subjective consciousness or the social field that has encountered the event. The conceptual threefold of event, decision, and

political reproduction is well known to political theory, and closely associated
with the name of Carl Schmitt. A number of scholars have pointed out the
theoretical proximity of Luhmann's decisional reproduction of sense in the
event and Carl Schmitt's political theology, where a particular social formation, that of the political sovereign, reproduces itself through the decision
on the evental exception (Thornhill, 2007; Fischer-Lescano and Christensen,
2012; Schütz, 2000; Wirtz, 1999).

Luhmann himself rejects this theoretical association in a, for him,
uncharacteristically direct manner. Luhmann is "indeed not convinced"
(Luhmann, quoted in Wirtz, 1999; my translation) by Schmitt's foundational
presumption of a static structural antagonism that underpins all political
power. For Luhmann, "a good politics is precisely one that is able to combine a maximum of realizability with a minimal genesis of enemies. It has
to try and convince enemies and conquered to not remain those forever"
(Wirtz, 1999). Luhmann's assessment of Schmitt certainly seems based on
a somewhat simplistic engagement with his theory that might prevent him
from acknowledging a certain common ground between their theoretical
projects (Wirtz, 1999). However, more importantly, Luhmann's postfoundational ontology where the decision on the event produces not only the
political power of the decision-making entity, but rather the world that this
expression of political power is embedded in and acts on, lays the ground
for a political reading of the decision on the event that is significantly more
nuanced, and more far reaching, than it is the case in Schmitt.

The particular contribution of Luhmann's decision on the event, read as
political theory, comes to the fore when we situate Luhmann more fully in
the "philosophical tradition from Benjamin to Agamben" (Schütz, 2000, p.
116) that explores sociopolitical reproduction in the event of the exception.
Schmitt's theory of politics is decisionist insofar as political legitimacy is
here not derived from democratic support or "overwhelmingly convincing
arguments" (Schmitt, 1996, p. 46; my translation) but from an authoritative
decision that provides "judgement by means of the authoritative setting
aside of doubt" (p. 46; my translation). In the sovereign decision on the
exception, judgment "is born out of nothingness" (Schmitt, 1979, p. 41; my
translation). The decision from which the sovereign derives their legitimacy
is the twofold decision on the exception. The sovereign has the authority
to declare a state of exception, and can then decide about the exceptional
means that need to be deployed in order to overcome it (Weber, 1992, p.
12; Thornhill, 2007, pp. 500–501). The state of exception is evental insofar
as its unprecedented, extraordinary happenings disrupt and threaten the nor-

mal workings of social relations within the political community. Declaring
a state of exception, which lies outside the normal political-legal order, the
sovereign reproduces the ordinary realm of governmental authority through
the exception's constitutive outside (Schütz, 2000, p. 118; Weber, 1992,
pp. 9–12). The exceptional event functions as the hinge of a self-referential
Schmittian politics where the decision on the exception invigorates the
sovereign authority making it (Schmitt, 1912, p. 86; Fischer-Lescano and
Christensen, 2012, p. 94).

Agamben's *Homo Sacer* series makes Schmitt's decision on the exception
the centerpiece of a political theory where continuous decisional reproduction allows a sovereign power that lacks all ontological essence to exist, and
to be exercised. The decision on the exception renders manifest a political
power that in fact did not pre-exist this exceptional use of force, but is
created by the former *ex post facto* (Agamben, 2003, pp. 28–34; 2011,
pp. 99–105; p. 127). The political sovereign needs the exceptional event.
For this reason, political governance has developed an intricate mechanism
of ideas, symbols, objects, and bodies spanning all areas of social life that
ensures the continuous return of the exception and effectively stages its
political resolution. Governance requires smoke and mirrors to conceal that
the sovereign throne is ultimately empty. It operates through "an oikonomia,
an administrative praxis that governs the course of things" (Agamben, 2011,
p. 50) in which "government and [. . .] the state of exception coincide"
(p. 50). The exception is here not a genuine outside to the social relations
it is set to reproduce, as is the case in Schmitt. It is rather produced as
such through an "inclusive exclusion" (Agamben, 2003, p. 22). It stages a
threatening externality that can then be internalized and resolved in the
political decision that allows sovereign politics to renew or even transgress
its established boundaries. In this sense, the "suspension of the norm does
not mean its abolition, and the zone of anomie that it establishes is not
(or at least claims not to be) unrelated to the juridical order" (p. 23).[5] Far
from being truly "exceptional," Agamben's exception-event is the regulated,
standardized output of an industrial "ontologico-political machine" (Agamben, 2016, p. 239) that ensures there is always a manifest emergency that
needs political resolution. Agamben's political power functions autopoietic
insofar as it continuously brings forth the exception-events it needs for its
reproduction.

Walter Benjamin's iteration of the political decision on the exception
developed in *The Origin of the German Tragic Drama* (1998) evokes first
and foremost the tragic loss of genuine political power (Benjamin, 1998,

pp. 60–68; Weber, 1992, p. 8; Lindroos, 1998, pp. 76–77).[6] Like Agamben, Benjamin exposes the dramatic production of a political power that lacks substance and the capacity for actual executive control. Like Machiavelli's prince, the political sovereign can only exist as such in and through the "chaos" (Lindroos, 1998, p. 159) of the exceptional event. As Benjamin suggests in the eighth thesis of *On the Concept of History* (2003), the modern sovereign must govern through a state of exception that "is not the exception but the rule" (p. 392)—which Agamben (2005, p. 57) will later borrow for his conceptualization of political exceptionalism at the dawn of the twenty-first century. Politics must reproduce itself as the agent of salvation in a continuously returning exceptional event. At this juncture, Benjamin emphasizes that the constitutive potentiality of the event does not endow the sovereign with the power to fully resolve the threatening chaos of the exception through executive decision. The exceptional event must rather be thought together with "the indecisiveness of the tyrant. The prince, who is responsible for making the decision to proclaim the state of emergency, reveals at the first opportunity, that he is almost incapable of making a decision" (Benjamin, 1998, p. 71).

In Benjamin, there is no one-off, forceful decision that produces the exception to be politically resolved, and thereby the constituent power resolving it. The decision is instead broken down, multiplied, repeated, and drawn out. The final decision that conclusively ends the chaos of the exception never takes place. As Weber (1992, p. 12) highlights, Benjamin does not speak of a sovereign decision on the exception in the sense of deciding what is to be constitutively excluded from the realm of sovereign legality. The task that Benjamin's sovereign faces is instead the task of excluding the exception, of containing the chaos that allows sovereign power to exist but at the same time threatens it with its presence. Benjamin not only questions the foundation of political power but also appears doubtful that its dramatic staging in the face of this ontological void functions in the manner of Agamben's smooth, faultless onto-political machine.[7] The continuous return of the decisional moment is here not just strategically manufactured, as in Schmitt, or economically automated, as in Agamben. It rather speaks of the sovereign's genuine inability to contain the constitutive exception-event through a political decision that can only ever be "temporary, problematic and limited" (Benjamin, 1998, pp. 116–117).

Benjamin's sovereign is not absolutely powerful, not even as the hero of their own political drama that is the decision on the exception. The "state of exception is excluded as theatre" (Weber, 1992, p. 17). But Benjamin's

Baroque German *Trauerspiel* "diverges both from classical tragedy and from the Schmittian theory of sovereignty in that it leaves no place for anything resembling a definitive decision. Rather, it is precisely the absence of such a verdict and the possibility of unending appeal" (p. 17). The *Trauerspiel* is marked by the recurrence of fate as an evental force of accident that continues to threaten every resolution achieved through decision (Benjamin, 1998, p. 137). Compared to Schmitt, but also to Agamben, Benjamin's political reproduction in the exceptional event is imperfect and reactive and reveals the essential weakness and dependency of a sovereign order that relies on constant legitimization in the exception. Here, the political sovereign does not rule through the exception they create but rather is cornered by it. The "dilemma of the sovereign in baroque drama" (Weber, 1992, p. 16) that Benjamin draws out is its dependency on "forces that are independent of it, that buffet and drive it from one extreme to another" (p. 16).

Benjamin reveals the ambiguity that characterizes the functional relationship between event and sociopolitical order. The "temporally limited" (Benjamin, 1998, p. 117) emergence of the event interrupts social order in time and thereby creates the opportunity for its reproduction. But the exception's evental rupture has to be excluded by the sovereign in order to reproduce the status quo of ordinary politics (Benjamin, 1998, pp. 129–130; Weber, 1992, pp. 12–14). Benjamin shifts the focus of the politically reproductive event from the staging of the evental exception to its decisional resolution, which is here not guaranteed, and not easily achieved. What distinguishes the *Trauerspiel* from the tragedy and renders its political symbolism so powerful is that it entails a double tragedy, or a double loss. Lost is not only the ontological foundation of political power but also the possibility of a sovereign decision fully able to resolve the chaotic complexity of the event (Benjamin, 1998, pp. 163–169). As a consequence of this double loss of actual and enacted decision-making power, Benjamin's decision in the event cannot take place *ex nihilo*, as is the case in Schmitt and Agamben. The always only temporarily powerful sovereign requires a structural auxiliary. In Benjamin, this auxiliary is history. Historical timelines provide orientation in the chaotic emergency of the event and facilitate its political exclusion (Lindroos, 1998, p. 76).[8]

Luhmann's decision on the sense-event is noticeably closer to Agamben's than to Schmitt's. In Schmitt, the exceptional event is a tool deployed at will by a political sovereign looking to renew or extend their power. The exception that allows for this political creation *ex nihilo* is here a transcendental, quasi-mythical moment of emergence. In both Agamben and Luhmann, the primacy and externality of the exceptional event is on the contrary not absolute. The exception is here the product of a socio-historically evolved, intricate functional mechanism. It continuously brings forth the events that allow the social structures it is embedded in to persist (Fischer-Lescano and Christensen, 2012, pp. 98–100). Luhmann's event appears only as the "outside" of informational complexity within the nexus of sense relations that endow it with this particular actuality. Externality can only be understood as the ontological quality of evental complexity insofar as it is produced as such within the nexus relations that render the information-event, or complexity-event, actual.

Agamben's reproductive decision, however, remains tied to the big drama of politics—the event that is here politically staged and publicly perceived as a serious crisis in or lethal threat to the political community, and the demonstrably powerful swing of the sovereign sword that defeats the threat to restore order and, in the same breath, give reality to the hand holding it. In Agamben, the onto-political mechanism of the decision on the exception works only insofar as the politically productive exception is also given ontological reality *as such*. Agamben leaves no room for an event that ruptures established order to constitutively reproduce it—but is not actualized as exceptional in sense. Scholarship analyzing the the U.S. Prison in Guantanamo Bay (Aradau, 2007; Johns, 2005), the EU refugee crisis (Richter, 2018), or Gaza (Tuastad, 2017) in their exceptional quality points to the necessity to decouple the idea of an ungrounded, self-productive politics that functions through the decision from an exceptional emergency. On the one hand, exceptions can exist, and function reproductively, in the absence of a singular, clear sovereign decision. A sociopolitical status quo can be maintained through a multiplicity of decisions on how sense is made of new happenings, encounters, and conditions; it can be facilitated and upheld by practices and tacit agreements rather than a sovereign will. These decisions in sense are political in their ontogenetic implications—but not all of them are ever perceived as sovereign decision.

On the other hand, not all self-reproductive instances of sovereign decision making follow an exceptional logic. What Whitehead shows, and Luhmann's decision in the event captures, is that existing conditions, which can be manifest social inequalities and structures of political control, can be reproduced through the evental production of business as usual—the actual occasion drawn from its evental potentiality can be that of stillness and continuity. Luhmann's decisional resolution of complexity in sense makes it possible to appreciate the political quality of contingent actualization in sense. This continuation in sense has political implications, but does not necessarily take the form of a decision or action made sense of as "political"—as executed by a political sovereign. The reproduction of sovereign power in the expressly political decision is but one very specific case of the former. Politics, and the exercise of power that its structures allow for, is amongst the social formations reproduced through the continuation of sense in the event. It is output, not operator, of the evental decision.

Like Benjamin, Luhmann views the evental complexity that allows for the reproduction of a certain social status quo in sense as a genuine threat to the integrity of the relations reproduced. Evental complexity must thus be decisionally excluded from a system of sense-relations to make any continuation in sense, for example the reproduction of political power, possible. But, as in Benjamin, the resolution of evental complexity through the decision in sense is always only temporary. The event must continuously return to allow social relations built on sense and ordered in time to continue autopoietically. In a sense, Luhmann subverts rather than echoes the decisionist politics of Schmitt and Agamben, where the decision on the exception securely reproduces the social formation of sovereign authority (Fischer-Lescano and Christensen, 2012, pp. 97–102). In Luhmann, the decision "is always partial, differentiated, and revocable" (Thornhill, 2007, p. 504) and never total because "modern society can never confront itself totally in a decision, and it can never be brought into an exceptional or total account of itself" (p. 504). For this reason, Luhmann can only be understood as a decisionist "who sought to demystify decisions and who saw the dramatic totalization of decisions as a modern absurdity" (p. 504). The event is not the variable constituent of a political order that remains stable through the former. Rather, because the return of the complexity event that must be resolved is a stable functional feature of an autopoiesis in sense which grounds all social order, the particular order produced, including that of sovereign politics, must remain flexibly adaptable to the requirements of autopoietic reproduction through the decisional continuation of sense in the event.

In Benjamin, history helps to contain the chaos of the exception and facilitates political reproduction. Luhmann's decisional reproduction in sense functions through structures of expectation that order the complexity of the event and prepare the continuation of a particular line of sense. Any conceptualization of the exceptional event—as political emergency (Luhman, 1991b, 1984) act of God, natural disaster, or no event at all—already makes use of particular structures of expectation to classify evental complexity and thus prepares its decisional resolution. Luhmann's systems "cannot grasp their own complexity (even less that of their environment) and yet can problematize it" (Luhmann, 1995a, p. 28) by giving the complexity-event a particular actuality. While Schmitt's exception must be politically acted on in order to function productively, in Luhmann, the diagnosis of a an evental exception itself sets in motion a process of complexity-reduction that prepares for the reproduction of sense. The political quality of the exception here lies in its contingent actualizations of evental complexity, which has consequences for the lines of sense made available for the decisional response. The remainder of this book will be dedicated to exploring the relationship between the evental continuation of sense and the realm of modern politics.

Chapter 5

The Politics of Orientation

Deleuze's "Postscript on the Societies of Control" is arguably his most explicitly political piece of writing. The short essay offers a dystopian vision of life in highly technologized, hyper-capitalist societies where subjects are governed not by clearly differentiated social institutions but by networks of algorithmic control spanning all areas of social life. Here, the disciplinary institutions so "brilliantly analyzed" (Deleuze, 1992a, p. 4) by Foucault have lost the monopoly to reproductively exercise control.[1] This leads to a "crisis" (p. 4) that all institutional "environments of enclosure" (p. 4) are subject to: "everyone knows that these institutions are finished, whatever the length of their expiration periods. It's only a matter of administering their last rites and of keeping people employed until the installation of the new forces knocking at the door. These are the societies of control, which are in the process of replacing the disciplinary societies" (Deleuze, 1992a, pp. 4–5). Deleuze argues that institutions have lost their importance as centers of governmental control because contemporary societies are characterized by a mode of governance that is dislocated and unconfined. This control is technologically mediated and exercised in the form of an automated, algorithmic modulation rather than an institutionally situated subjectivation (Lazzarato, 2006, pp. 179–180). Societies of control modulate the "dividuals" that populate them as mere sets of data without the binding center of a subjectivity through codes and passwords. In the societies of Deleuze's postscript, "control is made of codes that mark access to information" (Deleuze, 1992a, p. 5) and exercises an automated governance over digital subjects for which "surfing has already replaced the older sports" (Deleuze, 1992b, pp. 5–6).

For political theory, Deleuze's account of post-institutional control constitutes a puzzle. Deleuze does not mention the institutions of democratic politics as such here. He uses the term "institution" in a slightly ambiguous way. Beyond Anthony Giddens's classical conceptualization of institutions as the "more enduring features of social life" (1984, p. 24), Deleuze's Foucauldian institutions are complex, dynamic social forms comprised of multiple intersecting relations that produce not only the actions, ideas, and values of the subjects they mold but also the integrity of their institutional grid as a whole (Rouvroy, 2011, pp. 120–124). However, the institutional crisis that Deleuze diagnoses must certainly affect the institutions of democratic politics, whose foundational claim lies in the capacity to effectively regulate and steer social distribution and evolution in response to topical issues, long-term developments, and the will of the electorate. The question that arises is how this supposed crisis can be reconciled with the fact that, despite some signs of post-democratic fatigue, voter manipulation, and anti-democratic political attitudes, the institutional political systems of Western democracies are remarkably intact. If contemporary political institutions retain only little effective steering power in the societies they govern, if they are "finished" in a political sense, as Deleuze argues, how and on which basis do they function and persist as political authorities?

Luhmann's ideas offer an answer to the question that Deleuze's postscript poses for political thought. Here, institutional politics persists because the entirety of its intricate, functional system, steadily developed and differentiated further as modernity unfolded, is geared toward one aim only: the self-legitimation of politics. Different from Agamben's sovereign economy of glory, this political self-legitimation does not operate through smokes and mirrors only: a functionally differentiated politics can exist only as long as it fulfills a certain social responsibility. The particular social role of politics is a steering one: it must produce collectively binding decisions in exchange for functional legitimacy. The conditions of functional differentiation, which echo Deleuze's societies of control, however, render such rationalist political steering extremely difficult. Societies are governed by relational dynamics that are no longer those of sovereign politics. Political institutions lack the control, and also lack the knowledge they would require to effectively govern what lies outside of them. But, thought with Luhmann, the production of political steering need not end here, ending institutional democratic politics as we know it with it. Instead, politics can adapt: it now provides collective steering not through effectively governing decisions but by decisionally resolving complexity in sense to diagnose and identify the state and quality of a political community, the challenges it faces, and the prospects it can realize. The speculative argument developed in this chapter is that the democratic politics that survives in contemporary capitalist societies is such a politics of orientation.

The Impossibility of Modern Politics

Luhmann dedicates two books to the condition of democratic politics in the social present he analyzes: *Political Theory in the Welfare State* and the posthumously published, yet to be untranslated *Die Politik der Gesellschaft*.[2] In both, Luhmann theorizes a modern politics whose social status, operation, and functional challenges must be understood in the context of a socio-historical evolution toward functional differentiation. While primitive societies were horizontally segmented into a number of distinct realms, such as families or clans, Luhmann argues that increasing social complexity reduces the binding power of kinship relations and causes societies to be reorganized. Now, territorial segmentation along a center-periphery division allows for cultural, economic, and political advancements, such as the emergence of political Empires increasing in size, international trade relations, professionalized manufacturing and a developed moral-theological system of ideas. These socio-evolutionary advancements produce differences in status and wealth, which in time condition a shift to hierarchically stratified societies. This social stratification does not happen without a parallel political centralization that institutes a sovereign authority as the political, financial, cultural, and theological center of pre-modern societies. A further drastic increase in the complexity of social relations at the brink of modernity then leads to the formation of autopoietically closed, functionally differentiated social systems (Luhmann, 2013, pp. 27–107). Now politics operates as an autopoietic, sense-based system that reproduces its own relations through the continuous distinction between systemic inside and environment. In a Luhmannian spin on the Aristotelian distinction between *oikos* and *polis*, external differentiation is here constitutive of the "something" that is producing its own sense as political. Under these conditions, the political sovereign is no longer able to effectively control all social realms because these operate autologically according to their own logics of sense (Luhmann, 2002, pp. 72–76: 2013, pp. 13–21).

The particular social role and responsibility of the functionally differentiated political system lies in "satisfying the need for collectively binding decisions" (Luhmann, 1990b, p. 101) or "holding ready the capacity for collectively binding decision-making" (Luhmann, 2002, p. 84; my translation) for society and its subjects.[3] The decision on how to continue lines of sense in the encounter with the information-event's complexity, which underlies all self-reproduction in sense, has a double relevance for Luhmann's political system. It is not only necessary to sustain its own sense-relations by continuously excluding complexity to a co-produced environment, but for the political system, the capacity for steering decision making is also what sustains its existence as a distinct functional system within complex modern societies. The political system exists only insofar as it is effective as society's decision-making authority. For Luhmann, the social contract theory of the Enlightenment, and particularly the figure of Hobbes's *Leviathan*, illustrates this modern turn to politics as an automated, self-reproductive decision-making machine. Here, the essence of politics is now explicitly

> not virtue, justice and equal distance to all particular values, but a particular political capacity to decide, which consolidates peace and furthers the common good. [. . .] The mechanistic conception of the State must further be understood in this context [. . .] The State was only supposed to produce the effects it was created for, and at the same time the allegory of the machine illustrates that it cannot be effective without strictly functioning according to its own internal rules. (Luhmann, 1990b, p. 86; my translation)

Luhmann's political decisionism shifts the focus away from the exercise of power in the sovereign decision to a decision-making capacity that is the product of political sense-making and sustains the integrity of politics as autonomous functional system. For Luhmann, decisions are the means "by which politics constructs itself as differentiated and autonomous" (Thornhill, 2007, p. 504). Political reproduction in the decision is here not *per se* tied to the figure of the sovereign as either the author or the product of the decision. The political system reproduced can be centered on a single political ruler, but can equally be a system of democratic institutions, actors, and practices composed of loosely cooperating, local grassroots collectives—or take a shape yet to be imagined and put into practice. The only constant is that whatever system of sense-relations is being reproduced as political must fulfill the social function assigned to it in the process of functional differentiation—the production of collectively steering decisions.

As shown in the previous chapter, Luhmann's political decision does not, as in Agamben, conceal the empty throne of sovereign power, but has replaced the former: "the monarch is already dead and after him there is nothing but decisions" (Luhmann, 2002, p. 431; my translation). However, at the same time, political self-reproduction cannot happen entirely *ex nihilo*, as is the case in Agamben. The autopoietic existence of the political system necessitates the effective production of collectively binding decisions. The self-reproductive functioning of politics does not absolve politics from the necessity *to do something* for the society in which it sustains itself. Only the way in which politics fulfills its collectively steering function, and the structures it develops and makes use of to do so, are radically contingent. The indeterminacy with regard to the form of the political reproduced is, for Luhmann, a "structural gain" (1990b, p. 234) that allows self-reproductive politics to adapt to changing social conditions. In Luhmann, the pluralization of the political form is the "modern solution to the political problem" (Rasch, 1997, p. 110).

The functional closure of a politics sustained in this way is closely connected to the notion of democracy. While it is certainly thinkable that various types of political regimes reproduce themselves by expressing their capacity for collectively binding decision making on the level of sense, Luhmann's interest is focused on the intricate institutional structures, roles, and procedures that democracies have developed to achieve functional reproduction (Thornhill, 2006, p. 89). For Luhmann, the "universalism of the presumption of decision [Entscheidungsunterstellung] is perfected in the democratic scheme" (2002, p. 86; my translation), where "everything politics wants to see as a decision can be presented as such" (p. 86; my translation). Following Luhmann, democracy "is thus nothing else but the completion of politics' functional differentiation. The system grounds itself on decisions which it has instituted itself" (2002, p. 105; my translation). Luhmann's tripartite democratic system is divided into politics, administration, and public (Luhmann, 1990b, p. 47; p. 110). This division, and here particularly the separation of politics and democratic public, allows the political system to deparadoxify its self-legitimizing functioning. While both are part of an autopoietic politics, the politics/public distinction allows for a political self-observation where sovereign power is legitimized by a (democratic) force external to it, as it is for instance the case in the ideas of Enlightenment political philosophers (Luhmann, 1990b, pp. 120–129). In Luhmann, the "political system is rigorously directed toward the environments created within itself" (p. 48).

As a specific form of the decisional continuation of sense in the information-event, the political decision requires the perpetual bridging of invasive complexity in sense. In order to continue its own sense-relations in such a way that collectively steering decisions for society can be continuously produced, politics has developed a range of auxiliary expectational structures. Elections, for example, are a sociostructural program specific to democratic politics that gives manageable form, and a regular temporal structure, to the return of complexity to the political system. At the same time, elections ensure that evental openness does regularly interrupt the ordinary workings of politics and allow the former to adapt to changing social conditions (Luhmann, 1990b, pp. 181–186). In a society that observes itself as increasingly disrupted by environmental challenges, for example, elections make it possible for ecological themes and green parties to become included in the processes of political decision making. Of particular importance for complexity management in the democratic political system is, for Luhmann, the binary code government/opposition. Within a democracy, all political actions and suggestions that do not fit the government/opposition scheme can be legitimately excluded as "undemocratic" complexity. In this sense, the government/opposition binary also streamlines evental complexity while at the same time ensuring it remains available to charge structural change (pp. 175–179).

However, the smoothly running autopoietic machine of Luhmann's political system has an in-built flaw—and it is a decisive one. A functionally differentiated politics continuously faces the problem of its own impossibility. Its self-reproduction relies on the ability to serve as the effective decision-making authority for a "society that *it itself cannot regulate any longer*" (Luhmann, 1990b, pp. 151–152; original emphasis). Luhmann's self-reproductive political system is embedded in a social context characterized by functional differentiation. Individual social systems are closed off toward each other's relations of sense. This autopoietic closure allows social systems to sustain a high level of internal complexity. But it also means that the functioning and products of other systems can be made sense of only as external complexity and never understood on their own term, which renders intervention in the sense of rational planning and effective steering impossible for any external authority (p. 125). The economic system, for example, has no access to art or education in their own distinct logics of sense but can only understand the former through its own parameters—of capital, competition, and profit. Luhmann's understanding of modern politics is precisely anti-Weberian. Modern politics is here not characterized by its monopoly for the exercise of control—but, on the contrary, by the fact that it has lost exactly this monopoly. Functionally differentiated social systems govern and steer their functioning autologically without the need, and without any place, for external steering. As Vincent August observes, the consequence is an "algorithmic" (2021, p. 333) governance that renders political control redundant. Mirroring Deleuze's societies of control closely, the consequence is a society "in which we are no longer governed by people but rather by codes" (Luhmann, 1987, p. 168).

It is categorically impossible for an autopoietically closed political system to understand the social systems and subjects it is designed to govern, rendering precarious any possibility of effective political steering through collectively binding decision-making (Luhmann, 2002, pp. 52–55; 2009c, p. 332; Thornhill, 2007, p. 511). The issues and challenges politics is confronted with "are unsolvable problems, because they reflect the functional-structural differentiation of the social system into the political system, but at the same time are based on the fact that the political system is only a subsystem in this functional differentiation of society" (Luhmann, 2002, p. 216; my translation). At the same time as the political capacity of effectively responding to the information-events of social challenges is called into question, the autopoietic functioning of politics means that it continuously, and increasingly, must expose itself to the complexity of other social systems. Politics requires the functional coupling with other social systems and subjects in order to ensure a steady supply of complexity to decisionally resolve, which Thornhill refers to as the "dramatic politicisation" (2007, p. 512) of other sense-based systems. In order "to maintain society's differentiation politics must sporadically de-differentiate its own relation to other systems of society, and it must deploy cognitive resources which are adequate to the internal communications of a plurality of different social systems" (p. 512).

Autopoietic politics reproduces itself through a programmatic overburdening that endangers exactly those connective decisions through which it functionally persists (Clam, 2006). Having little effective political control, it politicizes everything it comes into contact with—turning everything into an opportunity for demonstrating decisional steering capacity. Democratic politics at the end of the twentieth century, which Luhmann, from a distinctly German perspective, captures with the label of the welfare state, functions according to "the sociological principle of *inclusion*" (1990b, p. 34). In the absence of effective steering capacity, politics precariously "secures its autopoiesis through the re-definition of unsolvable problems. There is certainly always something to do" (p. 34). The introversive politicization that politics performs in order to continuously demonstrate its collective steering capacity increases the need for complexity-reducing programs and codes. Contemporary politics thus marks "a self-reflexive condition of politics itself, in which the political system maximizes its own ability to address its own constantly escalating complexity" (Thornhill, 2006, p. 97).

The evolution, and evolutionary adaption, of self-reproductive modern politics is illustrated powerfully by Luhmann's analysis of power. For Luhmann, power is a symbolically generalized medium of communication whose expression is particular to politics. Other examples for such symbolically generalized media of communication that play a key role for their respective functionally differentiated system are money, scientific truth, and love (Baraldi, 2021c, pp. 229–233). All symbolically generalized media render sense-expression understandable with the help of a binary code, which is here the distinction between legitimate power, prompting acceptance, and the use of illegitimate power, inciting resistance and a reproduction of political authority along different lines (Thornhill, 2006). Where programs and codes reduce complexity to render the decision in sense possible, the medium of power completes its expression by ensuring it is received and understood by those governed (Luhmann, 2002, pp. 11–15; 2012b, pp. 18–27). A number of secondary readings focus on the expressive, relational quality of Luhmann's power as a starting point to draw out its parallels to the Foucauldian iteration of the concept (August, 2021; Borch, 2005; Opitz, 2013).[4] Like Foucault, Luhmann objects to understanding power as an actor capacity with a pre-given ontological essence and emphasizes that power exists only insofar as it functions productively (Borch, 2005, pp. 156–159).

Within an autopoietically closed political system, the productive capacity of power is oriented toward self-reproduction: power expresses, and thereby reproduces, the decision-making authority of politics. The political sovereign does to *have* power—but is on the contrary bound and limited by its workings. Power "does not instrumentalize [instrumentiert] a pre-existent will, it only produces this will and it can obligate it, bind it, can make it absorb insecurities and risks, can even tempt it and make it fail" (Luhmann, 2002, p. 29). At the same time, like Foucault, Luhmann insists on the materially real quality of an expressed power that is "not just an analytical summary" (Luhmann, 2012b, p. 20). For Luhmann, the exercise of violence, or at least the threat of the former, has historically been the most effective way to express politically reproductive power. But social evolution, and particularly the completion of functional differentiation, does not leave a medium of power, which is "ambiguous and fluctuating 'by nature' " (p. 52), unaffected. Luhmann mirrors Foucault closely when he argues that as modern societies evolve, power shifts away from a mode of direct exercise on the body of the governed and becomes increasingly depersonalized and symbolic (pp. 45–55), or technologized (Baraldi, 2021c, p. 233). The programs and codes of the democratic system now organize the distinction between legitimate and illegitimate power, and facilitate the transition from one to the other. Mirroring the evolution of democratic politics toward Luhmann's welfare state of the late twentieth century, the medium of power is forced to continuously extend its boundaries and incorporate more and more themes (Luhmann, 2002, pp. 128–130).

On the one hand, this extension can be seen as an increase in scope for a power now strongly reminiscent of Foucault's governmentality, operating as a politics of life that spans all areas of society. In Luhmann's late modern societies, "welfare provisions provide regular forms of assistance that incorporate people into a system of social advantages, then the possibilities of negative sanction in the form of the potential power of withdrawal of such advantages grow" (Ashenden, 2006, p. 138). On the other hand, the power of Luhmann's welfare state "operates in a diffuse and productive manner, and is not amenable to centralized control" (p. 138). The functionally necessary reactivity of the political system diffuses the medium of power. August speaks here of an "inflation" (2021, p. 338) of power that decreases its societal value. As Luhmann puts it, "the symbiosis of environmental sensitivity and the practice of power—i.e., the unlimited capacity to politicize themes—becomes a problem with a new kind of urgency. The ruler cannot in fact care about everything. Absolute power is little power. Autonomized, underdetermined, self-determining political power is dangerous in an entirely different way" (Luhmann, 1990b, p. 140)—it endangers the self-reproduction of politics mediated by power.

The perpetual widening of the political system's decisional scope, paralleled by its declining ability for effective decisional steering, throws the expectational structures of the political system into a loop. The codes it is comprised of—power/powerlessness for political actors or organizations, progressive/conservative for political parties, legitimate/illegitimate for decisions—are multiple, increasingly variable, and increasingly unsuccessful in communicating the message of an effectively governing political sovereign (August, 2021, p. 335). Politics is society's problem-solving system. It fulfills its responsibility of "uncertainty absorption" (Luhmann, 1993, p. 530) through the provision of collectively binding decisions for society. But exactly this message is no longer expressed and understood unambiguously by those governed. Luhmann dismisses the governmental powers of politics in the welfare state with uncharacteristically strong words. Any "attempt to downplay this problem with self-deception and the deception" (1990b, p. 114) on the part of politics is, for Luhmann, "illusory. Its style of practice fools no one" (p. 114).

The effect that Luhmann prophesizes seems to describe the context of twenty-first-century politics aptly: society is characterized by a decline of trust in the political system. In the "political system's public . . . skepticism about the possibilities of forming a politics is widespread" (Luhmann, 1990b, p. 114). Declining trust in the effectiveness of political governance, together with an unresolved, high level of uncertainty that follows from manifest, publicly recognized governmental failures, impedes socially reproductive processes of sense-making/worldmaking (Luhmann, 1993b, pp. 530–531, 538–539; 2002, pp. 67–68; Brunczel, 2010, pp. 168–170; Clam, 2006, pp. 145–147). The "narrow scope of the at all possible" (Luhmann, 2002, p. 102; my translation) effective governance "relocates politics to predominantly verbal conflicts which only accidentally lead to creative innovations" (p. 102; my translation). As a consequence, many "political concerns and interests thus remain unrepresented . . . and seek out alternative means of expression, or fall into the apathy feared particularly by democrats, which can, if at all, only be reinvigorated with exaggerated rhetoric" (p. 102; my translation). The radical structural contingency of Luhmann's self-reproductive politics, which includes the political expression of power itself, however means that the story of modern political power does not have to end in continuous decline. Luhmann's autopoietic politics can adapt to the increasingly visible impossibility of producing collectively binding decisions over matters and for parts of society that it can neither know nor steer. Luhmann himself does not flesh out a political theory *beyond the welfare state* and for twenty-first-century societies of control—but his theory offers us a glimpse of the former.

Marxist Interlude

Before further investigating the functioning of autopoietic politics in societies of control, we should pause briefly to ask, how did we get here in the first place? As shown above, Luhmann views the autopoietic closure of politics as the contingent but irrevocable consequence of the particular social evolution that is functional differentiation. But there is another way of telling the same story—one that reveals, and renders usable, what Laurindo Dias Minhoto identifies as a "crypto-normative pretension" (2017, p. 63) in Luhmann's theory. It is directed against, I suggest with Dias Minhoto, advanced capitalism or neoliberalism not as an economic model but as a form of social relation that has become generalized beyond its economic location of origin in late modern societies. The social relation of capitalism is, I suggest, the "elephant in the room" of Luhmann's theory of functional differentiation.

As laid out in the Introduction, Luhmann can, if at all, be only cautiously identified as a critical thinker. At all times he retained a mocking attitude toward what he described as "the muscly metaphysics of materialism" (Luhmann, 1991c, p. 91), especially the historical materialism of the Frankfurt School kind, which Luhmann rejects not for its political implications, but rather for lacking in theoretical radicality and creativity (1990b, p. 28). However, a small body of scholarship has drawn out parallels in the way Marx and Luhmann imagine the functioning of the societies that they live in and analyze. In both thinkers, history and productive distinction form important component parts of their theoretical frameworks. Both imagine social life as ordered by self-reproductive structures and as ultimately directed toward the maintenance of a certain status quo (Pahl, 2008; Thornhill, 2013; Hessinger, 2015; Prien, 2013; Renner, 2013). Luhmann justifies his commitment to the discipline of sociology with a reference to Ricœur's masters of suspicion: Nietzsche, Freud, and Marx. For Luhmann, they embody the sociological commitment to move beyond an ontological level of analysis and reveal the productive mechanisms that lie behind, and work through, ontological statements (Luhmann, 2009a, pp. 14–20, 68–82).

In *Observations on Modernity*, Luhmann himself speaks surprisingly favorably of the theoretical purchase of Marx's thought, albeit that the thinker would need to be re-imagined as a "non-Marxist Marx" (1998, p. 7) stripped of, one can only assume, the radical political implications of his ideas. For Luhmann, the central achievement of Marx's theory is that it reveals the socio-evolutionary contingency of a capitalism that is only necessary insofar as it continuously produces its own necessity for the social relations it is embedded in. Marx's political economy performs

> the shift of a knowledge previously justified through nature to a social context. The economic order of capitalism does not, according to Marx, follow a natural economic action with an innate trend toward individual and collective rationality. It is,

rather, a social construct. The reference to nature is presented as "reification"; that is, it is analyzed as a moment of social construction. Economic theory's claim to represent an extrasocial objectivity is contested. It only reflects the logic of a social construct. (Luhmann, 1998, p. 8)

Both Luhmann and Marx are not just interested in describing the social status quo they observe but also want to understand its particular historical evolution (Pahl, 2008, pp. 113–115). In Marx, history unfolds in four stages from a primitive society to antique and medieval classed societies and finally industrial capitalism. Luhmann's socio-historic evolution toward functional differentiation shares a significant common ground with Marx's materialist history. In his *Theory of Society*, Luhmann divides the history of functionally differentiated, Western industrialized societies into four distinct stages: segmented societies, societies characterized by a center-periphery differentiation, hierarchically stratified societies, and functionally differentiated societies. To be clear, what characterizes a particular historical stage and provokes evolution is not the state of material production or distribution in Luhmann. Rather, decisive is here how social relations are organized, and through which inside/outside distinctions they reproduce themselves (Baraldi, 2021d, pp. 66–68; Luhmann, 2013, pp. 7–12).

However, somewhat through the backdoor, Luhmann seems to reintroduce the state of economic development as a decisive factor for the shift from one form of social organization to the next. While discussed comparatively little for horizontally segmented societies, the economic realm appears to become more central in the transition to hierarchically stratified societies. While Luhmann suggests that "current status of research leaves it open" (2013, p. 52) to what extent we are to understand economic advancements as causes for sociopolitical evolution, he attributes significant importance to economic factors in rendering the reciprocal relations of segmented societies one-directional, leading to the establishment of fixed social hierarchies (pp. 52–54). A further leap in social complexity then leads to the differentiation of society into epistemologically segmented functional realms whose relationality of sense becomes unprocessable for any central authority. As Otto Bode (2000) points out in his economically situated analysis of Luhmann's theory, the functional logic of the autopoietic system is that of the liberal *homo economicus*. Both are machines that use particular codes to ensure that their diagrammatic relations operate toward whatever constitutes functional gain—for Luhmann's system, this gain is not financial profit but autopoietic existence (Bode, 2000, p. 184).

Luhmann himself never explicitly states that the logic of functional differentiation is capitalist. However, he does liken functional differentiation to a "division of labour" (Luhmann, 1984, p. 65) between different social systems for the purposed of increased efficiency, which clearly echoes the theoretical foundations of capitalism in the works of Adam Smith and David Ricardo. Luhmann's functional differentiation constitutes a shift from the primacy of the political to a primacy of the economic. The economic realm thus holds a particularly influential position with regard to how sense is made in functionally differentiated contemporary societies (Barben, 1996, p. 128; Schimank, 2015). In Marx, capitalism is marked by the extension of the functional logic of capital to the whole of society. Something similar seems to be underpinning Luhmann's functional differentiation—society becomes divided into functional realms with respectively increased performance. Atomistically detached from their environment, these functional realms solely operate toward their own goals.[5] Beneath its alien, technical language and conceptual framing, Luhmann's theory of functional differentiation produces an account of society under the conditions of advanced, industrialized capitalism with its "underlying processes of rationalization and commodification" (Dias Minhoto, 2017, p. 57) that "configure a social context marked by a deepening of the forced division of labour, the spreading of the inversion of means and ends, the crystallization of systemic blind tautologies and colonizations" (p. 57.).

In Luhmann, money is just one form that the reproductive medium of sense can take, and that is particular to the economic system. Politics, for example, reproduces itself in the expression of power, and science through the medium of truth. While Luhmann rejects a theoretical focus on capital and its reproduction as reductionist, I suggest this rejection is based on Luhmann's own, reductionist understanding of Marx's capital (Luhmann, 1990b, pp. 68–69). Under the conditions of capitalism, capital, in Marx, is not just a medium of transaction—it is the operational mode of social relations. In the *Grundrisse*, Marx identifies three distinct functions of money in pre-capitalist societies. Money is first a measurement for the value of a particular commodity. Second, it is a medium through which exchange can take place to generate value, and third a means of aggregating wealth—but, importantly, not yet of increasing value through aggregation (Marx, 1973, pp. 221–224). All three forms of money have in common a certain quantitative limitation. Even though use and value fluctuate with social conditions, money is materially limited, both by the availability of the material it is made from, such as gold, or by the labor necessary to produce the commodity for which it is exchanged (Paulani, 2014, pp. 282–286; Choat, 2016, pp. 67–73).

This material limitation is suspended when the commodity is fully replaced by its price and, together with its use-value, detaches financial transfer from the process of economic production. The gradual expulsion of money's material basis "is precisely what makes it autonomous from circulation" (Paulani, 2014, p. 287). Capital now operates through self-valorization, reorganizing the social function of money according to its self-reproductive logic (Marx, 2000, pp. 556–557; Nelson, 1999, pp. 117–119). In Marx, the shift toward capitalism is thus not merely a change in the mode of economic production. Capitalist circulation rather fundamentally alters the functioning of social life. Capital relations, no longer bound to material conditions of production or exchange that fix the value of the circulated money, are characterized by nothing but their own capacity for self-production—they reproduce capital as a relationality able to constantly integrate new events in its internal logic (Nelson, 1999, pp. 104–109). Marx captures the unbound, totalized, and self-productive functionality of capital with his concept of fictitious capital. Fictitious capital is devoid of any external basis and limit, and directed by nothing but its internal logic of self-production. Fictitious capital "is everything that isn't capital, wasn't capital and will not be capital but works as such" (Paulani, 2014, p. 291) and renders everything consumable in the process of capitalization (Choat, 2016, pp. 83–84). Under capitalism, capital, for Marx, is first and foremost a mode of organizing social relations. Everything produced under the conditions of capitalism must be understood as produced from "a specific relation of capital to itself" (Marx, 1973, p. 259).

Marx's capital indeed functions analogous to Luhmann's autopoietic sense: both are the medium in which all social relations are expressed, both operate self-reproductively, and both do so by introversively embedding all novelty encountered into their own particular logic. Marx's capital relations and Luhmann's sense relations reproduce themselves by independently generating the elements necessary for their reproduction, and thereby also create their own flexible and constantly widening limits. Marx's famous image of capital as a vampire must be understood in this sense. Capital persists through constantly interiorizing something from its environment. It "only lives by sucking living labour, and lives the more, the more labour it sucks" (Marx, 1976, p. 342; see also: 367). But Luhmann's autopoietic systems are equally vampiric. Their reproduction relies on their ability to continuously internalize the new information they are exposed to in the event.

For Luhmann's political system, this vampiric functioning holds true in a more specific sense. Because it's autopoiesis is tied to its capacity to provide orientation on all collective issues that emerge within a particular society, a self-reproductive politics must expose itself to ever-new social complexity, must introversively absorb ever new aspects of society in order to persist in its collectively steering function. But Luhmann, more than Marx, draws attention to the vulnerability of the vampiric system. The failure to internalize constitutes a permanent, existential threat for the vampiric system. Marx's capital relations are endangered when they no longer have anything to extend themselves to and financialize—markets, industries, or bodies. Luhmann's autopoietic system, and particularly his overburdened politics of the welfare state, is lethally threatened when it no longer succeeds at coding and reducing complexity.

Marx's capital operates dialectically—its reproduction necessitates a constitutive difference. The totalized unity of capital must produce its own outside from which it can differentiate itself (Kurz, 2012, pp. 52–53). In his fourth thesis on Feuerbach, Marx criticizes Feuerbach's assumption of a pre-given split of the world into a material and a spiritual sphere. For Marx, both the worldly-material sphere and the theological-normative "realm in the clouds" (2000, p. 172) are rather co-produced through a constitutive disruption of the material-social world, a contingent and artificial splitting-in-two (Jal, 2009, pp. 223–224; Nelson, 1999, p. 7). When money becomes capital, it ceases to be the representation of a fixed material value and instead autologically produces value. Capital's self-productivity is deparadoxified through an analogous splitting-in-two that allows capital to differentiate itself from a theological, political, or normative outside which it in fact co-produces. In this sense, the self-reproduction of capital in Marx takes place "via a *Umweg*, a detour that is built on the schizophrenic characteristics of capitalism: the individual and the social, the subject and the object, use-values and value, the material and the ideal, the concrete and the abstract" (Jal, 1994, p. 224).

Marx's reproductive splitting between material base and ideological superstructure functions equivalently to the constitutive system/environment distinction that grounds autopoietic world- and self-making in Luhmann. Like Marx's societies, Luhmann's systems reproduce themselves through the dialectic distinction between system and environment. In both Marx and Luhmann, the reproductive split conceals its own contingency by ontologizing the distinction it produces. As Dias Minhoto observes, "the way in which the system-environment relationship presents itself in Luhmann seems to configure a very special type of real abstraction, i.e., one that does not merely run along the lines of the real abstraction of the commodity-form"

(2017, p. 60) but aims "to preserve a non-identity" (p. 60) of a different kind. This non-identity is that of the autopoietic system produced through the constitutive split between materiality and ideas which, reproduces the capitalist society as a self-observing system (Pahl, 2008, pp. 47–50).

The strong family resemblance between the social conditions of Marx's capitalism and Luhmann's functional differentiation certainly does not render Luhmann a critical thinker. However, there is a certain critical potential to the way Luhmann approaches functional differentiation. Like Marx's analysis of capitalism, Luhmann's theory of functional differentiation is motivated by an interest in revealing the fundamental contingency of the system reproduced. For this reason, even if social theory might discard all other Marxist ideas, Luhmann insists that it should "keep this and proceed with Marx" (1998, p. 8): "the capitalistic economy is founded not on an extrasocial objectivity but rather on itself, and that all references to interests, needs, necessities, or advantages of rationality are internal references to external situations" (p. 8). For Luhmann, different from Marx, there can be no revolutionary big bang that overcomes functional differentiation—and it is not clear whether Luhmann would even regard the end of functional differentiation as something to be wished for.

But on the inside, functional differentiation, the way individual systems operate and how they are coupled, can be radically reimagined—and there is ground to suggest that Luhmann endorses such change. Luhmann views the challenges faced by a society and a politics with little capacity for steered adaption and central governability as historically unprecedented and urgent—never before has society been so complex, and so maneuverable. Under these conditions, Luhmann's emphasis on contingency amounts to a critical intervention intended to highlight that change is always possible. Luhmann's theory, read in this sense, offers not only "an analytically consistent description of [the] pathologies" (Dias Minhoto, 2017, p. 63) of capitalist societies, but also, "simultaneously, the potential for illuminating some of the blocks in the way of the promise of overcoming these pathologies" (p. 63).

Post-Mortem Despotism after Control

Against the background of this Marxist interlude, it is now possible to enfold Luhmann's theory of autopoietic politics with the way Deleuze and Guattari conceptualize the functioning of politics under the conditions of capitalism in *Anti-Oedipus*. The starting point for this enfolding is Deleuze and Guattari's evolutionary history of social machines. Even more so than Marx's own materialist history, it parallels social evolution in Luhmann, albeit with an obvious Marxist undercurrent. In *Anti-Oedipus*, Deleuze and Guattari employ the concept of the abstract machine to describe the mode in which social relations are organized within a particular society at a particular point in time.[6] Here, social evolution begins with the savage territorial machine as the most primitive form of social organization. Like Luhmann's segmented society, the savage territorial machine operates through immediately productive, clear and distinct relations between states, families, producers, and consumers or speakers and audience (Deleuze and Guattari, 1983, pp. 146–164).

Gradual centralization, through which different territorial entities become enveloped by the despotic machine of the state, transforms this flat, territorial social organization into a hierarchical order. The despotic machine of the sovereign state exercises control through a totalizing overcoding that subsumes the formerly distinct modes of social production under the logic of politics (Patton, 2000, pp. 91–92). Analogous to the pre- or early modern sovereign described by Luhmann, the despotic machine exercises control through the inscription of its own authority in all social relations, producing the socius it governs as a hierarchically stratified political unity. But in the course of further social evolution, this political overcoding becomes, just like in Luhmann, impossible. The coded flows break open and give way to a state of free-flowing complexity that can no longer be contained by a territory or state, but instead oscillates freely, self-referentially, and self-reproductively. In Deleuze and Guattari, this is the mode of social production and relational interconnection determined by the capitalist machine. The capitalist machine "begins when capital ceases to be a capital of alliance to become a filiative capital. Capital becomes filiative when money begets money, or value a surplus value" (1983, p. 227). Under the capitalist machine, "capital becomes the full body, the new socius or the quasi cause that appropriates all the productive forces" (p. 227).

While the material-economic roots of the capitalist machine are obvious, it is more than a particular mode of economic production defined in a narrow sense. The capitalist machine creates a social field that follows the relational logic of "filiative capital." Here, relational self-reproduction unfolds in multiple, conjunctive flows that oscillate simultaneously without affecting each other in a way that is strongly reminiscent of Luhmann's functionally differentiated social systems. Like Marx's capital and Luhmann's autopoietic systems, Deleuze and Guattari's filiative capital operates introversively—it constantly produces new capital flows. The machine of capitalism is "always ready to widen its own limits so as to add a new axiom to a previously saturated system" (Deleuze and Guattari, 1983, p. 238). Deleuze and Guattari's socio-historic evolution of machinic capitalism is thus "a Marxist theory . . . but one that has been transformed and adapted to new conditions" (Smith, 2011, p. 38). Its analytical focus is not capital, but rather the way social relations operate and are reproduced under conditions where they have adopted the operational mode of capital. Deleuze does not explicitly link his postscript to the capitalist machine. *However*, the "ultrarapid" and "free-floating" (Deleuze, 1992a, 4) "capitalism of the product" (p. 6) that drives the algorithmic modulation and total control of dividuals here folds neatly into the workings of free-flowing, deterritorialized capitalism sketched out in *Anti-Oedipus* (Sotiris, 2016).

In both, control is no longer exercised, let alone monopolized, by the disciplinary institutions of the state (Deleuze and Guattari, 1983, p. 228). The productive primacy of decoded flows is thus catastrophic for the state's despotic machine: it can no longer reproduce itself through overcoding. Importantly, however, it is not lethal for the former. "Decoded flows," Deleuze and Guattari suggest, "strike the despotic State with latency; they submerge the tyrant, but they also cause him to return in unexpected forms; they democratize him, oligarchize him, segmentalize him, monarchize him, and always internalize and spiritualize him" (p. 222). The despotic machine is adaptive. In the absence of genuine control, it "is now up to the State to recode as best it can, by means of regular or exceptional operations, the product of the decoded flows" (p. 223). Under the conditions of vampiric capitalism, a turn of phrase which Deleuze and Guattari adopt from Marx, the political sovereign becomes a retroactive "*post-mortem* despotism" (p. 228; original emphasis). Post-mortem despotism is effectively powerless because it cannot steer the flows it codes (Smith, 2011, p. 48). But rather than becoming obsolete, it establishes is a certain symbiotic relationship to free-flowing capital.

The capitalist machine reproduces itself through deterritorialization. Equivalent to the perpetual financialization performed by Marx's fictitious capital, the reterritorializing force of Deleuze and Guattari's capitalist machine turns everything it touches into free-flowing capital. But to be able to do so, the capitalist machine requires a steady supply of territories to reterritorialize. Under the conditions of machinic capitalism, the symbiotic function of politics "consists in reterritorializing, so as to prevent the decoded flow from breaking loose at all the edges of the social axiomatic. One sometimes has the impression that the flows of capital would willingly dispatch themselves to the moon if the capitalist State were not there to bring them back to earth" (Deleuze and Guattari, 1983, p. 258). Self-extensive capitalism works only if there is always new land to be conquered, something to be financialized—and for this to happen it requires a counterweight, a balancing force that, at least for a moment, at least as a pretense, places parts of society under a different logic—which can then be yet again broken up by capital flows. In this sense, Keynesian welfare state politics do not so much distort the social effects of capitalism but unfold a force of reterritorialization that ensures there is always something to be subsumed under the logic of self-expansive capital. Political coding is included in the relationality of capital flows as a socially evolved, protective mechanism against the "nightmare of every society" that is "the terror of a non-coded or decoded flow" (Smith, 2011, p. 44).

While unable to control and steer the flows of capital, Deleuze and Guattari's post-mortem politics reproduces itself through momentary reterritorialization—the reproduction of coded ordering structures against the chaos of capital flows. Like Luhmann, Deleuze and Guattari theorize contemporary politics as functioning self-reproductively. But while this self-reproduction is focused on the production of manifest governmental steering through collectively binding decisions in Luhmann, Deleuze and Guattari's reterritorialization is conceptually more open. The territories produced through political coding must be understood as distinct and stable structures of sense where "the emergence of matters of expression (qualities)" (Deleuze and Guattari, 1987, p. 315) take places. As lines of sense, territories are actualized through the "semi-stable selection from chaos" (Kleinherenbrink, 2015, p. 212) and prepare for the expression of meaning. While the political coding of territories can involve decision making with manifest effects on the lives of citizens, or the exercise of physical violence by the executive, first and foremost, it takes place on the level of sense. Against this background, Deleuze and Guattari's political (re-)territorialization makes it possible to conceptualize a self-reproductive politics where this self-reproduction is directly tied to an ordering sense-making performed by it.

Recoding Luhmann's Political Theory

How can Luhmann's political system adapt to the societies of control? How can it reproduce itself, in its functional responsibility to provide collective steering, in a world it has no insight to, and which renders effective steering precarious and unlikely? Against the background of Deleuze and Guattari's post-mortem despotism whose purpose lies in performing ordering recoding on the level of sense, I suggest that Luhmann's theory offers an answer if taken beyond Luhmann's political theory of the welfare state. A functionally differentiated politics can persist in the societies of control as a *politics of orientation* that guides society and its citizens in making sense of their increasingly complex, increasingly globalized social lifeworld. In the posthumously published *Die Politik der Gesellschaft*, a project Luhmann was working on up to his death and which therefore can be viewed as his "last word" on the political system, Luhmann phrases the functional responsibility that sustains the former in a curiously passive way.[7] An autopoietic politics reproduces itself by "holding ready the capacity for collectively binding decision-making" (Luhmann, 2002, p. 84; my translation).[8] For Luhmann, effectively steering, collectively binding political decisions do not actually have to be produced in order for politics to fulfill its social function. Rather, *holding ready* such decision-making power in the eyes of the democratic public is what allows an autopoietic politics to exist.

While Luhmann's rephrasing of politics' functional responsibility compared to his older political works (see for example Luhmann 1990b, p. 101) seems slight, the theoretical consequence is significant. To reproduce politics, the decision on how to continue sense in the complexity-event does not actually need to be expressed as a political decision with collectively steering effects. The decision in sense merely needs to produce the idea that governance is *per se possible*, that there is a clearly defined issue, problem or threat to be politically addressed, and that it can be addressed via a select number of alternative political routes. Applying Luhmann's new definition of the social function of politics, a decision in sense that reduces evental complexity in order to describe and diagnose the state of a society in its qualities, achievements, and the most urgent challenges it faces is sufficient to reproduce a political system hinged on collective steering. An autopoietic politics reimagined in this way can provide collective steering in the absence of effective governmental control. The social function of politics now lies in producing collective orientation on the level of sense through the decisional reduction of complexity.

A politics of orientation might not effectively govern, but its decisions offer guidance for how subjects and social systems make sense of themselves and the social world they inhabit. It carves out where threats and opportunities to be governed lie—even if these are currently not acted upon by a particular politician, government or institutional system. While the responsibility of the political system has, for Luhmann, always been the authoritative representation of society, a Luhmannian politics of orientation functions by literally producing representations of society for its subsystems and subjects. The political questions are now: "Who is specifically authorized to speak on behalf of society? Who really, as part of the whole, can represent the whole?" (Luhmann, 1990b, p. 13). Luhmann allows us to understand contemporary "post-control" politics as functioning as a "politics of understanding. Understandings are negotiated provisos that can be relied upon for a given time. They do not imply consensus, nor do they represent reasonable or even correct solutions to problems. They fix the reference points . . . in which coalitions and oppositions can form anew. Understandings have one big advantage over the claims of authority: they cannot be discredited but must be constantly renegotiated" (Luhmann, 1998, p. 69). In functionally differentiated societies, sense-relations in all areas of social life are faced with a multiplicity of alternative trajectories. As a consequence, the autopoietically reproductive continuation of sense has become insecure—for society as a whole as well as for its social systems and subjects (Luhmann, 2002, pp. 69–74). As Luhmann observes in *Political Theory in the Welfare State*, the inflation of communicative sense-expression under social conditions dominated by sense-based self-reproduction "apparently perversely" (Luhmann, 1990b, p. 206) has the consequence of "a loss of orientation for individuals" (p. 206; see also: p. 217). This resulting insecurity over how to continue sense in the information-event when a pervasive social complexity makes it possible to identify concrete alternatives for autopoietic continuation provides politics with a new *raison d'être*. Society needs a politics of orientation so that subjects and social systems have available reference points for the continuous complexity-reduction required for their autopoietic self- and worldmaking. The political system, on its part, relies on the decisional production of orientation in sense to "actualize itself as *something* (and specifically as *something political*)" (Thornhill, 2007, p. 504) under social conditions where it has lost the monopoly for regulation and steering. Against this background, the functioning of politics shifts from an effectively controlling governance to the management of a continuously encroaching social complexity no longer concealed by the socially cohesive meta-ontologies of religion and morality. A politics of orientation fulfills the social function of "contingency control" (Luhmann, 2002, p. 68; my translation) and "uncertainty absorption" (Luhmann, 1993b, p. 530). Completing a process that began at the dawn of modernity, contemporary post-control politics has fully replaced religion and morality as the authority that produces collectively binding diagnostic observations on the state of society that orient subjective and sociostructural sense-making (Luhmann, 2913, pp. 176–220; Folkers, 1987, pp. 48–49, 62–63; Barben, 1996, p. 104).

It must be made clear at this point that the political system's operational turn to the provision of orientation does not mean, and that Luhmann does not argue, that politics does not make decisions that profoundly affect the lives of citizens. "That politics has effects cannot be denied," (Luhmann, 2002, p. 110; my translation), Luhmann emphasizes. But at the same time, "it cannot be denied that it is unable to determine systemic conditions (and be it its own ones) in a particular direction" (p. 110; my translation). For Luhmann, the modern-liberal fiction of a rationalist sovereign politics whose decisions produce intended governmental outcomes through a linear cause-effect relationship cannot be sustained under conditions of high social complexity and complete functional closure. Rendered inoperative as the institution of collective planning and steering in the course of functional differentiation, politics legitimizes its existence and powers directly through the decision on the sense-event. A politics of orientation reproduces itself as the authoritative source of society's self-observation (pp. 168–169).

The "delegation of self-description" (Luhmann, 1984, p. 67) to the political realm absolves the political system from the responsibility for effective decisional governance—but self-reproduction as a politics of orientation comes with its own challenges. A politics that reproduces itself by providing orientation still requires "some kind of control, and if not organized control at least semantic one" (p. 67). The issue of complexity-overburdening already prevalent in Luhmann's welfare state politics is heightened further for a politics of orientation whose functional responsibility, and thus autopoiesis, rests on being able to produce orientation regarding all matters arising within a society. Speculating about the future of politics in *Political Theory in the Welfare State*, Luhmann suggests that a politics sustained through the provision of social self-descriptions would need to "politicize," and offer distinct lines of sense-making, even on issues formerly regarded as private. Such a politics "would have good reason to take up topics like love and marriage and view them as more than a mere exercise field of demands for equality and support. It would have to be able to presuppose possibilities of enriching the meaning of personal life to which it could contribute nothing" (Luhmann, 1990b, p. 102). The political responsibility to guide social sense-making on a constantly increasing range of issues means that a politics of orientation, even more so than its effectively governing predecessor, exists autopoietically only as it perpetually endangers its autopoiesis by exposing itself to an escalating external complexity. It therefore requires a highly developed and robust structural apparatus for complexity reduction that facilitates the decisional production of sense in the information-event. At first glance, Luhmann's political works appear to offer insight into exactly this detailed apparatus of complexity-reducing expectational structures available to the political system: the symbolically generalized medium of power and its evolution, the programs and codes of politics. However, it is precisely Luhmann's detailed, miniscule account of this structural apparatus that, as many have observed (August, 2021; Borch, 2012; Brunczel, 2010), constitutes the weakness of his political theory. Luhmann's systemic politics exudes a certain datedness and is compromised by its rigidity, hindering adaptive, creative readings of his political theory as exemplified by the politics of orientation of this book.

Luhmann's politics is a politics of clear lines: internally, the political system is divided into government, administration, and public (Luhmann, 2002, p. 117). Political parties are structured according to the binary code conservative/progressive, and there is a binary polarization between government and opposition within democratic institutions (pp. 95–96). This stringent, orderly ideal of institutional democracy modeled in the image of the Western German Republic after the Second World War seems at odds with the current practice of democratic politics. Political parties have multiplied in many countries, and even binary systems have differentiated further through divisions between right and left camps within both progressive and conservative parties. At the same time, parties move across the ideological spectrum more flexibly—in the span of less than a decade, a general tendency toward centrism has been replaced by severe ideological polarization in many Western democracies. Single issues and political personalities shape political outcomes more decisively than party ideology, and do so in part across government/opposition lines. Elections produce political stability, but no longer ensure political legitimacy in the eyes of the democratic public. In short, the political programs and codes Luhmann describes in miniscule detail no longer seem to fit the current state of his functionally differentiated democracies. As Balázs Brunczel observes, "the characteristics of the functional subsystem" (2010, p. 241) Luhmann specifies for the political system "describe the most important features of politics less plausibly than they do in the case of other subsystems" (p. 241).

The highly formalistic and somewhat anemic expectational structures of the political system also seem peculiarly at odds with Luhmann's insistence on the radical adaptivity of autopoietic politics. The programs and codes Luhmann outlines appear too narrow, small-scale, and specific to register and accommodate more profound shifts in the autopoietic functioning of politics; a program, for example, is something that is "assigned to the administration" (Luhmann, 2002, p. 261; my translation) or guides the actions of a political party (p. 265). But can the dramatized absence of political substance à la Boris Johnson in the United Kingdom, or conspiracies on the "stolen" 2020 election victory of Donald Trump, be accommodated in this framework of political programs and binary codes? Christian Borch makes a similar observation in his discussion of power in Luhmann. Following Borch, Luhmann, on the one hand, emphasizes the radical contingency of power—not just how it is expressed, but even of power as the symbolically generalized medium that sustains the autopoiesis of politics (1990b, p. 104). But on the other hand, Luhmann's analysis of power seems to fall short of his own repeatedly formulated standards of theoretical radicality. His discussion of power as something transmissible is "encumbered with ontological formulations" (Borch, 2005, p. 160) and his insistence that communication through power works only through the threat of negative sanctions implies a degree of political control no longer available to a functionally differentiated politics (p. 161).

For Borch, it is possible to salvage the radicality of Luhmann's thought from his theoretically conservative structuralism if we once again read Luhmann beyond Luhmann (Borch, 2012, pp. 156, 162–163). While Borch proceeds with Foucault, I suggest that Deleuze and Guattari's concept of the code offers a way to capture how a politics of orientation reduces complexity to make collectively guiding sense, but without the overly restrictive requirements of Luhmann's programs and binary codes. Deleuze and Guattari's political sovereign operates through territorializing coding, both under the conditions of the despotic machine where it forms the authoritarian center of social life, and as a post-mortem despotism where it has lost all manifest control to the free-flowing relations of the capitalist machine. Political coding, importantly, adapts to the changing conditions under which it operates. In Deleuze and Guattari, codes territorialize sense (Smith, 2011, p. 49). Codes reproduce the "unity of a socius: an organism, social or living, is composed as a whole, as a global or complete object" (Deleuze and Guattari, 1987, p. 342) on the level of social self-description, which, under the capitalist machine, has become the functional domain and survival mechanism of politics. Smith suggests that the code should therefore be understood as the functional correlative of capital flows. It is "a form of inscription or recording" that is " 'applied' to a flow" (2011, pp. 43–44) and stabilizes its sense, allowing for meaning to be drawn from it. James Williams's concept of the sign developed in *A Process Philosophy of Signs* can lend further definition to a Deleuzian account of the code.[9]

Williams's signs function by initiating a "process of selection" that produces "a fixed relation" (Williams, 2016a, p. 77) to guide the expressive production of sense. Signs make the continuous, processual production of reality possible by providing a creative force with ordered lines of actualizations. The code as sign theorized by Williams constitutes a less rigid Deleuzian counterpart to Luhmann's code. Beyond Luhmann's binary coding, Deleuzian codes are *internally multiple*. While codes appear fixed and singular, they draw their ordering power from their internal multiplicity of diverse relational associations. Following Williams, a "cup of tea as a sign . . . made up of tea, breakfast, Britishness and tradition, but it could also be tea, tea leaves and the hills of Sri Lanka, the history of plantation life, the exploitation of young women" (2016a, p. 2). The relational sets of codes can interrelate, overlap, conflict, and change, as distinctions between particular codes are always contingent. It "does not matter where we draw the line" (p. 25), Williams suggests, because each time we delineate a particular code "the limit will prove to be porous" (p. 25).

Second, beyond the latent determinism of Luhmann's codes, Deleuzian codes are historically developed and thus *path-dependent but never determined*. The code is not ontologically external to the process it guides but is rather a product of its processual use developed over time (Williams, 2016a, p. 25). The relations of the code are themselves meta-stable and subject to "a process of intensive unfolding" (p. 76). While the code establishes structural path-dependencies, their application remains open—"selections are free" (p. 80) and can change the set of the code itself. Each instant of coding thus "remains an unconditioned selection despite prevalent patterns" (p. 82). The cup of tea, as a code, can guide selection by ordering the complexity of sense so effectively because its composition is not static, but flexible and conjunctive, allowing it to adapt to the social conditions under which it helps to territorialize sense.

Deleuzian codes are further *synthetic* and include material as well as epistemic constituents (Williams, 2016b). The synthetic quality Luhmann's structures of expectation is implied but never made explicit, such as when he defines the ordering function of political programs, which require actors and written manifestos as well as ideas (Brunczel, 2010, pp. 148–149). However, Luhmann's detailed unpacking of epistemic programs and codes—for example, in the four volumes of *Gesellschaftsstruktur und Semantik*—suggests that Luhmann at least latently prioritizes the epistemic components of expectational structures. Against this background, the Deleuzian code as sign safeguards against a reductionist understanding of the code as achieving complexity-reduction primarily through the use of signs and symbols, bracketing the ordering power of objects, bodies, and spaces. Beyond Luhmann's neatly ordered, lifeless coded programs, Williams's Deleuzian codes achieve complexity-reduction as internally multiple and synthetic, path-dependent but nevertheless flexible structures. This conceptual flexibility can sustain a speculative exploration of how political coding has transformed beyond Luhmann's welfare state politics, and which codes sustain a contemporary democratic politics of orientation.

Chapter 6

Post-Truth Populism as a
Politics of Orientation

"We have entered an age of post-truth politics" (2016), William Davies declares gravely in the opening passage of his 2016 *New York Times* think piece with the same title. In a year that saw both the United Kingdom's Vote Leave campaign and Donald Trump's run for the office of U.S. president succeed in mobilizing a majority of voters through a blend of openly counterfactual claims and affective appeals to xenophobia and nationalist authoritarianism, Davies's piece was one of the first to give a clear descriptor to the widespread sense that something rather fundamental had changed in the functioning of a contemporary democracy where formerly "sacred" (Davies, 2016) facts "seem to be losing their ability to support consensus" (Davis, 2016) and, rather "than sit coolly outside the fray of political argument . . . are now one of the main rhetorical weapons within it" (Davis, 2016): post-truth. Since 2016, post-truth politics continues to function as a buzzword designed to capture the political zeitgeist within both mainstream media and the wider public political discourse they inform (Snyder, 2021; McIntyre and Rauch, 2021; Kakutani, 2018; Dimmock, 2018). But it has also become the focal point of a quickly growing body of scholarship that seeks to unpack what exactly it is that has changed in contemporary democratic politics (Speed and Mannion, 2017; Harsin, 2015; Singer, 2021; Porpora, 2020).

Different accounts vary considerably in how they describe, and what they deem responsible for, the rise and prevalence of anti-democratic sentiments within the public discourse of twenty-first-century industrialized and digitalized democracies. However, at their common core is the diagnosis of an amalgamation of "right-wing populisms and post-truth politics" (Harsin, 2015) characterized by an outright rejection of scientific findings and expertise as well as "a unique distrust for professional journalism" (Harsin, 2015), which renders them distinct from the populist movements of the nineteenth and twentieth centuries (Speed and Mannion, 2017; Harsin, 2015). Within both public discourse and academic literature, the question whether there really is anything new and significant about contemporary populist politics, and to what extent they should be considered anti-democratic, is certainly contested. Scholars and political commentators complicate the all too "appealingly simple tale" (Gray, 2017) of a post-truth populism that has subverted a formerly rational-liberal democracy. Highlighting that strategic voter manipulation, conspiracy, and irrationality were already common features and instruments of twentieth-century democracy (Hofstadter, 1964; De Cleen, 2017; Gray, 2017), they caution against the simplistic assumptions that the turn to anti-technocratic post-truth politics expresses a new, general mistrust in scientific expertise (Dommett and Pearce, 2019). On the other hand, scholars interrogate the problematic bias of accounts that dismiss the voices and concerns of those deemed irrational from the perspective of an educated middle-class while failing to apply the same critical gaze to left-wing movements that primarily seek to appeal through affect and via the demonization of the political opponent (Gerrard, 2021; Powell, 2017).

For a starting point, the considerations developed below side with those scholars who insist that there is something new and significant about the post-truth populism that has come to shape democratic politics toward the end of the twenty-first-century's second decade with no clear end in sight. However, I suggest that the theoretical lens of a Deleuzian-Luhmannian politics of orientation can offer what is currently absent from the scholarship on post-truth populism: a nuanced account that unpacks the former in its social conditions of emergence and its functioning at the intersection of citizen perceptions and democratic institutions to reveal both evolutionary changes and continuities with twentieth-century democracy. Understood as a politics of orientation, the post-factual, affect-based appearance of post-truth populism does not take away from the fact that it continues the autopoietic functioning of modern politics, which is hinged on the provision of collective steering for society. It only offers collective steering with different means—through the provision of complexity-reducing orientation for sense-making. The task is then to unpack why contemporary social conditions render populist orientation a particularly successful mode of collectively binding steering for both politics and citizens. In order to show how this book's Deleuzian-Luhmannian theory can engage existing analytical lenses on post-truth populism while also advancing beyond them, the reading of post-truth populism as a politics of orientation will be developed against the backdrop of two prominent alternatives: the thought of Wendy Brown and Chantal Mouffe.

The Dredge and the Iron Cage

The central claim of Brown's *In the Ruins of Neoliberalism* is that neoliberalism, not as a paradigm for economic policy but as an ideology, is to be held responsible for the rise of post-truth populism within the contemporary Western democracies that have all embraced it, albeit to varying degrees. For Brown, the "composite Left account" (2019, p. 3), according to which the neoliberal flexibilization of labor markets and the parallel erosion of social security networks has created an uprooted, precarious working class whose legitimate albeit misguided anger is mobilized by the anti-democratic forces of post-truth populism, only reveals the most superficial layer of the complex link between neoliberalism and post-truth populism. Brown unpacks how neoliberalism, in the shadows of its immediate economic effects and thus dangerously hidden from view, has directly undermined the democratic social community on a theoretical and ethical level by installing a moralized market that folds neatly into traditional family, gender, or religious values in place (Brown, 2019, pp. 7–8, 29). Brown turns to the writings of Friedrich Hayek to show how neoliberalism directly targets the idea of a democratic collective marked by equality as the equal political capacity to engage "in modest self rule" (p. 27). Even a democratically anchored political sovereign, Hayek fears, is a self-interested executive force with an appetite for expansion. It will use all collectively produced rules to "make itself true" (p. 71) by inscribing the need for, and thus legitimacy of, political rule in the ontological vision of society itself. Against the "dangerous ontological error" (p. 106) of liberal democratic theory, Hayek seeks to "dereify society" (p. 106). Collectively binding rules can and should be thought without the always-already politically stained social—as a set of self-regulating, adaptive ordering principles "borne by tradition" (p. 96), whose operational logic is that of the liberal market. The products of Hayek's neoliberal marketplace of social rules are contingent on socio-historically proven usefulness and limited by personal freedom, rendering individual choice absolute. The consequence is, Brown suggests, the inflation and transcendentalist of an economically conceptualized freedom that here becomes the foundational principle for social life (pp. 16–17) and undermines social rules based on, and focused on creating, political equality (p. 44).

Brown draws out the paradoxical quality of neoliberalism's bloated, introversively self-extensive concept of individual freedom. Obsessively focused on warding off the dangers of collectively (democratically) produced coercion, neoliberal freedom disregards any infringements on individual freedoms produced by the market, or indeed as a consequence of who wins in the marketplace of ordering principles. Brown cites landmark constitutional court decisions on the rights of business owners to treat customers unequally based on political or sexual orientation from the United States and the United Kingdom. Here, the protection of a private sphere that is economically expanded into the political community produces manifest social inequality, but legitimizes this production in the name of individual freedom. Protected here is not the freedom of artistic expression, for example of those cake-makers refusing to provide services for gay weddings, but the supremacy of the private over the social (Brown, 2019, pp. 124–160; 2020, p. 21). Within the neoliberal logic, "free speech takes free exercise by the hand, pulls it into the public and commercial world, and uniquely empowers it there" (Brown, 2019, p. 140). Against this background, anti-immigrant sentiments using home-owner analogies, as popularized by the French and Italian far-right, become legitimate beyond any possibility of political intervention or critique. Because neoliberalism regards those rules which have proven successful according to a marketplace logic as legitimate, neoliberal freedom exists symbiotically with conservative traditionalism, as the above cases illustrate (Brown, 2019, pp. 92–93; see also: Cooper, 2017).

For Brown, the democratic community's erosion by the neoliberal expansion of freedom creates a political culture of nihilistic *ressentiment* which manifests itself in the rise of post-truth populism. This becomes visible first of all in the populist rejection of expert opinions and scientific facts, exemplified by "the British tabloids whipping up Brexit support" (Brown, 2018, p. 27) or "Trump's manifest indifference to truth, consistency, or affirmative (as opposed to grievance-based) political or moral convictions" (p. 27). Instead of a positive political program or social vision, post-truth populist ressentiment attracts supporters in the logic of a wounded attachment. Subjects are mobilized and bound together by the belief in a fundamental violation of individual freedom cooked up behind closed doors by social and political elites and enacted by the State. Trump, Brown suggests, is the ideal-typical embodiment of post-truth populist ressentiment: "[I]t does not matter what policies he pursues, only that he opposes those they hold responsible for their suffering" (2019, p. 179) because the support of his followers is based not on "moral rectitude, let alone political competence, but for revenge against the wound of nothingness by destroying the imagined agent of that wound" (p. 179). The danger of post-truth populism lies in the fact that the fight against the sovereignty of the democratic community itself has become the new *raison d'être* for its otherwise aimless, entirely negative political expression. It cannot easily be countered and redirected by a democratic politics whose social roots neoliberalism has weakened dangerously.

Like Brown, Mouffe retraces the rise of post-truth populism within democratic heartlands to a fault inbuilt into contemporary democracy. Mouffe, however, does not limit her critique to the neoliberal strain of liberal democracy but extends it to the very idea of the former. The issue, for Mouffe, is not the erosion of democratic collectivity performed by a liberal freedom that subsumes everything it touches under its economic logic. The democratic social as such has rather never existed in the first place—it always has to be made from radically diverse, competing conceptions. As Mouffe and Laclau write in *Hegemony and Socialist Strategy*, "the social only exists . . . as an effort to construct that impossible object" (2012, p. 112)—society. Society has no ontological existence and can only maintain actuality against this ontological void if it is continuously produced in social relations (Mouffe, 1993, pp. 10–12). Radical pluralism, from which any social totality can only be made contingently in the face of numerous competing alternatives, is Mouffe's ontological starting point and the "axiological principle" (Mouffe, 2000, p. 19) of her democratic theory. This foundational pluralism is essentially political. Different accounts of the social to be actualized stand in Schmittian antagonistic relation to each other, and struggle for hegemony. This struggle against the constitutive others of alternative social visions is here an intrinsic part of the conflictual political process of social formation (Mouffe, 2000, pp. 20–22; Laclau and Mouffe, 2012, pp. 153–160).

A democratic politics which, following Mouffe, cannot escape the antagonistic nature of socio-political actualization is left with two alternatives. It can either establish a set of democratic institutions which contain but safeguard nonviolent political contestation, which Mouffe draws out as a radical democratic alternative to contemporary democracy (Mouffe, 2000, pp. 121–124). Or, alternatively, democracy can implement and universalize one particular, hegemonic vision of rights and freedoms at the expense of all others, suppressing ontological and social pluralism. Any singular democratic ideal, if actualized conclusively, is so through such a hegemonic exclusion of alternatives, which is fundamentally incongruent with democratic political equality. For Mouffe, contemporary liberal democracy, which claims to have overcome political antagonism in favor of the aggregate representation of political will, rational centrism and political compromise, is guilty of exactly this hegemonic exclusion of genuine pluralism (Mouffe, 2000, pp. 106–114; Mouffe, 2005, p. 126). This suppressed antagonism is what now comes back to haunt liberal democracy in the form of post-truth populism (Mouffe, 2019).

For Mouffe, the idea of liberal democracy is based on a foundational paradox—it encompasses and intertwines two incompatible logics. On the one hand, liberal democracy institutes popular sovereignty in which every citizen participates with equal political weight as the highest authority. But the liberal paradigm, on the other hand, requires limitations to the popular will in the name of an individual sphere of freedom and protected rights that always has to be defined in a certain fashion—and is thus always the freedom of some, never the freedom of all, equally (Mouffe, 2000, pp. 39–43). Mouffe again draws on Schmitt to argue that liberal democracy, if applied in practice, requires an illiberal constitutive distinction (pp. 40–42). Protecting certain freedoms automatically requires an infringement on the absolute political equality of all, as the implementation of a particular set of rights and freedoms privileges the political will of some over alternative visions. Liberal democracy thus sustains its social reality against the background of another sphere in which substantial inequalities prevail, such as the economic sphere (Schmitt, 1979, pp. 15–18).

For Mouffe, the liberal-democratic suppression of political multiplicity is not only normatively problematic because it violates political equality but also because it endangers the functional integrity of democracy. A rational-liberal democracy that has excluded all avenues for identity-building adversarial demarcation becomes trapped in the iron cage of its own making when the democratic community begins to disintegrate as a consequence of lacking opportunities for antagonistic constitution. Politically, liberal democracy does not maintain itself against outside alternatives but rather seeks to absorb them. The aim is, as per Francis Fukuyama, a liberal democratic end of history where all dialectic opposition is resolved in unity. However, unlike Fukuyama, Mouffe views the pursuit of ultimate liberal-democratic unity as futile. Rational-liberal consensus politics without an adversary must backfires because the pretense "to include everybody in 'the people'" (Mouffe, 2000, p. 121) makes the lack of actual political representation and economic opportunities glaringly obvious to those who are not part of the socioeconomic elite whose interests are currently hegemonic. Liberal democracy cannot make the political antagonism foundational to social integration disappear. It only forces it to the margins, and stipulates political contestation to surface here in anti-democratic form (Mouffe, 2000, p. 114).

One important consequence of the liberal democratic eradication of political conflict is the *moralization* of antagonism. When "frontiers between us and them [. . .] can no longer be defined in political terms—given that the adversarial model has supposedly been overcome—these frontiers are drawn in moral categories, between 'us the good' and 'them the evil ones'" (Mouffe, 2005, p. 129). Excluded from the political sphere, conflict reappears within the realm of morality, institutionally unguarded and thus open to excess. For Mouffe, "Sade [. . .] cannot be separated from Rousseau, whose idea of a transparent community he reproduces in a perverted form: the general will becomes the voluptuous will and the immediacy of communication becomes the immediacy of debauchery" (2000, p. 131). With Mouffe, post-truth populism must be understood as an expression of this bastardized, extra-political antagonism breaking open the frontiers of the democratic community that liberal democracy has rendered fragile (2019). A left-wing rejection of the populist underpinnings of this new right-wing politics is consequently misguided. An effective response to the challenge of right-wing populism must, on the contrary, take the form of a left populism that facilitates the return of actual but nonviolent contestation to democratic politics and opens the iron cage of centrist neoliberal democracy to the multiplicity of alternative political visions it has so far contained (Mouffe, 2019).

The Dilemma of the Dividual:
Neoliberalism and Post-Institutional Control

Despite their differences, Brown's and Mouffe's accounts of post-truth populism reveal a certain common ground in how they outline the phenomenon at stake, and where their theories place emphasis. The first one of these shared presumptions is that the emergence of post-truth populism is the result of developments and decisions internal to the democratic political sphere. For Brown, the structural fault within democratic politics that allowed post-truth populism to emerge was caused by the democratic embrace of neoliberalism, whose unseen normative effect was the gradual erosion of democratic collective sovereignty. For Mouffe, the liberal democratic presumption that political conflict can be resolved in rational bargaining or democratic deliberation conditions the return of political antagonism in the extra-democratic form of post-truth populism. The engineers and representatives of the neoliberal post-democracy paved the way for post-truth populists not only to become the only political force that challenges its status quo, but also to do so in a manner that is unguarded by democratic institutions and norms, and therefore violently anti-democratic. For both Brown and Mouffe, the rise of post-truth populism is politically conditioned. For this reason, it can, and must, be resolved on the level of democratic politics, albeit that such resolution is in considerably closer reach in Mouffe.

The second presumption that Brown and Mouffe share is that the post-factual component of post-truth populism,[1] expressed for instance as the rejection of scientific insights and recommendations in the COVID-19 pandemic, the negation of research findings on anthropogenic climate change, or the anti-expert sentiments fueling support for the United Kingdom's Vote Leave campaign (Marshall and Drieschova, 2020) and Trump's presidential ambitions to "drain the swamp" (Toles, 2017) of U.S. politics, is an effect and symptom of, rather than a contributing factor to, the rise of post-truth populism. "Frightened by the loss of values and goods heretofore secured by the nomos of the earth" (Brown, 2019, p. 187), Brown's uprooted and atomized subjects inhabiting the ruins of neoliberalism turn their back on the political, scientific and social elite they deem responsible for this loss, and instead cling to the "affective remains" (Brown, 2019, p. 188) of "nation, family, property, and the traditions reproducing racial and gender privilege" (p. 187).

In Mouffe, the negation of Enlightenment rationalism must, like the attack on the elites and institutional bodies of liberal democracy, be understood as an expression of unhinged political antagonism which, suppressed by the liberal democratic hegemony for too long, now comes to the fore in pure, all-encompassing form as an attack on the rational-liberal human condition itself. Because of the nihilistic, violent excess of post-truth populism, both Brown and Mouffe view it as inherently tied to the anti-democratic political right, which forms their third shared presumption. While Mouffe suggests that a left populism is not only possible, but rather the only way forward for democratic politics to counter the anti-democratic right, the make-up of left populism is clearly distinct from the former. Mouffe's left populism targets the institutional-procedural design of democracy where it seeks to recover social pluralism against "a common adversary: the oligarchy" (Mouffe, 2017, p. 18) and through "the establishment of a chain of equivalence among the demands of the workers, the immigrants and the precarious middle class, as well as other democratic demands, such as those of the LGBT community" (p. 18).

Understanding post-truth politics as a Deleuzian-Luhmannian politics of orientation ties in with elements of Brown's and Mouffe's analyses, such as the conditioning role of the logic of capital extended to the social sphere, or the necessity for social production to have a constitutive outside in post-truth populism. However, understanding post-truth populism as a politics of orientation also necessitates departing from their accounts in a number of ways. First, the origins of post-truth populism understood as functioning toward and through the provision of orientation are socio-historical and lie in the escalation of complexity within functionally differentiated societies. Post-truth populism is here not the avoidable product of decision making in the liberal democracy, and thus cannot be undone through political course correction. Second, because the issue of drastic complexity-reduction is central to the rise of post-truth populism, the turn to the post-factual is here key to understanding its rise and prevalence. Third, post-truth populism is only one particular coding of an autopoietic politics that functions through the provision of orientation for sense-making can take. The danger posed by right-wing post-truth populism lies in the fact that its codes are *more effective at providing orientation* than the actors and institutions of liberal democracy and therefore has considerable appeal within a democratic context where public support is based on orienting complexity-reduction.

If we seek to understand post-truth populism as one particular effect and symptom of a more general, socio-historically conditioned shift to a politics of orientation at the intersection between political actors and institutions and the needs and preferences of democratic citizens, the deterritorialized complexity of contemporary globalized, capitalist and digitalized democratic societies is an important staring point. The last chapter unpacked how functional differentiation, to say it with Luhmann, or the rise of the capitalist social machine, in Deleuze and Guattari's words, created an effectively powerless, retroactively self-productive politics. This post-mortem despotism needs to expose itself to an ever-increasing range of social issues to "recode" through political decision making in order to reproduce itself, in the eyes of citizens, in its function as society's collective steering authority. Politics can only offer steering in the form of orienting frameworks, narratives and problem constellations made through selective decision in sense which orient citizens in the continuous self- and worldmaking that sustains their existence.

The conditioning role of capitalism in driving this shift toward a politics of orientation folds smoothly into Brown's discussion neoliberalism as the social root cause of post-truth populism. What allows neoliberalism to act as a widening crack in the fabric of the democratic social is, for Brown, not the manifest material inequality it creates and cements, but the shift in the functioning of social norms which it initiates. Brown's reading of Hayek reveals how Hayek's neoliberalism seeks to shift the provision of social steering through collectively binding rules away from a (democratically legitimized) political authority and toward the market-logic of autopoietic self-production. In Hayek, markets and morals parallel each other insofar as both form ordering systems that are socially conditioned but ultimately groundless, flexibly adaptive to the needs of changing social environments, and operate as *autopoietic* functional systems (Hayek, 1979, pp. 134–149; 2011, pp. 75–81). This functional parallelism between neoliberal markets and morals creates a social sphere governed by autologically self-extensive normative orders centered on the concept of individual freedom (Hayek, 2011, pp. 58–59). Where Luhmann focuses on welfare state democracy to emphasize how the functional overburdening of an autopoietic politics hinged of demonstrating effective governance intensifies its functional crisis, neoliberalism must be understood as its parallelly operating underside. It removes collective steering from the singular hinge of a political authority and subjects it to the market-logic of decentered, socially multiplied self-production.

The addition of Brown's Hayekian neoliberalism to our Deleuzian-Luhmannian framework invites a change in perspective. It stipulates an exploration of how the conditions of a functional differentiation driven by the logic of (neoliberal) capital not only forces politics to adapt its functioning to the provision of orientation but at the same time creates a social context in which complexity-reducing orientation has particular political *appeal* for democratic subjects. A return to Deleuze's postscript makes it possible to zoom in on the experience of the subject within societies of control that are shaped by an institutionally unconfined capitalism, but also by the rise of digital technology. In Deleuze, algorithmic modulation is a central feature of the post-institutional societies of control. A number of scholars have employed Deleuze's references to the "ultrarapid forms" (1992a, p. 4) and "numerical logic" (p. 4.) of the new control he sketches out to read the postscript as an essay on the human condition in digitalized societies (Galloway, 2004; Rouvroy, 2013; MacKenzie and Porter, 2019; Hui, 2015). The majority of Deleuzian scholarship here focuses on the quality, extent, and operational mode of this new control brought forth by the digital "technologies which have transformed twenty-first-century production into a vital mass of immaterial flows and instantaneous transactions" (Galloway, 2004, p. 20).

While Alexander Galloway draws out the logic of algorithmic modulation in Deleuze's societies of control as that of the computational protocol operating on decentralized networks (2004, p. 25), Antionette Rouvroy suggests viewing digital control as the next evolutionary stage of Foucault's governmentality. Algorithmic modulation no longer produces self-governing subjects, but rather functions desubjectivizing (or, as Yuk Hui [2015] suggests with reference to Simondon, disindividuating). The subject is broken apart into digital "dividual" pieces required to participate, and maximize performance in a multiplicity of different processes without the hinge of an identity to recuperate agency (Rouvroy, 2013, pp. 5–7). Algorithmic control "does not need to tame the wilderness of facts and behaviours" (Rouvroy, 2013, p. 11), as institutional subjectivization did, but operates through technological shortcuts and commands on a dividual that exists on the level of digital communication alone. The behavior of the dividual is not coercively constrained but rather pre-emptively modulated on the basis of aggregate data and algorithmic prediction, which ultrarapidly anticipates and controls the future at the same time as the present is unfolding (Rouvroy, 2011, pp. 13–14).

In their essay "Totalizing Institutions," Iain MacKenzie and Robert Porter (2019) examine the functioning of algorithmic control in comparison to the disciplinary institutions it replaces. Bringing Deleuze's postscript into conversation with Erving Goffman's theory of social institutions, they suggest that digital control does in fact not end the workings of disciplinary institutions like the workplace, school, church, or the family—rather, it totalizes them. Within the new, totalized, institutionally unlocalized spheres of control, "one is always, to some degree, a child, a school pupil, an apprentice, a university student, a worker, a consumer, a parent, a patient, a prisoner, a free person etc. but one is never merely one of these things at any one time (a disciplined subject of an institution)" (MacKenzie and Porter, 2019, p. 13). While it is unclear to what extent Deleuze, and with him MacKenzie and Porter, view the rise of digital technology as solely responsible for the blurring of boundaries between the different social institutions, its role is certainly decisive. The interface of a smartphone allows one to stay in touch with their parents, learn a language, read an academic paper on a certain topic, answer work emails and check the baby monitoring system in in the adjacent room—all within the span of minutes. But, and this is the precisely the point of Deleuze's postscript, these technological possibilities are not so much opportunities as they are the source of obligations. The dividual in the control society is simultaneously exposed to the information, demands and requirements of all institutions of modern society at the same time, which now permeate the entire social sphere. For Mackenzie and Porter, the control theorized in Deleuze's postscript is thus not just algorithmic, it is multilayered, and thus exponential (2019, pp. 21–23). To cope with the impossible demand of the control society, the dividual needs to reduce complexity—they need means to select, prioritize and focus.

The experience of the dividual who has "to occupy several stages all at once, perform several roles all at once, construct several scenes all at once . . . with no backstage as a site of retreat" (MacKenzie and Porter, 2019, p. 15) is equivalent to the dilemma which the subject faces in Luhmann's functionally differentiated systems. They have little choice but to participate in several social systems if they want to live in the societies they shape—education, the family or the economy. But this participation means exposing themselves to the vast complexity of each social system, which can never be understood adequately but yet must be managed to the extent that this participation does not interfere with continuous self- and worldmaking in sense. The subject inhabiting Luhmann's functionally differentiated systems thus equally requires means for complexity-reduction. However, the timelines do not quite seem to fit. Deleuze links the shift to societies of control to the digital revolution at the end of the twentieth century. For Luhmann, on the contrary, functional differentiation is a characteristic of modern society, and fully developed in the twentieth century. The subject's dilemma of having to face the complex workings of multiple systems it is functionally coupled with is thus nothing new, and cannot readily be identified as the cause of political shifts taking place in twenty-first-century democracy. However, if we turn to the role of second-order observation for producing complexity in Luhmann, it is possible to draw out how the rise of digital media has changed the social experience of the subject.

Functional differentiation is accompanied by a shift to second-order observation. As Moeller suggests, for Luhmann, "the crucial shift that constitutes modernity not merely consists in the 'differing out' of function systems, but, within these systems, in the eventual emergence of communication that operates pervasively as second-order observation" (2016, p. 31). The "shift of a consciousness of reality to a description of descriptions" (Luhmann, 2012a, p. 100) that characterizes second-order observation is a necessary component of the autopoietic closure of social systems. Autopoietically closed sense-based systems do not create self and world in sense *ex nihilo*. They rather auto-poietically distinguish both on the basis of existing observations produced by other subjects or social systems and expressed in sense—they observe observations (Moeller, 2016, pp. 26–30; Luhmann, 2012a, p. 148). While functionally differentiated systems draw on always-already expressed sense for processes of self- and worldmaking all throughout modernity, the means available for second-order observation certainly do not remain unchanged.

Luhmann himself here mainly focuses on the rise of mass media as a distinct social system to which the production of new observational data for sense-making is socially outsourced in the nineteenth and especially the twentieth century (Luhmann, 1996a). Mass media do not replace other media of communication but rather multiply their effect—for instance, "morality is and remains available, both in face-to-face interaction and in communication by the mass media. Television, in particular, has led to the conspicuous everyday topicality of moral communication" (Luhmann, 2012a, p. 241). The continuous production of new information, as news, becomes the functional requirement that allows the mass media to exist as an autopoietic social system (Luhmann, 2012a, pp. 121–122, 332–343; Luhmann, 1996a). To fulfill its functional responsibility of informing society, the media system must constantly produce the new observational information it expresses (Luhmann, 1996a). The differentiation of an autopoietically closed mass media system creates a society that observes itself—directly through the media, and indirectly through other systems it is coupled with, such as politics, the economy, and, importantly, subjects—as subject to a never-ending series of new events from international conflicts to natural disasters, security crises or changing economic forecasts (p. 59). Paradoxically, the collective social need for observational data to maintain processes of self- and worldmaking against an outside of complexity sets in motion a socio-historical evolution at the end of which a functionally differentiated mass media system bears a significant responsibility for creating the complexity that processes of self- and worldmaking then need to overcome.

A functionally differentiated mass media system, in short, has made twentieth-century societies observe themselves as more complex. And because reality is produced in sense on the basis of past observations expressed, it *has made them more complex*. Although Luhmann, like Deleuze, witnessed at least the dawn of digitalization and the early days of the internet, unlike Deleuze he had very little to say about its transformative potential (or lack thereof) (Moeller, 2016, p. 37). But using Luhmann once again beyond

Luhmann, it is possible to unpack the effect of digitalization on second-order observation as that of exponential expansion. Elena Esposito's (2011; Esposito and Stark, 2019) work on financial markets as second-order observation structures illustrates powerfully, for the case of the economic system, how digital technology proliferates second-order observation. The economy's health and productivity, to a large extent, is now a product of its second-order observation performed by financial markets. Using algorithmic predictions for high-frequency trading, the observations produced by digitalized financial markets are no longer based on a direct observation of economic processes but produce predictions based on previous observations of the former—on second-order observations (Esposito, 2011).

The effectiveness of political steering, whose observation was previously primarily the responsibility of mass media, is now also being observed by social media in the form of a "third-order" observation of what the mainstream media discourse is missing out, getting wrong or deliberately excluding. The accusation of "fake news," coined by Donald Trump (Woodward, 2020) and now a common trope within post-truth populist discourse, is exactly that—an observation of how mass media observes society. At the same time, social media, as Moeller notes, have also "taken on the shape of a sort of 'peer review system' of private life" (2016, p. 35). Different from Luhmann's mass media, social media, and digital communication more generally, do not fulfill a particular, clearly delineated function for society as a whole. They do not form a separate social system but must rather be understood as a technological means that drastically expands and accelerates communicative second-order observation for all social systems and subjects. It is hence hardly surprising that traditional media outlets from established newspapers to public broadcasting companies are fighting for survival in the digital age. Their fate is that of the disciplinary institutions of Deleuze's societies of control—"they are finished" because they have lost the monopoly for what once legitimized their existence as a functionally differentiated social system, in this case the second-order observation of society.

For the dividuals living in the societies of control, the digitalization and de-institutionalization of second-order observation significantly adds to the experience of complexity. Digital media, both news media and social media, is omnipresent in all social systems, diverse in its sources (at least as the subject perceives it), and constantly changes due to the speed of delivery. Social self-observation is no longer centralized in a mass media system, and thus no longer forced into palatable bites by its analogue limitations, such as the length of the evening TV news or the pages of a newspaper. The entropic digital second-order observation is experienced as complex, fractional, and transitory. The second-order observer cannot help but notice that what is actually being observed is only a small part of the observational data available, and an even smaller part of the information that could be available through first-order observation—if only one could actually know what politicians and CEOs decide behind closed doors, what scientists discover in their labs, what family members disclose to others in private messages. Informational entropy places the observer in a position of insecurity—they do not know how to select from the multiple informational sources available, but they do know that every selection will leave their knowledge incomplete, and thus forms an insufficient basis for performing world- and self-making in sense. Under these conditions, the political appeal of post-truth politics, as it will be argued in the following, lies in the fact that it is particularly effective as a politics that offers orientation for sense-making.

Post-Truth Populist Orientation

When complexity has become the most urgent challenge requiring social steering, and managing it a central need for democratic subjects, politics adapts—and becomes the locus of a socially centralized, autological production of orientation. It is in the form of orientation that reduces complexity and offers citizens narratives, explanatory frameworks, issues, and values to guide self- and worldmaking in sense that politics fulfills its collectively steering function. And it is here that politics, if the orientation it offers is accepted as fit for purpose, receives the public recognition of its social effectiveness that allows it to persist. The theoretical lens of a politics of orientation renders the radical discontinuity of post-truth populism, usually illustrated with the many surreal details of Trump's presidency, from his tweets to his public appearances and the grand finale of the storming of Capitol hill, congruent with an exploration of its continuities. Like Mouffe, the politics of orientation suggests that the underlying patterns of modern politics continue within the superficially disrupted contemporary democracies. But what continues is here not a Mouffian antagonism essential to the political but rather the autopoietic functioning of modern politics that *still works* as a politics of orientation—it still provides collective steering for society and its citizens.

The turn to populism and post-factual political content can in this sense not be understood as antithetical to a liberal democratic politics where citizens trade freedoms and rights for certain social advantages. It also is not the Frankensteinian creation of a neoliberal political economy where all democratic processes and values have been dissolved. A politics of orientation, including post-truth populism, can sustain itself only because it offers citizens something in return for their political support, which is not merely the product of ideological manipulation on the side of populist demagogues. Citizens marching in support of Trump, or against state-mandated pandemic measures, are democratic subjects in the sense that they exchange political support for the provision of a social good that is lacking. Only the appearance of democratic politics has become monstrous because the social good desired is not a Hobbesian collective security or a Lockean protection of individual rights but a collective orientation where successful complexity-reduction trumps both of the former, or even legitimizes their complete disregard.

When the production of orientation for sense-making in society has become the functional mechanism of political autopoiesis, a politically produced orientation, not absolutely but increasingly, becomes the code under which the remnants of expectational structures—ethics, scientific truth, religion—become subsumed. These alternative ordering frameworks do not lose their power but are blended with the lines and frameworks of orientation offered by politics. Whether or not citizens accept the truth of scientific studies evidencing the reality of the COVID-19 pandemic, and the effectiveness of vaccines in pro-tecting individuals from contracting it, depends on whether an anti-social, anti-democratic conspiracy theory has been adopted as the orienting framework. The prioritization of ethical guidelines regarding sustainable consumption and the relationship to nonhumans is conditional on the adoption of ecological politics as an orienting code. On the other side of the political spectrum, the politics of the new right are characterized by an overarching concern for an economically framed private sphere freedom. Religious orientation and traditional views on gender and sexuality seamlessly blend with the former, but less so with the ordering framework of green politics.

As the medium of political autopoiesis expressed in sense, political orientation is neither limited to particular actors or institutions on the inside of the apparatus of parliamentary democracy nor to particular kinds of political content. Governments might often be centrally involved in the production of political orientation—Agamben's state of exception can be understood as an orienting code dominating democratic politics following the 9/11 attacks—but they can never monopolize the former. Understood in this sense, exceptionalism does not only characterize how executive force is produced and reproduced through the epistemic creation of a lethal threat to the political community, but the perspective of a politics of orientation allows us to move beyond the simplistic assumption that this takes place against the background of the state's strategic manipulation of a public perception that it fully controls.

Understood as code within a politics of orientation, the state of exception offers citizens complexity-reduction and guidance for sense-making in return for accepting the executive force of the orienting power. The external threat, and the "otherness" of its source, be it Islamic terrorism or migration for Western democracies, provides citizens with a framework through which they can make sense of their own self as well as the current state of the world in which they act. Using exceptionalism as orientation importantly does not equate to supporting of exceptional measures—it can equally take the form of a self- and worldmaking that is deliberately anti-xenophobic and suspicious of executive power and extensive state surveillance. Agamben, in his infamous comment from the early days of the pandemic, expresses worry that COVID-19 will replace the threat of Islamic terrorism as the hinge of the exceptional political apparatus (Agamben, 2020). Viewed through the lens of a politics of orientation, what appears to be taking place within democratic societies at the dawn of the twenty-first century's third decade is a shift of a rather different kind.

Exceptionalism, as a politics of orientation, produced legitimacy for the institutions and actors of the (democratic or authoritarian) state. It does so in the tradition of conspiracy theories that have shaped twentieth-century democratic politics, such as ideas of secret mason lodges, McCarthy's conspiracy of a communist infiltration of U.S. politics, or suspicions of secret machinations directed against "Catholics and Mormons later, Negroes and Jews" (1964), as Richard Hofstadter outlines in his seminal "The Paranoid Style in American Politics." But in a world that seems only inadequately ordered and controlled by political authority, the state's politics of orientation, including exceptionalism, appear to have lost at least some of their draw. As Roberto Esposito observes contra Agamben on the occasion of Italy's response to the COVID-19 pandemic, "it seems to me that what is happening . . . has more the character of a breakdown of public authorities than that of a dramatic totalitarian grip" (2020). The actors and institutions of liberal democracy, which can no longer rest their political claim on effective steering through decision making, also fail to clearly and unambiguously succeed as a politics of orientation.

After exceptionalism, there is no one challenge, issue, ideal, or aim that singularly captures the attention and guides the political imagination of citizens—political orientation lacks a unifying code. Rather, what we find is a network of competing, disconnected and often directly contradictory frameworks of orientation available to guide sense-making on the part of citizens. Clear lines between government and opposition are replaced by ad-hoc coalitions, and many party systems witness the rise of new political players, such as the increasingly popular green parties. Formerly more or less unitary centrist parties, both on the left and on the right of the political spectrum, are now fragmented into different wings whose frameworks of orientation at times stand in direct tension with each other (Santucci, 2020; Somer and McCoy, 2018; Zollinger, 2021). One might think of the U.S. Democrats after Joe Biden's election victory against Trump. While the moderate Democratic majority advocated for a return to the orienting status quo of twentieth-century politics, a smaller, progressive circle promoted radical change, insisting that precisely this status quo had caused the current anti-democratic perils.

Collective orientation for self- and worldmaking is not just offered by actors or topics conventionally understood as political. Under conditions where such orientation has become the defining product of the political system, topics and actors *become politicized through their provision of orientation*. In this sense, the politics of orientation continue the proliferation of the political that characterized twentieth-century welfare state politics for Luhmann (1990b, pp. 102–103). Political claims surrounding sex and sexuality, for example, have become political because they provide orientation for sense-making, and not just for those whose identity is being represented, as do conspiracy theories regarding the shape of the Earth, or the origin and reality of the coronavirus. Again, to be clear, neither political factions nor conspiracy theories or activist movements are exclusive to twenty-first-century democratic politics. What is new, I suggest through the lens of political orientation, is the extent to which the provision of orientation for self- and worldmaking takes priority over, or in some cases fully replaces, concrete and ideologically fleshed out political demands, programs, and action points.

Simple messages of making America great again, in the case of Trump's first presidential campaign, or taking back control for Vote Leave, do not function to condense and sell a political manifesto but rather replace it. The complexity-reducing coding of post-truth populism functions through the bloated but empty signifiers of nationalist or traditional values, accompanied by a general suspicion against everything not already well established in common sense or immediately obvious to the eye. For post-truth populism, Brown identifies this as the nihilistic ressentiment of the political right. But the same focus on self- and worldmaking through a radically single-issue complexity-reduction underpins progressive "identity politics" (Barkhoff and Leerssen, 2021; Besley and Persson, 2020). The conflict between an "open" versus a "closed" outlook on society has become one of the central lines of division in many Western democracies (Zollinger, 2021). It is a conflict that plays out on the level of *worldmaking*, of how the social status quo is perceived and which direction of development is viewed as favorable on this basis. Political support is not exchanged for a political program that represents and resonates with a subject's interests and aims—but rather for the provision of a world- and identity-making vision.

While the shift toward a politics of orientation is theorized as general-social, it is argued that the upheavals of democratic politics labeled as post-truth populist here follow from the fact that established democratic actors and institutions are, not absolutely but also not insignificantly, losing political traction vis-à-vis these new political forces. Post-truth populism, understood as a politics of orientation, is more effective at providing orientation because of two distinct qualities: the use of *negation* and the *control of intransparency*. Brown draws attention to the role of apolitical, contentless negation in the politics of the new right. For Brown, post-truth populism appeals to and draws together political supporters merely as a "wounded attachment" lacking any positive claim and offering nothing but a universal rejection. But importantly, there is certainty in this rejection. The political appeal of Brown's wounded nihilism lies in that it offers a powerful way of reducing complexity to guide sense-making. The negation of sense—of all existing values, explanatory frameworks, and political claims, is also a way to make sense. Sense-making through negation has the specific advantage that it can take place under conditions of high complexity and uncertainty with little knowledge of the context in which it is taking place.

As Luhmann writes in the first volume of *Theory of Society*, "negation permits the domestication of the determinate/indeterminate schema, one of the fundamental distinctions enabling us to deal with [sense]" (2012a, p. 133; my translation)—negation tames sense insofar as it always allows us to transform complete indeterminacy into determinacy: "Through negation we can indicate something in such a way that it remains uncertain what is actually going on. 'No one in the desert' does not tell us what else there is in the desert, or where people really are, or who is meant at all. The communication is nonetheless immediately comprehensible and ready to be dealt with further—for example, as a warning. [. . .] For this purpose, negative reference builds bridges to normality" (Luhmann, 2012a, p. 133).

In this sense, libertarian rejections of mask-wearing and lockdown restrictions, of racial and gender-based equality or of economic redistribution are appealing not because those they appeal to hold a rationally developed, opposing political stance but because they offer "bridges to normality"—they allow citizens to make sense of the world they inhabit, even under conditions where the former remains largely unknown. The negation that characterizes post-truth populism hence does not aim at convincing or even defeating a political opponent, but purely at negation itself, which excludes the complexity of what is negated to the outside of non-engagement and non-acknowledgment.

While exclusionary negation as a means of complexity-reduction is certainly a prominent feature of post-truth populism, it is not exclusive to the former but also visible in mainstream and left-wing politics, again particularly on the part of progressive identity politics. Denying structural racism or the patriarchal quality of society is here not so much an incorrect view to be critiqued and countered but a position that simply cannot be held, that can only be negated (Gerrard, 2021). In the debate surrounding trans-rights, those arguing for the (either biologically or socially rooted) stability of the category "woman" are similarly met not with counterarguments but only with negation, such as through terms like "TERF." Here, it is not post-factual content but rather individual experience that offers complexity-reducing certainty. Political support is derived from the attachment to the experience of racialized, gendered, or classed inequality and the creation of political space for critiquing former. Negation here offers subjects orientation for self-making—for example as an anti-sexist, anti-racist "ally"—but also for the production of the social world as centered on a particular inequality. For ecological politics, the recognition of environmental shaping power as real, but not fully understandable and governable, becomes a way of giving form to, and thereby excluding, complexity as environmental. Luhmann presciently references Climate anxiety, which has become a prevalent social phenomenon (Taylor and Murray, 2020), to argue that it is, for the subject experiencing it, a way of reducing uncertainty because it gives anxiety a form, cause, and course of action through which to respond to it. It transforms "the uncertainty of the situation into the certainty of anxiety" (Luhmann, 1989, p. 130; see also: 1993b, p. 535) induced by an environmental shaping power that we cannot comprehend or control.

Beyond a negation that functions effectively complexity-reducing, post-truth populism is particularly effective as a politics of orientation because it offers means for the control of intransparency. In Wiener's cybernetic theory, control describes the functional necessity of managing uncertainty in the face of information overload, which is experienced by all self-observing second-order machines. Because second-order machines constantly observe their own, changing observational position vis-à-vis their environment, they are subject to a constant escalation of informational complexity. Against this background, Wiener likens the systemic control of feedback, information resulting from self-observation, to the fire-control system of a plane (Wiener, 1985, pp. 10–12). Both need to function in such a way that they automatically ward off the most pressing danger the machine they are integrated in can face to preserve its functioning. For a plane, this means protecting the engines in the event of a fire. The second-order system must maintain its ability to selectively produce output by controlling entropy (p. 17). Control is thus a functional necessity for the second-order machine.

In his essay "Control and Control Societies in Deleuze" (2016), Bruce Clark suggests that the cybernetic connotation of control is at work, at least implicitly, as "cybernetic subtexts" (Clark, 2016, p. 1) in Deleuze's postscript. The dividual of the digitalized control society is not only free from institutional disciplining but also from its subjectivized, internalized continuation in the form of self-disciplining (Rouvroy, 2013). The pressure that the dividual faces is of a different kind: it arises from the impossible task of fulfilling their role effectively in all institutional logics at one (Clark, 2016, pp. 11–12; MacKenzie and Porter, 2019, pp. 15–16). The dividual can succeed as an informed participant in all social realms only if they find a way to condense the flows of information—through control, which means the adoption of internal rules to select information and thereby counteract entropy. Dividuals must select to reduce complexity—but this has already been established. In "The Control of Intransparency" (1997b), Luhmann offers a definition of control that adapts Wiener's cybernetic conceptualization to the context of his social systems theory, and specifies its meaning beyond selective complexity-reduction. For Luhmann, control describes the structurally evolved skill of social systems and their psychic observers to deal with the complexity that has become a functionally necessary aspect of autopoietic existence in modern societies (Luhmann, 1997b, p. 363). Control involves complexity-reduction, but importantly is also a way to make sense of the fact that this complexity-reduction is always partial and temporary. The functionally differentiated society as a whole can be experienced only as a "symphony of intransparency" (p. 360) that must be absorbed by mechanisms of control.[2]

The necessity to control for intransparency fleshes out the challenge that living in a society composed of autopoietic systems poses for the subject. Not only do the inhabitants of functionally differentiated societies need to find ways to reduce the perpetually escalating complexity that multiple couplings with different social systems expose them to, but at the same time, they need to control observational insights into their lack of steering success resulting from complexity-induced intransparency. In other words, subjects also need to come to terms with the insufficiency of any means for complexity-reduction they might employ in a world filled with autopoietically closed systems where all they know, and can direct, are ultimately the insides of their systems of sense. The fact that a society with a developed, now digitalized, media system observes itself as increasingly unknowable only exacerbates the issue at hand. The interlinked requirements of complexity-reduction and control drive what subjects expect from a politics of orientation, which is to fulfill its social steering function effectively. Against this background, the anti-elite, anti-technocratic stance of post-truth populism does more than justify the absence of a rationally developed claims or a political program—it controls for intransparency by putting the blame for the instransparency experienced on political and scientific elites that are deliberately trying to conceal their machinations.

In this sense, the Vote Leave campaign's success might not solely be explicable through affective appeal to the latent xenophobia of the British public. The outcome of the Brexit referendum also reflects the desire to counter the social complexity embodied by the EU's intricate bureaucratic design with a more transparent, simpler social arrangement symbolized by the value of British sovereignty simplified and absolutized to an extent that it is "closer to that used by North Korea than to that of any other free-trading western nation" (Westcott, 2020). COVID-conspiracy theories about the origin of the virus, its nonexistence, or the supposed effects of the vaccine are a way to reduce and manage complexity and make sense of individual agency vis-a-vis a society at the receiving end of the spread of a highly infectious and unpredictably evolving virus. Subjects turn to conspiracy theories for their simplicity and orienting effect in times of uncertainty or threat, not only in the context of the COVID-19 pandemic. But added to the orienting function of COVID-conspiracy theories is an anti-elitist suspicion that controls for the ensuing individual powerlessness—the lab origin of the virus is not widely know because of a strategic political cover-up. The public is being manipulated with false information and data by a sinister conglomerate of governments, scientists, and pharmaceutical companies. Post-factual content gives the lack of subjective knowledge and agency a cause, and thereby renders it manageable.

Conclusion

In the preceding pages, I have attempted not only to generate but, more importantly, to put to work a theoretical enfolding of the conceptual worlds of Luhmann and Deleuze for political theory. I hope that this enfolding has substantiated this book's presupposition of a kinship not between the thinkers Luhmann and Deleuze but between the conceptual personae emergent from their works, the impersonal thinkers who "are closely linked to the diagrammatic features of thought and the intensive features of concepts" (Deleuze and Guattari, 1994, p. 69). Both Luhmann and Deleuze reverse our common-sense understanding of order and chaos. They reveal the latter as the productive continuity behind everything, always present, always shining through the cracks of our ordering systems, and the former as the fragile, radically contingent, and laboriously upheld exception to be explained. While many philosophies begin from the question, "Why are things the way they are?," both Luhmann and Deleuze instead wonder, "How come things are not constantly changing?" and set out to expose and unpack the forces that impose a particular continuity on the world. This taming of multiplicity or complexity, for both thinkers, takes place in sense. The concept of sense thus forms the center of the Deleuzian-Luhmannian conceptual world drawn out in this book. Sense is the immanently creative medium of world- and self-making. Sense creates and actualizes a contingent border between what is and what is not as the distinction between expressed sense and the underside of nonsense, which drives the mechanism of sense-making as constitutive outside and creative reservoir.

Because the outside of nonsense always remains present in every instance of sense-making, sense tames chaotic nonsense only ever for an instant. The production of stable selves and continuous worlds not constantly taken apart and put back together differently whenever sense and nonsense collide again requires the emergence of ordering structures in sense. The most fundamental, and most important, of these ordering structures, for Deleuze and Luhmann alike, is time. It was shown how both thinkers conceptualize time not as an *a priori* structure framing sense-making from the outside, but as a form of self-ordering immanent to sense, which changes and adapts together with the worlds it orders in sense. Because time functions ordering only insofar as it renders itself transitory, it requires its own mechanism of self-reproduction that allows ordering time to continuously return to relations of sense. In both Luhmann and Deleuze, the continuation of time is made possible through the eternal return of the rupturing event. Reintroducing the motor of complexity or multiplicity to the otherwise lifeless circle of passing time, the event allows time, and with it the worlds and selves it stabilizes in sense, to be made again, and thus to continue.

While it is Deleuze who theoretically captures the eternal return of the rupturing event most clearly, Luhmann allows us to see a different side of Deleuze's creative event. The event is both productive and conditioned; it does not return by chance but is actively produced by a creative mechanism of sense-making-in-time that functionally requires it to remain in motion. The "immanent externality" of the event does not take away from its rupturing force. But it unfolds, and becomes evental, only in relation to the order of sense upon which it acts. For this reason, the particular link between evental singularity and the nexus of sense that enfolds it determines how evental creativity plays out in the continuum between exact reproduction and radical change. While Deleuze's theoretical and political interest, unlike Luhmann's, lies with the revolutionary event, the former must be conceived of as a special case of the creative event that always has to be made, or rather, counter-effectuated. The event is always productive, but does not necessarily produce change. The eternal stillness of the Great Pyramid is also an event.

The conceptual fold of Deleuze's and Luhmann's event marked the transition from ontology to political theory in this book. Counter-effectuating the revolutionary event is the great political act, and task, in Deleuze. But in a more abstract sense, Deleuze and Luhmann reveal every event as political. It is in the evental continuation of sense that the decision on *which world exactly* will emerge from the event takes place. Every subject is continuously faced with the task of deciding on the pathway that carves out the contours of the world that continues in sense. But Luhmann shows that authoritative worldmaking in sense, which offers this decision in a collectively binding fashion, is the social function of modern politics. Luhmann's theory puts a spin on the idea of political decisionism: politics does not so much directly produce its constitutive power in the sovereign decision. Its social role and authority is rather legitimized by the function it fulfills for its citizens, which is the decision on the continuation of sense that continuously actualizes a particular world. However, this social function causes a dilemma for the political institutions that govern late twentieth- and early twenty-first-century democracies because it is exactly such worldmaking authority that they can no longer effectively exercise.

Luhmann, and Deleuze and Guattari, in *Anti-Oedipus*, draw out how the disjointed flows of neoliberal capitalism, which Luhmann captures as functionally differentiated social relations, are responsible for the dilemma of politics. Capital, not political authority, is the principle that guides social organization and thus worldmaking in sense. The despotic machine of politics no longer has the authority to govern worldmaking through state overcoding; politics can merely govern what is internal to its own functional system but lacks both insight and controlling capacity regarding the rest of society. While this does not mean that politics is completely powerless, the political system can no longer readily perform collective steering in the form of a demonstratively effective governmental worldmaking. This functional dilemma, however, does not cause the processes and institutions of modern politics to disintegrate—it causes them to adapt. Politics becomes, to borrow Deleuze and Guattari's term, a "post-mortem despotism" that proves its social use through the re-territorializing provision of collective orientation. While politics can no longer function collectively steering by governing worldmaking, it can offer subjects with frameworks of orientation they can draw on to make sense of the world they inhabit, and their own position within it.

In societies where citizens have to participate in multiple different functional systems or dislocated institutional realms at once, their experience of the social world is one of intransparent complexity, which threatens subjective processes of world- and self-making in sense. This experience of complexity is heightened by the digitalization of sense-expression, which has led to an implosion of second-order observation and thus a multiplication of available lines of sense. Under these conditions, complexity-reducing orientation becomes a public demand—and its provision a new basis of democratic politics. This book has argued that this underlying shift to a politics of orientation, which characterizes twenty-first-century democratic politics, is the fertile ground on which the political forces of post-truth populism flourish. It codes and thereby reduces complexity through a combination of negation, oversimplification, and affective-normative appeal, which render post-truth populism particularly effective at offering orientation, and, at least currently, decisively more so than the actors and institutions of established parliamentary democracy. The task for democratic politics is thus to reimagine itself for the age of a politics of orientation for which, because it is rooted in the social conditions of neoliberal capitalism, no end is in sight.

Political theory has a part to play in such a process of reimagining. And Deleuze and Luhmann do not leave us completely without guidance for how it can be achieved. To posit the re-imagining of democratic politics as an achievement, however, implies the possibility of a subject achieving it, and thereby crystallizes the question of subjective agency that has surfaced at different points in this book. In its established sense, the notion of the acting subject is alien to the works of both Deleuze and Luhmann. For Luhmann, this is a fairly uncontentious claim, as the structural determinism of his theory, where the subject is dissolved into a set of self-reproductive psychic relations not controlled by either reason or will, and themselves unable to intervene in the steering of autopoietic social systems, has always been amongst the most widely criticized implications of his general systems theory (Habermas, 1971; Brunczel, 2010). Whether or not there is space for an intentionally acting subject in Deleuze is a more controversially discussed question within the secondary literature. As shown in chapter 4, on the topic of how revolutionary events unfold, Stengers (2011, pp. 270–273), and in a more nuanced way Ansell Pearson (1997) and Widder (2008, pp. 95–98), maintain that actual change follows only from the subjective ethical commitment of willing the event. On the other side of the Deleuzian agency spectrum, Gavin Rae, in *Poststructuralist Agency*, argues that Deleuze's philosophy "affirms pre-personal structures and processes to the extent that any agential action [. . .] is explicitly undermined" (2020, p. 5), leading him to conclude that "subjective agency is the question where Deleuze's differential ontology (purposely) runs up against its limits" (p. 55).

This book unfolds a Deleuzian theory that aligns with Rae's conclusion; like Luhmann's, Deleuze's thought cannot account for subjective agency because its entire conceptual apparatus is intended to reveal what lies behind and beyond the "uninteresting and useless" (Rae, 2020, p. 55) conceptual façade of the subject. Like the world in which they act, the individual subject is contingently produced from relations of sense, and their becoming is continuously shaped by their self-reproductive unfolding. Of course, it would be absurd to assume that Deleuze and Luhmann think subjects don't act, or act with no meaningful consequence. Subjective action is rather a blind spot of their theories, which they set up in explicit contrast to a modern philosophy and social theory where subjective agency has unquestionably been placed center stage. At this juncture, I believe Sean Bowden's idea of expressive agency offers a useful account for the kind of subjective agency that Deleuze's and Luhmann's theories permit, albeit that this subjective agency always remains hidden from their theoretical gazes.

Bowden develops his expressive agency through a reading of Deleuze's *Logic of Sense*, which, against the background of the arguments developed above, renders it applicable to Luhmann's work. As shown in chapter 1, the bodies and actions of *The Logic of Sense* are never the causes of expressive sense-events, but only their quasi-causes. This is the case because productive sense unfolds from the autological interplay of sense and nonsense where subjective action is linked to past happenings, present contexts, and lines of thought to function creatively. However, as Bowden emphasizes, this does not take away from the fact that subjective agency is present in the vicinity of the creative sense-event unfolding, and that it adds something to it. In the expressive event, "the agent with his or her intentions is not so much behind her actions as 'out there' in her actions such as these are interpreted or made sense of in a shared expressive medium" (Bowden, 2014, p. 243). Subjective action can neither bring forth nor intentionally shape events. However, because events are unfolding in sense, and thus always only insofar as they are made sense of, the presence of an acting subject linked to the event as part of this sense-making process *ex post facto* can be decisive for the quality and direction of the productive force that unfolds (Bowden, 2014, pp. 244–246). Similar to what was argued in chapter 4, subjective action does not possess a pre-given power over the event, but depending on the relational links established in the event it can become powerful in making a—rupturing or reproductive—event happen after the fact. As Deleuze puts it, actors are the "offspring of one's events" because "action is itself produced by the offspring of the event" (1990, p. 150) and not by subjective intent. Subjects can never be certain of their evental contributions, but their actions nevertheless have importance and value because of the interpretational links they offer to the relationally productive sense-event. It is in this sense, I suggest, that the agential speculations of philosophers have a place in Deleuze's and Luhmann's conceptual worlds.

In *What is Philosophy?*, Deleuze and Guattari identify concept creation as the purpose of philosophy. For Deleuze and Guattari, concepts "are like multiple waves, rising and falling" (1994, p. 36), which break on the plane of immanence from which new thought emerges. Concept creation aims at opening sense-relations to the evental multiplicity that forms their underside in order to create an opening for the counter-effectuation of new thought, or new politics (Mengue, 2013). "The task of philosophy when it creates concepts," Deleuze and Guattari write, "is always to extract an event from things and beings" (1994, p. 33; see also Deleuze, 1990, pp. 196–170). Concepts are thus not created *ex nihilo* but emerge in sense relations and work in the former—they have a history and a past in sense. For this reason, Deleuze and Guattari prefer to speak of concept extraction rather than of concept creation. Because of their intrinsic relational interconnectedness, concepts cannot be understood as isolated forms. A concept includes the way it affects the network of sense relations it is situated in. It is "a heterogenesis—that is to say, an ordering of its components by zones of neighborhood. [. . .] The concept is in a state of survey [sur-volt] in relation to its components, endlessly traversing them according to an order without distance" (Deleuze and Guattari, 1994, p. 20).

Due to the connective nature of the concept, the method of extractive concept creation must take the form of a productive dialogue between different ideas, frameworks, and philosophies. On the contrary, "those who criticize without creating . . . are the plague of philosophy" (Deleuze and Guattari, 1994, p. 28). Concept creation is hence the diametrical opposite of a dogmatic use of philosophy pre-directed by a particular school of thought and its leaders (p. 80). Like the counter-effectuation of the event, the success of the exploratory investment of concept creation is never guaranteed, and there is no easy way to even measure its success without a pre-given rule to determine "whether this is the good plane, the good persona, or the good concept" (p. 82). But for Deleuze and Guattari, it is always worth risking. I suggest that this aim of deliberately venturing beyond all established philosophical rules, framework, and lines of interpretation for the uncertain opportunity of developing a pathway for sense-making through which the world can be thought, and thus can be made, differently, also lies at the heart of Luhmann's mode of theorizing. So much so that Luhmann devised a methodological tool to assist his concept creation: the Zettelkasten.

Luhmann's Zettelkasten is a collection of 90,000 numbered note cards that he started using in 1951 and continuously updated until 1996. Luhmann viewed the Zettelkasten as vital to his work (Schmidt, 2012, 2014). In an interview published in a major German newspaper, he stated, albeit certainly with a dose of his characteristic humor, that "the Zettelkasten takes up more time than writing books" (Luhmann, quoted in Erd and Maihofer, 1985). Luhmann's academic intimate Dirk Baecker (2012, p. 2) recalls that Luhmann turned down visiting fellowships at the most prestigious universities in Europe and North America because he did not want to risk losing his Zettelkasten in transit. The notes collected in the Zettelkasten contain bibliographical references, indices of keywords, and, most importantly, Luhmann's reading notes. While Schmidt observes that Luhmann's earlier notes remain close to their reference texts, and only make sense as comments on the former, over time Luhmann's notes took on a life of their own (2014, p. 169). They became theoretical statements and arguments in their own right, which were inspired by the source text but clearly independent of it.

Even more important than the content of the Zettelkasten is, however, the way in which Luhmann organized it. Borrowing from the terminology of *A Thousand Plateaus*, I suggest that the organizational structure of the Zettelkasten is rhizomatic. In Luhmann's own words, the note cards form a "spider-like system" (1987, p. 143; my translation). While Luhmann organized his note box around themes with multiple subcategories, these subcategories are not linked to the overall theme in a linear, arborescent manner that follows and reproduces an underlying ordering principle. On the contrary, the nonhierarchical and mutually interconnected subcategories of the Zettelkasten allow for the emergence of conceptual networks beyond pre-given interpretive lines. Schmidt describes the rhizomatic organization of the Zettelkasten's note cards in the following manner:

> [T]he way they were organized meant that the initial decision on an ordering theme did not produce a monothematic sequence of notes. Whenever there is an interesting secondary object, it is explored (now or later) on note cards added to an already noted thought which were inserted immediately behind the note they relate to. There can be several points like this on an original note, which led to several inserted cards, cross-referencing further notes. This procedure can then also be applied to the inserted notes themselves, generating a sequence of notes which—if read in a linear fashion—becomes further and further removed from the original topic. This organizational method means that the preliminary categorization into themes is in part abolished within those thematic categories themselves. It produces a particular structural depth [. . .] which means that on the one hand a topic or concept can be accessed via different routes. On the other hand, the different contexts which situate a topic produce divergent information [on this topic] which is relative to the comparative grounds on which it is based. (Schmidt, 2014, p. 172; my translation)[1]

What, then, is the purpose of Luhmann's laboriously assembled and upheld Zettelkasten? In Luhmann's own words, the complex structure of spontaneous associations and multiple thematic cross-references renders it significantly more than just a "second memory" (Luhmann, quoted in Schmidt, 2014, p. 168)—a "tool for thinking" (p. 168). The nonlinear order of the collected notes not only preserves theoretical connections once drawn in thought but, more importantly, at the same time forces the thinker to discover and consider new links, thematic connections, and lines of thought. Whenever you look for something in the Zettelkasten, Luhmann explains, whenever you try to establish a particular connective relation, you always find more than you are looking for, and more than you could even have anticipated (Luhmann, 1981, p. 226; see also: Luhmann et al. 2000). "The Zettelkasten finds combinatory opportunities which have never been planned, never been thought, never been conceptualized in given occasions" (Luhmann, 1981, p. 226). It is a theoretical-methodological tool "whose effects are the genesis of chance" (p. 228).

The methodological tool of the Zettelkasten forces an encounter with the openness immanent to sense but tamed by philosophical canonization and cultural tastes. It eclipses the figure of the thinker in favor of a creative thought-production that takes place in the open interplay of sense relations themselves. "I don't think all of this on my own," Luhmann insists in this sense, "but this indeed happens in the Zettelkasten [. . .] my productivity must mostly be attributed to the Zettelkasten" (1987, p. 142).[2] Is the lesson to be drawn here that all critical theorists should immediately get to work, either with wooden planks and cardboard or a software that can achieve the equivalent, to build a Zettelkasten that assists them in the radical reimagining of democratic politics? I certainly would not want to go this far. However, I do think that Luhmann's Zettelkasten makes an urgent case for forcefully retaining openness toward exploratory work that transgresses established interpretive trajectories to provoke an encounter between a philosophy and its outside, be it in one's own reading and writing, be it as a reviewer, a graduate supervisor, a member of a hiring panel, or in a public discussion, even if the immediate gut reaction tempts one toward the otherwise. Of course, not all of these open-ended explorations are fruitful—as not all conceptual links produced by the Zettelkasten make sense. But in a democratic present that seems to urgently require new ideas, they indeed seem always worth risking.

Notes

Introduction

1. This link came to my attention through Regan Burles's paper "Orienting World Politics: The Measure of the Earth," presented at the "Geopolitics and Planetary Boundaries" workshop in Sigtuna, Sweden, in 2022.

2. A more detailed breakdown of these theoretical parallels, including concepts that Luhmann develops with explicit reference to Deleuze, will follow in chapter 1.

3. In 2009, a picture of Luhmann's membership card that identified him as a member of the German National-Socialist party (NSDAP) was publicly circulated and received much attention. However, neither the authenticity of the document nor the fact that Luhmann, who was a teenage soldier in the Second World War, even knew about his possible party membership, can be sufficiently verified (Steinbacher, 2009).

4. While a number of short papers engage with Deleuze and Luhmann together (Philippopoulos-Mihalopoulos, 2013; Guy, 2019; Pottage, 1998) there is no book-length, substantial work that interlinks both theories.

5. Luhmann persistently refused to identify as a philosopher—or classify his work as philosophy. Belying the obvious philosophical ambitions of his work, this refusal seems to be rooted in Luhmann's disdain for what he perceived as philosophy's disciplinary arrogance and performative intellectualism. Luhmann's feelings vis-à-vis philosophy shine through in occasional mocking remarks, such as the following, borrowed from Jean Paul, which he made in a lecture on Husserl: "[T]he analysis just presented [. . .] was neither intended as a 'critique' nor [. . .] as a philosophy. For a sociologist, the windows are located too high above in philosophical auditoriums" (Luhmann, 1996b, p. 56; my translation).

6. Beyond the examples provided here, the Facebook page *Luhmanns Humor* contains numerous examples of humorous or absurd remarks in Luhmann's writings and his personal as well as professional correspondence compiled by the sociologist David J. Klett (2018).

7. In a radio interview with *Radio Bremen*, Luhmann reveals a deeply rooted and rather personal interest in the idea of order and its relationship to chaos. He reflects on the origins of his academic interest beginning with his studies of law after the Second World War, which he attributes to a commitment to "ordering all the chaos" (Luhmann, 1997a).

8. Deleuze's rejection of the Hegelian dialectic does not equate to an altogether dismissal of the dialectic method. As Widder convincingly shows in "Thought after Dialectics: Deleuze's Ontology of Sense" (2003), Deleuze's theory of sense, which functions generative through self-differentiation, can be understood as an iteration or even completion of Hegel's productive dialectic, but importantly without the final resolution in absolute unity.

9. The Deleuze scholarship remains divided on whether, and to what extent, his early works written prior to his encounter with Guattari can be classified as political. However, a number of scholars have shown how the combination of a genealogical critique that reveals the artificiality of philosophical truths and recovers the creative multiplicity they conceal and an affirmative exploration of how the creative multiplicity uncovered can be used to make a manifest difference to the world we live in constitutes a red thread that runs through all of Deleuze's work from his early philosophical commentary on selected grand figures of modern thought to his late experimental writings with Guattari (Widder, 2012; Demers, 2008; Buchanan and Thoburn, 2008; Patton, 2000).

10. Against such a democratic reading of Deleuze. Phillippe Mengue (2005) argues that Deleuze's radical politics is fundamentally anti-institutional and hostile toward the idea of democracy.

Chapter 1

1. In both quotes from Luhmann, the German "Sinn" has been translated as "sense," not as "meaning," which is the chosen expression in the English translation of *Theory of Society*. A longer discussion of this choice of translation will follow further in the chapter.

2. What is more, only a few of those recent publications are actually driven by an interest in Deleuze's philosophy of sense as such. James William's (2008) reader guide seeks to provide an accessible introduction to *The Logic of Sense*, but thereby mainly fills a hole in the secondary literature on Deleuze's work. Guillaume Collet (2016) and Piotrek Świątkowski (2016) use *The Logic of Sense* to draw out a hidden, psychoanalytic undercurrent in Deleuze's work. Only Sean Bowden and Widder, whose work is akin to some of the arguments developed in this book, place the concept of sense at the center of Deleuze's philosophy. Like Bowden and Widder, this book argues that the central contribution of *The Logic of Sense* is that it allows us to think a thoroughly immanent mode of ontogenesis. The pure event of sense is transcendental insofar as it is "not external to the conditions of

knowledge" (Bowden, 2011, p. 69). Thought and world are made in one and the same creative sense expression, which is not externally charged or conditioned but emerges on the inside of sense itself (pp. 108, 122, 185; Widder, 2012, pp. 21–22; 2008, pp. 34–36).

3. Bowden hints at the potential fruitfulness of such a political application of the ideas that Deleuze develops in *The Logic of Sense* at the very end of his *The Priority of Events*, where he suggests that they can "be brought into a fruitful conversation with political . . . thought" (2011, p. 277).

4. In *The Crisis of the European Sciences and Transcendental Phenomenology*, Husserl later re-orients his philosophy of sense to move even closer to Deleuze's account in a more radical phenomenology of sense. Now, sense-making is no longer anchored in and pre-ordered by the faculties of subjective consciousness. It is rather made at the boundary of subjectivity and material environment as the open-ended "possibility space" (Ratcliffe, 2013, p. 74) that the subject inhabits, and that shapes ideas and perceptions.

5. These arguments relate to Bowden's discussion of Deleuze's psychoanalytic sense as an "intersubjective or social space" (2014, p. 235) in "Willing the Event."

6. Just as Luhmann will do later, Parsons breaks up social reality into a compound of different systems such as psychic, social, or cultural. The medium of systemic organization, however, is action in Parsons—interaction systems relationally emerge between actor and situation or actor and object. For Parsons, a system is "the structure of the relations between the actors as involved in the interactive process" (1991, p. 15). Because systemic structures are generalizable for Parsons, they can be used to analyze how social interactions function, adapt, and change on a macro-level.

7. This book uses the term "subject" in the context of Luhmann's theory—in full awareness of the fact that the subject not only does not feature in Luhmann's own theoretical register, but that it rather is one of the philosophical categories that Luhmann seeks to do away with in order to understand what "lies beneath"—a set of particular social and epistemological conditions that lead to consciousness systems describing themselves, and others, as subjects (Luhman, 2013, pp. 266–267; see also: Luhmann, 2008b, pp. 142–154 for a similar discussion on the concept of "person"). This book can speak of a Deleuzian-Luhmannian "subject" insofar as both Deleuze and Luhmann reject the idea of the rational-individual subject as the unit of human action. For both, creative processes take place within and through the subject without requiring the agency of the former. Important here are the sense-making processes discussed in this chapter, and in the next one, but also Deleuze and Guattari's famous insistence that the unconscious should be understood not as a theater but as a factory (1983, p. 24). This "non-subjective subject," made up of and acting productive through creative sense-relations is the subject this book refers to. The motivation for holding on to the concept of the subject, rather than insisting on Luhmann's consciousness system or psychic system, is simply that of rendering Luhmann's thought accessible, and palatable, for a broad audience of philosophical readers by avoiding Luhmann's system theoretic jargon wherever possible.

8. While Luhmann never explicitly limits the epistemic horizon and social context to which his theory can be applied to, the central role that modernity plays in Luhmann's writings suggests that this specification is indeed apt. As Baecker notes, Luhmann "tried to be as explicit about his circumstances as one possibly could be. He searched descriptions of modern society in literally all European languages save Russian. But he knew that circumstances in Slovenia, Japan, Italy, Mexico, Brazil, and Denmark must be quite different from those he was referring to when working on his theory. So he did not venture to find out why researchers from all over the world developed an interest in his theory. . . . he did not insist on their using his theory correctly or even at all" (1999, p. 11).

9. This dimension of Luhmann's work offers fruitful connections to recent post-humanist and new materialist scholarship that, beyond the works of Philip-popoulos-Mihalopoulos (2011; 2014) and Bryant (2014), remain unexplored.

10. At this point, the objection could be made that I carelessly abandon the established translation authorized by Luhmann himself in order to facilitate the theoretical connection to Deleuze's logic of sense. I believe this argument has little purchase for two reasons. First, as I pointed out in the Introduction, Luhmann himself references Deleuze's *The Logic of Sense* (in the French original) when developing his account of "Sinn" in *Die Gesellschaft der Gesellschaft*. Thus, it can be assumed that Luhmann himself saw at least a close relationship between his "Sinn" and Deleuze's sense, which attributes equal status to linguistic and material singularities in the production and productivity of sense. Second, evidence suggests that Luhmann is not overly concerned with either the translation of his concepts and conceptual coherence in his own works and their reading. The editor of his translated works at Stanford University Press recalls that Luhmann regularly advised her not to "worry too much about the choice of words in the translation. I could always have chosen differently" (Tartar, 1999, p. 88). A former student of Luhmann similarly recalls that Luhmann found it perfectly acceptable to connect his older with his newer writings, even if the change in concepts and their meaning is sometimes considerable (Thyssen, 1999, p. 149). A number of Luhmann scholars who have known or worked with him thus insist that a creative use of his theory to "make other and very different texts . . . speak" (Esposito, 1999, p. 66) is most in tune with his understanding of using and producing theory. "[T]o be a disciple of Luhmann you have to refuse to be a disciple" (Thyssen, 1999, p. 146).

Chapter 2

1. Interestingly, Maturana and Varela themselves disagree on whether their ideas are suitable for an application to social organizations (Beer, 1980). This disagreement is perhaps due to the fact that, different from Luhmann, especially Varela bases his analyses of neurological systems on a critical realist ontology. While

perceptions and knowledge are variable and constructed, systems must be empirically detectable and ontologically real in order to be studied through the theoretical lens of systems theory (Luhmann et al., 2000, pp. 114–115).

2. The term *poiesis* designates the capacity for creation and is opposed to *praxis* as a merely shaping, exhaustible force. As Maturana recounts in his introduction to *Autopoiesis and Creation* (1980), it is with reference to Cervantes's *Don Quixote* and the tautological, self-referential actions of its hero that Maturana and Varela created the concept of autopoiesis to designate a form of existence that is not static but autonomously self-creating.

3. At this point it should be noted that Guattari also employs Maturana and Varela's notion of autopoiesis in his work (1995, pp. 16–28). Guattari uses the concept of autopoiesis to describe the mode of self-productive subjectivation that takes place in a consciousness modulated by the capitalist machine. While Guattari's work, particularly his *Chaosmosis: An Ethicoaesthetic Paradigm* (1995), reveals a certain conceptual overlap with Luhmann's systems theory that appears as a fruitful starting point for further exploration (Guattari, 1995; Guattari and Alliez, 1984), such exploration is bracketed here.

4. Stefan Rossbach (2004) alternatively suggests that Luhmann's argumentation here is in fact mysticist: the reality outside of the system does not ground or in any way shape its internal relations, but its absence within the process of knowledge-production paradoxically conditions immanent sense-making. For Rossbach, a perpetually withdrawn and unknown outside is the condition of being and knowledge in Luhmann, where "only non-knowing systems can know; or: you can only see because you cannot see" (Luhmann, 2009c, p. 35).

5. In *Expressionism and Philosophy*, Deleuze reads Leibniz and Spinoza in an aligned fashion to argue that continuously unfolding becoming, not stable being, is the most suitable way to make sense of the world as it can be known. Spinoza's and Leibniz's "common project" is "a new "naturalism" (Deleuze, 1992b, p. 227) that offers a dynamic, materialist alternative to Cartesian rationalism. Much of the literature on Deleuze's use of Leibniz follows this Spinozist bend and focuses on a Leibnizian materialism to counter the above rationalism (Lærke, 2015; van Tuinen and McDonnell, 2010). There certainly are passages in *Expressionism in Philosophy* that support this materialist reading of Deleuze's engagement with Leibniz, for example, his suggestion that Leibniz "re-establishes the claims of a Nature endowed with forces or power" that "are no longer virtualities referred to occult entities, to souls or minds through which they are realized" (Deleuze, 1992b, p. 228). However, Leibniz himself very clearly does not equate the creative capacity of the monad with an anti-rationalist force of nature (Duncan, 2012; Jolley, 1998). While all monads are autonomous automata of perception, only the monads of the human mind produce sense-expression that function worldmaking (Jorgensen, 2015, pp. 53–54). Against this background, this book focuses on Deleuze's Leibnizian engagement with the body as a theory of conditioned grounding.

Chapter 3

1. We will see that regarding the nature of the past and memory, Luh-mann's and Deleuze's theories come very close to each other but have opposite focal points. Deleuze draws on Bergson to show how the past we produce in the present synthesis of habit is but one of multiple possible pasts. The multiplicity of the pure past can be re-accessed in the eternal return to change not only the future, but also history when a new past-future lineage is drawn. Luhmann, on his part, shows how the forgetting of the temporal multiplicity of everything that could be remembered, and the superimposition of a selective, active memory is necessary in order to allow for the continuation of sense in the present. While Luhmann, with the analytical gaze of the sociologist, is interested in why subjects and societies must forget, the critical philosopher Deleuze wants to change the refrain of what a particular society is forgetting and remembering. Deleuze's claim—made in both *Difference and Repetition* and *Proust and Signs*—that active forgetting can function as resistance must be understood in this sense.

2. In the context of this chapter, and the philosophical network it draws out, it is interesting to note that Vauvenargues is also referenced by Nietzsche (1988, pp. 646–647), who referred to him as one of the few philosophers with "real thoughts" (Broisson, 2009, p. 34).

3. Beyond Stegmaier's monograph, a number of publications draw out parallels and links between Luhmann's and Nietzsche's works (Cesaratto, 2013; Landgraf, 2013; Stegmaier, 1987). Exemplary here is their approach to creating innovation in thought: equally skeptical toward philosophical truth claims, ethics, and rationalism, both thinkers turn to scientific accounts of biological and informational networks as sources of theoretical inspiration (Landgraf, 2013, pp. 473–474).

4. Similar to what is the case for Luhmann, *Sinn* in Nietzsche is here usu-ally translated as "meaning." However, the context of the quote, where Nietzsche discusses contingencies and continuities in the function of punishment beyond a merely linguistic quality, justifies a translation as "sense," which also fits with Steg-maier's interpretation of the passage.

5. It is noteworthy how Luhmann here again draws attention to the contin-gency of his systemic ontology—it is merely one of several ways to respond to the need for orientation, in his case from the inside of the scientific system.

6. At this point a few clarifying remarks regarding the way Deleuze's philosophy of time is being used here are necessary. Throughout his work, Deleuze develops not one but indeed three different iterations of his theory of time—in relative isolation from each other. In *Difference & Repetition*, time is the product of three syntheses. In *The Logic of Sense*, Deleuze unpacks the genesis of time at the intersection of two presents, *Chronos* and *Aion*. The two *Cinema* volumes finally explore the genesis of time through the contrast between time-image and movement-image. The version of Deleuze's philosophy of time that is established and enfolded with Luhmann here mainly draws from *Difference & Repetition*. However, as suggested by James

Williams (2011, pp. 145–150), the former is read in conjunction with Deleuze's discussion of time from *The Logic of Sense*. While it is the former that provides insight to Deleuze's philosophy of time proper, the latter brings this theory of time into contact with sense and will make it possible to explore how an order of time that, in Deleuze just as in Luhmann, continuously ruptures itself impacts on the sense relations it grounds.

7. As Widder shows, Deleuze here departs from Bergson who posits memory, which he endows with a transcendent status, as absolutely primary to the present (2008, pp. 91–92).

Chapter 4

1. Even Grosz, who conceptualizes her incorporeal against reductive accounts of materialism that exclude or devaluate the productive capacity of epistemic relations, ultimately retraces evental creativity solely to the affective surface of the body that is charged by nothing else than the biological-physical becoming of life itself (Grosz, 2017, p. 7; pp. 66–67; pp. 206–208).

2. What exactly Deleuze draws from Whitehead and how relevant he is to his thinking, compared to those philosophers whom Deleuze dedicated a monograph to, is not quite clear. As Williams points out, "[t]here is no 'Deleuze's Whitehead' in the same way as there is 'Deleuze's Hume' or 'Deleuze's Nietzsche' " (2009b, p. 282).

3. Because of a certain ambiguity in the translation of the original French, counter-effectuation is sometimes also referred to, somewhat ambiguously, as counter-actualization (e.g., see Lundborg, 2009). For the context of this book I will use the term effectuation/counter-effectuation in line with recent scholarship (Widder, 2021) to make it clear that it differs from Deleuze's actualization from the virtual, which he unpacks in *Difference & Repetition*.

4. For a more detailed account of the example below, see Repo and Richter (2020).

5. Interestingly, Agamben describes this exceptional mechanism of producing an inside outside with a reference to Deleuze and Guattari's *A Thousand Plateaus*: "Sovereignty only reigns over what it is capable of internalizing" (1987, p. 360; as quoted in Agamben 1998, p. 18; see also: Richter, 2018).

6. Agamben (2005) in fact substantially draws on Benjamin's theory in addition to Schmitt to develop his of exceptional decisionism. However, in the context of this discussion I believe it makes sense to reverse this chronological and theoretical trajectory because the perspective developed in Benjamin is the furthest removed from Schmitt's sovereign determinism—and the closest to Luhmann's decision on the information-event.

7. Agamben reads the indecisiveness of Benjamin's sovereign in an ontological fashion. For him, it reveals that the distinction between the political-legal inside and the extra-legal anomie is fictitious and constitutively subverted in the political

figment of the exception. For Agamben, Benjamin's melancholy follows his realization that "the sphere of creatures and the juridical order are caught up in a single catastrophe" (Agamben, 2005, p. 57), which is the exception. There is no ordinary governance that is separate from exceptional violence.

8. Deleuze discusses the tragedy of the Baroque, which consists in the loss of a secure ontological anchor for reason and bleeds into the social fields of theology and politics, in *The Fold*. For Deleuze, the consequence of this loss is a turning inward, a becoming-immanent of power that now must operate through permanent, dramatically enacted relational continuation. While theology and politics have no means to avert the tragedy of foundational loss in Benjamin, Deleuze argues that it simply leads to a shift in their operational logic away from the exercise of manifest power to power relations that operate through internalization or enfolding. The "Baroque solution is the following: we shall multiply principles—we can always slip a new one out from under our cuffs [. . .] We will not have to ask what available object corresponds to a given luminous principle, but what hidden principle responds to whatever object is given" (Deleuze, 2006a, p. 76). The Baroque play of actualizing prescriptions in thought, religion, or politics "interiorizes not only the players who serve as pieces, but the board on which the game is played, and the material of that board" (p. 76). Deleuze mediates the pessimism of Benjamin's Baroque tragedy: the formlessness and dynamism of a groundless, decisionist politics here constitutes both loss and opportunity. The sociopolitical and epistemic relations actualized in the event are fixed only insofar as they are reproductive of a constituent power, of politics, but the form of this constituent power remains radically indeterminate—"we can always slip a new one out from under our cuffs." The event is here the operator of this politically productive variance.

Chapter 5

1. In Deleuze's account, Foucault's theory ends prior to his turn to biopolitical governmentality, which could indeed be understood as an alternative perspective on the phenomena Deleuze here describes as totalized, spatially unconfined control.

2. Luhmann's *Politische Soziologie* (2015), published even later, will be bracketed here as it is based on material written early in Luhmann's career. The book produces a detailed description of the semiotic technologies that structure the political system and keep it working but none of the innovative political analysis Luhmann develops in the later two books.

3. In *Political Theory in the Welfare State*, Luhmann suggests that he adopts this functional characterization of politics from Parsons (1990b, p. 73).

4. Nothing in Luhmann's work suggests he would have been unhappy to be associated with Foucault. His only direct comment on Foucault's work is a critique of his vague citation style, which Luhmann complains about precisely because it

prevents him from using cases from Foucault's work (Luhmann et al., 2000). As August notes, Luhmann's critique here is rather ironic considering that a cursory, ambiguous, and often eclectic use of source material is actually something that Luhmann has in common with Foucault (2021, p. 299).

5. The "economism" of Luhmann's functionally differentiated society, in combination with the absence of a central governmental authority, has led some scholars to identify Luhmann as a theorist of neoliberalism (Bröckling, 2016; Nabamowitz, 1988).

6. In *Foucault*, Deleuze develops an explicitly sociopolitical conception of the abstract machine of power relations that appears as a reiteration of the theory of machines presented in *Anti-Oedipus*. Every abstract machine of the social field relationally connects "discursive" and "non-discursive" (Deleuze, 1988, p. 37) formations to produce desire, which is equivalent to how sense is being conceptualized in this book. Despite the technological language used here, Deleuze's machines are "social before being technical. Or, rather, there is a human technology which exists before a material technology. No doubt the latter develops its effects within the whole social field; but . . . the tools or material machines have to be chosen first of all by a diagram and taken up by assemblages" (p. 40).

7. The precise phrasing of the political system's functional responsibility and its evolution in Luhmann have so far not been picked up in the secondary literature in Luhmann's political theory (August, 2021; Fischer-Lescano and Christensen, 2012; Thornhill, 2007).

8. In the original German: "das Bereithalten der Kapazität zu kollektiv bindendem Entscheiden."

9. Williams's book certainly goes beyond a secondary reading of Deleuze's philosophy in its theoretical scope and purchase. However, the theoretical proximity to Deleuze is, as in all of Williams's works, tangible, which justifies borrowing his concept in the context of a Deleuzian analysis. The way Williams applies his sign as an analytical lens is certainly different from Luhmann's code. He mentions family or sexuality (2016a, p. 103) as examples, which would be too broad to fit Luhmann's conceptualization of the code (sexuality, in Luhmann, is a socially generalized medium of communication, while family is an interaction system). However, precisely because I aim to broaden and de-rigidify Luhmann's concept of the code here this connection seems both plausible and fruitful.

Chapter 6

1. Brown and Mouffe would certainly reject the idea that politics was more rational and based on "facts" and "truth" before the appearance of post-truth populism. Both problematize the idea of political or scientific truth as the expression of a particular discursive regime or hegemony, which is that of modern-liberal ratio-

nalism. Truth, understood in this sense, does not signify epistemological progress or superiority but is rather the product of an epistemic-social network of power relations through which a socially dominant force cements its position on the level of ontology. Against this background, their interest in post-truth populism does not follow from the loss of political reason and a collective belief in facts. Rather, the now widespread contestation of modern-liberal rationalism signals a shift within the make-up of power relations that must be explored in its causes, and assessed in its risk for democratic societies.

2. As examples for the widespread social presence of intransparency to be controlled, Luhmann names "influences of worldwide financial speculation based on prognosis of prognoses," "the withdrawal" of science, for instance "the therapeutical profession towards constructivistic concepts and instructions" or "demotivating experiences with reform politics" (Luhmann, 1997b, p. 360)—the exact social areas and processes marked by escalating informational entropy on the level of second-order observation following the proliferation of digital technology.

Conclusion

1. In addition to its rhizomatically organized note cards, the Zettelkasten also contains a number of separate reference notes. These refer either to the number of a note card Luhmann viewed as particularly relevant to the topic where the reference note is located, or to the number of a note containing additional thoughts on the topic at hand, which would be inserted immediately after the reference note, further distorting the linearity of the collection (Schmidt, 2014, pp. 174–175).

2. This is strikingly similar to Deleuze and Guattari's suggestion that specifies it is not the philosopher who creates conceptual "thought-events" (1994, p. 70) but rather the conceptual persona emergent from their work. The conceptual persona can live within the work of a thinker, can appear to him- or herself, but it can also take the social context of a particular plane of immanence or the conceptual plane created by another thinker to actualize a conceptual persona. The conceptual persona is that which can become conceptually productive for sense-making within the work of a philosopher—that which "intervenes between chaos [of the diagrammatic outside] and the diagrammatic features of the plane of immanence" (p. 76).

References

Agamben, G. (1993). *Infancy & History: Essays on the Destruction of Experience* (L. Heron, Trans.). London & New York: Verso.

Agamben, G. (1998). *Homo Sacer: Sovereign Power and Bare Life* (D. Heller-Roazen, Trans.). Stanford, CA: Stanford University Press.

Agamben, G. (2003). *State of Exception* (K. Attell, Trans.). Chicago: University of Chicago Press.

Agamben, G. (2005). *The Time That Remains: A Commentary on the Letter to the Romans* (P. Dailey, Trans.). Stanford, CA: Stanford University Press.

Agamben, G. (2011). *The Kingdom and the Glory: for a Theological Genealogy of Economy and Government* (L. Chiesa and M. Mandarini, Trans.). Stanford, CA: Stanford University Press.

Agamben, G. (2016). *The Use of Bodies* (A. Kotsko, Trans.). Stanford, CA: Stanford University Press.

Agamben, G. (2020). The Invention of an Epidemic. *Coronavirus and Philosophers: European Journal of Psychoanalysis.* www.journal-psychoanalysis.eu/articles/coronavirus-and-philosophers

Alloa, E., & J. Michalet (2017). Differences in Becoming. Gilbert Simondon and Gilles Deleuze on Individuation. *Philosophy Today*, 61(3), 475–502. doi. org/10.5840/philtoday2017918167

Al-Saji, A. (2004). The Memory of Another Past: Bergson, Deleuze and a New Theory of Time. *Continental Philosophy Review*, 37, 203–239. doi.org/10.1007/s11007-005-5560-5

Amstutz, M., & A. Fischer-Lescano (2013). *Kritische Systemtheorie zur Evolution einer normativen Theorie.* Bielefeld: Transcript.

Ansell Pearson, K. (1997). Living the Eternal Return as the Event: Nietzsche with Deleuze. *Journal of Nietzsche Studies*, 14, 64–97.

Aradau, C. (2007). Law Transformed: Guantánamo and the "Other" Exception. *Third World Quarterly*, 28(3), 489–501. doi.org/10.1080/01436590701192298

Aristotle (1976). *Metaphysics* (J. Annas, Ed.). Oxford: Clarendon Press.

Arnoldi, J. (2010). Sense Making as Communication. *Soziale Systeme*, 16(1), 28–48. doi.org/10.1515/sosys-2010-0103

Ashenden, S. (2006). The Problem of Power in Luhmann's Systems Theory. In M. King & C. Thornhill (Eds.). *Luhmann on Law and Politics: Critical Appraisals and Applications* (pp.127–144). Oxford/Portland: Hart.

August, V. (2021). *Technologisches Regieren. Der Aufstieg des Netzwerk-Denkens in der Krise der Moderne. Foucault, Luhmann und die Kybernetik*. Bielefeld: transcript.

Badiou, A. (1999). *Deleuze: The Clamour of Being*. Minneapolis: University of Minnesota Press.

Badiou, A. (2005). *Being and Event*. London: Continuum.

Badiou, A. (2020, March 23). On the Epidemic Situation. Verso Blog. www.verso-books.com/blogs/4608-on-the-epidemic-situation

Baecker, D. (2012). Niklas Luhmann: Der Werdegang. In O. Jahraus, A. Nassehi, M. Grizelj, I. Saake, C. Kirchmeier, & J. Müller (Eds.), *Luhmann-Handbuch: Leben—Werk—Wirkung* (pp. 1–3). Stuttgart/Weimar: J. B. Metzler.

Barak, O. (2013). *On Time: Technology and Temporality in Modern Egypt*. Los Angeles: University of California Press.

Baraldi, C. (2021a). Interpenetration and Structural Coupling. In C. Baraldi, G. Corsi, & E. Esposito (Eds.), *Unlocking Luhmann: A Keyword Introduction to Systems Theory* (pp. 115–118). Bielefeld: Bielefeld University Press.

Baraldi, C. (2021b). Event. In C. Baraldi, G. Corsi, & E. Esposito (Eds.), *Unlocking Luhmann: A Keyword Introduction to Systems Theory* (pp. 87–89). Bielefeld: Bielefeld University Press.

Baraldi, C. (2021c). Symbolically Generalized Media. In C. Baraldi, G. Corsi, & E. Esposito (Eds.), *Unlocking Luhmann: A Keyword Introduction to Systems Theory* (pp. 229–234). Bielefeld: Bielefeld University Press.

Baraldi, C. (2021d). Differentiation of Society. In C. Baraldi, G. Corsi & E. Esposito (Eds.), *Unlocking Luhmann: A Keyword Introduction to Systems Theory* (66–70). Bielefeld: Bielefeld University Press.

Barben, D. (1996). *Theorietechnik und Politik bei Niklas Luhmann Grenzen einer universalen Theorie der modernen Gesellschaft*. Wiesbaden: VS Verlag für Sozialwissenschaften.

Bardin, A. (2015). *Epistemology and Political Philosophy in Gilbert Simondon: Individuation, Technics, Social Systems*. Dordrecht: Springer.

Barkhoff, J., & J. Leerssen (2021). *National Stereotyping, Identity Politics, European Crises*. Leiden: Brill.

Baum, A. L. (1977). Carroll's "Alices": The Semiotics of Paradox. *American Imago* 34(1), 86–108.

Beer, S. (1980). Preface to Autopoiesis. In H. Maturana & F. Varela, *Autopoiesis and Cognition: The Realization of the Living* (pp. 63–72). Dodrecht/London: Reidel.

Beistegui, M. de (2004). *Truth and Genesis: Philosophy as Differential Ontology*. Indianapolis: Indiana University Press.

Benjamin, W. (1998). *The Origin of German Tragic Drama* (J. Osborne, Trans.). London & New York: Verso.

Bergson, H. (1991). *Matter and Memory* (N. M. Paul & W. S. Palmer, Trans.). New York: Zone Books.

Besley, T., & T. Persson (2021). The Rise of Identity Politics: Policy, Political Organization, and Nationalist Dynamics. LSE working paper. www.lse. ac.uk/economics/Assets/Documents/personal-pages/tim-besley/working-papers/ the-rise-of-identity-politics.pdf

Bode, O. F. (2000). Die Ökonomische Theorie und die Systemtheorie Niklas Luhmanns. Möglichkeiten und Grenzen der Kompatibilität auf der theoretischen und praktischen Erklärungsebene. In H. de Berg & J. Schmidt (Eds.), *Rezeption und Reflexion: zur Resonanz der Systemtheorie Niklas Luhmanns ausserhalb der Soziologie* (pp. 179–208). Frankfurt a. M.: Suhrkamp.

Bogue, R. (2003). *Deleuze on Literature.* London: Routledge.

Böhler, A. (2010). The Time of Drama in Nietzsche and Deleuze: A Life as Performative Interaction. *Deleuze Studies* 4(1), 70–82. doi.org/10.3366/E1750224110000826

Borch, C. (2005). Systemic Power: Luhmann, Foucault, and Analytics of Power. *Acta Sociologica*, 48(2), 155–167. doi.org/10.1177/0001699305053769

Bowden, S. (2010). Deleuze's Neo-Leibnizianism, Events and The Logic of Sense's "Static Ontological Genesis." *Deleuze Studies* 4(3), 301–328.

Bowden, S. (2011). *The Priority of Events: Deleuze's Logic of Sense.* Edinburgh: Edinburgh University Press.

Bowden, S. (2014). "Willing the Event." Expressive Agency in Deleuze's Logic of Sense. *Critical Horizons: A Journal of Philosophy and Social Theory*, 15(3), 231–248. doi.org/10.1179/1440991714Z.00000000033

Braidotti, R. (2006). *Transpositions: On Nomadic Ethics.* Cambridge: Polity Press.

Braidotti, R. (2013). *The Posthuman.* Cambridge: Polity Press.

Brandom, R. (1981). Leibniz and Degrees of Perception. *Journal of the History of Philosophy*, 19(4), 447–479.

Bredekamp, H. (2008). *Die Fenster der Monade: Gottfried Wilhelm Leibniz' Theater der Natur und Kunst.* Berlin: Akademie Verlag.

Britt, B. (2012). The Schmittian Messiah in Agamben's "The Time That Remains." *Critical Inquiry*, 36(2), 262–287. doi.org/10.1086/648526

Bröckling, U. (2016). *Das unternehmerische Selbst. Soziologie einer Subjektivierungsform.* 6th ed. Frankfurt a.M.: Suhrkamp.

Broisson, I. (2009). Vauvenargues und der "Wille zur Macht." In. C. Pornschlegel, & M. Stingelin (Eds.), *Nietzsche und Frankreich* (pp. 33–46). Berlin & New York: Walter de Gruyter.

Brown, W. (2018). Neoliberalism's Frankenstein. Authoritarian Freedom in Twenty-First Century Democracies. In W. Brown, P. E. Gordon, & M. Pensky (Eds.), *Authoritarianism: Three Inquiries in Critical Theory* (pp. 7–44). Chicago: University of Chicago Press.

Brown, W. (2019). *In the Ruins of Neoliberalism: The Rise of Antidemocratic Politics in the West*. New York: Columbia University Press.

Brunczel, B. (2010). *Disillusioning Modernity: Niklas Luhmann's Social and Political Theory*. Frankfurt a. M.: Peter Lang.

Brunkhorst, H. (2012). Kritische Theorie. In O. Jahraus, A. Nassehi, M. Grizelj, I. Saake, C. Kirchmeier, & J. Müller (Eds.), *Luhmann-Handbuch: Leben—Werk—Wirkung* (pp. 288–295). Stuttgart/Weimar: J. B. Metzler.

Bryant, L. R. (2008). *Difference and Givenness: Deleuze's Transcendental Empiricism and the Ontology of Immanence*. Evanston, IL: Northwestern University Press.

Bryant, L. R. (2014). The Time of the Object: Derrida, Luhmann, and the Processual Nature of Substance. In R. Faber & A. Goffey (Eds.), *The Allure of Things: Process and Object in Contemporary Philosophy* (p. 71–91). London: Bloomsbury.

Buchanan, I., & N. Thoburn (2008). Introduction: Deleuze and Politics. In I. Buchanan & N. Thoburn (Eds.), *Deleuze and Politics* (pp. 1–12). Edinburgh: Edinburgh University Press.

Buchanan, I. (2008). Power, Theory and Praxis. In I. Buchanan & N. Thoburn (Eds.), *Deleuze and Politics* (pp. 13–34). Edinburgh: Edinburgh University Press.

Butler, A. (2009). Hume's Causal Reconstruction of the Perceptual Relativity Argument in Treatise 1.4.4. *Dialogue*, 48(1), 77–101. doi:10.1017/S0012217309090052

Butler, E. J. (2005). Stoic Metaphysics and the Logic of Sense. *Philosophy Today*, 49, 128–37. doi.org/10.5840/philtoday200549Supplement16

Calise, S. G. (2015). A Decorporealized Theory? Considerations about Luhmann's Conception of the Body. *Pandaemonium Germanicum*, 18(26), 104–125. https://doi.org/10.1590/1982-88371826104125

Carroll, L. (1995). What the Tortoise Said to Achilles. *Mind*, 104 (416), 691–693.

Carroll, L. (2001). *The Annotated Alice: Alice's Adventures in Wonderland and Through the Looking Glass*. London: Penguin.

Celis Bueno, C. (2020). The Face Revisited: Using Deleuze and Guattari to Explore the Politics of Algorithmic Face Recognition. *Theory, Culture & Society* 37(1), 73–91. doi.org/10.1177/026327641986775

Cesaratto, T. (2013). Luhmann, All Too Luhmann: Nietzsche, Luhmann and the Human. In A. La Cour & A. Philippopoulos-Mihalopoulos (Eds.), *Luhmann Observed: Radical Theoretical Encounters* (pp. 108–134). Houndmills: Palgrave Macmillan.

Chabot, P. (2013). *The Philosophy of Simondon: Between Technology and Individuation*. London: Bloomsbury Academic.

Choat, S. (2016). *Marx's "Grundrisse."* London: Bloomsbury.

Clam, J. (2006). What Is Modern Power? In M. King & C. Thornhill (Eds.), *Luhmann on Law and Politics: Critical Appraisals and Applications* (pp. 145–162). Oxford/Portland: Hart.

Clarke, B. (2016). Control and Control Societies in Deleuze and Systems Theory. www.academia.edu/31640128/Control_and_Control_Societies_in_Deleuze_and_Systems_Theory

Clisby, D. (2015). Deleuze's Secret Dualism? Competing Accounts of the Relationship between the Virtual and the Actual. *Parrhesia*, 24, 127–149.

Colebrook, C. (2002). *Understanding Deleuze*. Crows Nest, UK: Allen & Unwin.

Collett, G. (2016). *The Psychoanalysis of Sense: Deleuze and the Lacanian School*. Edinburgh: Edinburgh University Press.

Coluciello Barber, D. (2014). *Deleuze and the Naming of God: Post-secularism and the Future of Immanence*. Edinburgh: Edinburgh University Press.

Combes, M. (2013). *Gilbert Simondon and the Philosophy of the Transindividual*. Cambridge, MA: MIT Press.

Connolly, W. (2014). Immanence, abundance, democracy. In L. Tønder and L. Thomassen (Eds.), *Radical Democracy: Politics between Abundance and Lack* (pp. 239–255). Manchester: Manchester University Press.

Cooper, M. (2017). *Family Values*. Princeton, NJ: Princeton University Press.

Cordero, R., Mascareño, A., & Chernilo, D. (2017). On the Reflexivity of Crises: Lessons from Critical Theory and Systems Theory. *European Journal of Social Theory*, 20(4), 511–530. doi.org/10.1177/1368431016666886

Crockett, C. (2013). *Deleuze beyond Badiou: Ontology, Multiplicity, and Event*. New York: Columbia University Press.

D'Amato, P. (2019). Simondon and the Technologies of Control: On the Individuation of the Dividual. *Culture, Theory and Critique*, 60(3–4), 300–314. doi.org/10.1080/14735784.2019.1694211

Daly, G. (2004). Radical(ly) Political Economy: Luhmann, Postmarxism and Globalization. *Review of International Political Economy*, 11(1), 1–32.

Dammann, K. (1999). Wohlwollende Interpretationen. In T. M. Bardmann & D. Baecker (Eds.), *"Gibt es eigentlich den Berliner Zoo noch?" Erinnerungen an Niklas Luhmann* (pp. 24–28). Konstanz: UVK.

Davies, W. (2016, August 14). The Age of Post-truth Politics. *The New York Times*. www.nytimes.com/2016/08/24/opinion/campaign-stops/the-age-of-post-truth-politics.html

Debaise, D. (2016). The Dramatic Power of Events: The Function of Method in Deleuze's Philosophy. *Deleuze Studies*, 10(1), 5–18. doi.org/10.3366/dls.2016.0208

De Cleen, B. (2018). Populism, Exclusion, Post-truth. Some Conceptual Caveats. Comment on "The Rise of Post-truth Populism in Pluralist Liberal Democracies: Challenges for Health Policy." *International Journal of Health Policy Management*, 7(3), 268–271. doi.org/10.15171/IJHPM.2017.80

Dejanovic, S. (2014). Deleuze's New Meno: On Learning, Time and Thought. *The Journal of Aesthetic Education*, 48(2), 36–63. Doi.org/10.5406/jaesteduc.48.2.0036

De Landa, M. (2006). *A New Philosophy of Society: Assemblage Theory and Social Complexity*. London: Continuum.

Deleuze, G. (1954). Review of Jean Hyppolite's Logique et Existence. www.generation-online.org/p/fpdeleuze6.htm

Deleuze, G. (1967). The Method of Dramatization. https://ses.library.usyd.edu.au/bitstream/handle/2123/618/adt-NU20051202.14522707appendices.pdf;jsessionid=4E6C5C9EC001F750F646D59202F3B52D?sequence=2

Deleuze, G. (1980a). Les Cours de Gilles Deleuze: Sur Leibniz. Cours Vincennes—St Denis (15/04). www.webdeleuze.com/textes/48

Deleuze, G. (1980b). Les Cours de Gilles Deleuze: Sur Leibniz Cours Vincennes—St Denis (29/04). www.webdeleuze.com/textes/54

Deleuze, G. (1981). Spinoza: The Velocities of Thought (C. Stivale, Trans). Seminar 15, March 31, 1981. https://deleuze.cla.purdue.edu/seminars/spinoza-velocities-thought/lecture-15-0

Deleuze, G. (1984). *Kant's Critical Philosophy: The Doctrine of the Faculties* (H. Tomlinson & B. Habberjam). London: Athlone Press.

Deleuze, G. (1988). *Foucault* (S. Hand, Trans.). Minneapolis: University of Minnesota Press.

Deleuze, G. (1989). *Cinema 2: The Time Image* (H. Tomlinson & R. Galeta, Trans.). London: Athalone Press.

Deleuze, G. (1990). *The Logic of Sense* (M. Lester & C. Stivale, Trans.). New York: Columbia University Press.

Deleuze, G. (1991). Coldness and Cruelty. In *Masochism*. New York: Zone Books.

Deleuze, G. (1992a). Postscript on the Societies of Control. *October*, 59, pp. 3–7.

Deleuze, G. (1992b). *Expressionism in Philosophy: Spinoza* (M. Joughin, Trans.). New York: Zone Books.

Deleuze, G. (1994). *Difference and Repetition* (P. Patton, Trans.). London & New York: Continuum.

Deleuze, G. (1996). Foreword to "Capital Times." In E. Alliez, *Capital Times: Tales from the Conquest of Time* (pp. x–xiii). Minneapolis: University of Minnesota Press.

Deleuze, G. (2001). *Empiricism and Subjectivity: An Essay on Hume's Theory of Human Nature* (C. V. Boundas, Trans.). New York: Columbia University Press.

Deleuze, G. (2004). Desert Islands and Other Texts, 1953–1974 (D. Lapoujade, Ed.; M. Taomina, Trans.). Los Angeles: Semiotext(e)

Deleuze, G. (2006a). *The Fold. Leibniz and the Baroque* (T. Conley, Trans.). London: Continuum.

Deleuze, G. (2006b). *Nietzsche & Philosophy* (H. Tomlinson, Trans.). New York: Columbia University Press.

Deleuze, G., & F. Guattari (1983). *Anti-Oedipus: Capitalism and Schizophrenia* (R. Hurley, M. Seem, & H. R. Lane, Trans.). Minneapolis: University of Minnesota Press.

Deleuze, G., & F. Guattari (1986). *Kafka: Toward a Minor Literature* (D. Polan, Trans.). Minneapolis: University of Minnesota Press.

Deleuze, G., & F. Guattari (1987). *A Thousand Plateaus: Capitalism and Schizophrenia* B. Massumi, Trans.). Minneapolis & London: University of Minnesota Press.

Deleuze, G., & F. Guattari (1994). *What Is Philosophy?* (H. Tomlinson & G. Burchell, Trans.). New York: Columbia University Press.

Deleuze, G., & F. Guattari (2006). May 68 Did Not Take Place. In D. Lapoujade (Ed.). Gilles Deleuze. *Two Regimes of Madness: Texts and Interviews 1975–1995* (A. Hodges & M. Taromina, Trans., pp. 233–236). Los Angeles: Semiotext(e)

Demers, J. (2008). For a Political Gilles Deleuze. *Theory & Event*, 11(1). doi. org/10.1353/tae.2008.0001

Den Hollander, J. (2010). Beyond Historicism: From Leibniz to Luhmann. *Journal of the Philosophy of History*, 4(2), 210–225. doi.org/10.1163/187226310X509538

Descartes, R. (1968). *Discourse on Methods and The Meditations.* Harmondsworth: Penguin.

Dias Minhoto, L. (2017). Notes on Luhmann, Adorno, and the Critique of Neo-liberalism. *Thesis Eleven* 143(1), 56–69. doi.org/10.1177/0725513617741138

Dimmock, J. (2018, December 30). How Today's Post-truth World Can Be Tracked Back to a Remarkable 1995 Eric Cantona Quote. *The Independent.* www.independent.co.uk/voices/post-truth-alternative-facts-brexit-donald-trump-mainstream-media-eric-cantona-a8704246.html

Dommett K., & W. Pearce (2019). What Do We Know about Public Attitudes towards Experts? Reviewing Survey Data in the United Kingdom and European Union. *Public Understanding of Science*, 28(6), 669–678. doi. org/10.1177/0963662519852038

Doussan, J. (2013). Time and Presence in Agamben"s Critique of Deconstruction. *Cosmos and History: The Journal of Natural and Social Philosophy*, 9(1), 183–202.

Duffy, S. (2006). *The Logic of Expression: Quality, Quantity, and Intensity in Spinoza, Hegel, and Deleuze.* Farnham: Ashgate.

Duffy, S. (2010). Deleuze, Leibniz and Projective Geometry in the Fold. *Angelaki*, 15(2), 129–147. doi.org/10.1080/0969725X.2010.521401

Duncan, S. (2012). Leibniz's Mill Arguments against Materialism. *The Philosophical Quarterly*, 62(247), 250–272. doi.org/10.1111/j.1467-9213.2011.00017.x

Dziewas, R. (1992). Der M–nsch–ein Konglomerat autopoietischer Systeme? In W. Krawietz & M. Welker, M. (Eds.), *Kritik der Theorie sozialer Sy–teme–Auseinandersetzungen mit Luhmanns Hauptwerk* (pp. 113–132). Frankfurt a. M.: Suhrkamp.

Easton, D. (1957). An Approach to the Analysis of Political Systems. *World Politics*, 9(3), 383–400.

Erd, R., & A. Maihofer (1985, April 27). Der Zettelkasten kostet mich mehr Zeit als das Bücherschreiben. *Frankfurter Rundschau*, p. 3.

Esposito, E. (2011). *The Future of Futures: The Time of Money in Financing and Society.* Cheltenham: Edward Elgar.

Esposito, E. (2017). Critique without Crisis. *Thesis Eleven*, 143(1), 18–27. doi. org/10.1177/0725513617740966

Esposito, E., and D. Stark (2019). What's Observed in a Rating? Rankings as Orientation in the Face of Uncertainty. *Theory, Culture & Society*, 36(4), 3–26. doi.org/10.1177/0263276419826276

Faber, R. (2011). Introduction: Negotiating Becoming. In R. Faber & A. M. Stephenson (Eds.), *Secrets of Becoming: Negotiating Whitehead, Deleuze, and Butler* (pp. 1–59). New York: Fordham University Press.

Finlayson, J. N. (1975). Husserl's Analysis of the Inner Time-consciousness. *The Monist*, 59(1), 3–20.

Fischer-Lescano, A. (2012). Critical systems theory. *Philosophy and Social Criticism*, 38(1), pp. 3–23. doi.org/10.1177/0191453711421600

Fischer-Lescano, A., & R. Christensen (2012). Auctoritatis Interpositio: How Systems Theory Deconstructs Decisionism. *Social & Legal Studies*, 21(1), 93–119. doi.org/10.1177/0964663911423698

Folkers, H. (1987). Verabschiedete Vergangenheit. Ein Beitrag zur unaufhörlichen Selbstdeutung der Moderne. In D. Baecker, J. Markowitz, J. Stichweh, H. Tyrell, & H. Wilke (Eds.), *Theorie als Passion. Niklas Luhmann zum 60. Geburtstag* (pp. 46–83). Frankfurt a. M.: Suhrkamp.

Foucault, M., & G. Deleuze (1977). Intellectuals and Power. In D. F. Bouchard (Ed.), *Language, Counter-Memory, Practice: Selected Interviews and Essays* (pp. 205–217). Ithaca, NY: Cornell University Press.

Frege, G. (1993). On Sense and Reference. In A. W. Moore (Ed.), *Meaning and Reference* (pp. 23–42). Oxford: Oxford University Press.

Fuchs, P. (2012). Mensch/Person. In O. Jahraus, A. Nassehi, M. Grizelj, I. Saake, C. Kirchmeier, & J. Müller (Eds.), *Luhmann-Handbuch: Leben—Werk—Wirkung* (pp. 101–103). Stuttgart/Weimar: J. B. Metzler.

Galloway, A. R. (2004). *Protocol: How Control Exists after Decentralization*. Cambridge, MA: MIT Press.

Galloway, A. R. (2012). Computers and the Superfold. *Deleuze Studies*, 6(4), 513–528.

Gehring, P. (2007). Evolution, Temporalisierung und Gegenwart Revisited. Spielräume in Luhmanns Zeittheorie. *Soziale Systeme* 13 (1+2), 421–431. doi.org/10.1515/9783110509229-035

Geoghegan, B. D. (2011). From Information Theory to French Theory: Jakobson, Lévi-Strauss, and the Cybernetic Apparatus. *Critical Inquiry*, 38(1), 96–126. doi.org/10.1086/661645

Gerrard, J. (2021). The Uneducated and the Politics of Knowing in "Post Truth" Times: Ranciere, Populism and In/equality. *Discourse: Studies in the Cultural Politics of Education* 42(2), 155–169. Doi.org/10.1080/01596306.2019.1595528

Giddens, A. (1984). *The Constitution of Society: Outline of the Theory of Structuration*. Los Angeles: University of California Press.

Gray, J. (2017, May 19). Post Truth by Matthew D'Ancona and Post-Truth by Evan Davis. Review—Is This Really a New Era of Politics? *The Guardian*. www.theguardian.com/books/2017/may/19/post-truth-matthew-dancona-evan-davis-reiews

Greshoff, R. (1999). Lassen sich die Konzepte von Max Weber und Niklas Luhmann unter dem Aspekt "Struktur und Ereignis" miteinander vermitteln? In R. Greshoff & G. Kneer (Eds.), *Struktur und Ereignis in theorievergleichender Perspektive* (pp. 13–50). Vienna: Springer.

Grosz, E. (2017). *The Incorporeal: Ontology, Ethics, and the Limits of Materialism.* New York: Columbia University Press.

Guattari, F. (1995). *Chaosmosis: An Ethico-aesthetic Paradigm.* Bloomington & Indianapolis: Indiana University Press.

Guattari, F., & E. Alliez (1984). Capitalistic Systems, Structures and Processes. In F. Guattari (Ed.), *Molecular Revolution: Psychiatry and Politics* (pp. 273–287). New York: Peregrines.

Guy, J-S. (2019). Problems and Differentiation: A Deleuze-Luhmann Encounter. *Cybernetics & Human Knowing,* 26(1), 29–45.

Habermas, J. (1971). Theorie der Gesellschaft oder Sozialtechnologie? Eine Auseinandersetzung mit Niklas Luhmann. In N. Luhmann & J. Habermas, *Theorie-Diskussion. Theorie der Gesellschaft oder Sozialtechnologie—Was leistet die Systemforschung?* (pp. 142–290). Frankfurt a. M.: Suhrkamp.

Halewood, M. (2009). Language, Subjectivity and Individuality. In K. Robinson (Ed.), *Deleuze, Whitehead, Bergson: Rhizomatic Connections* (pp. 45–60). Houndmills: Palgrave Macmillan.

Harsin, J. (2015). Regimes of Posttruth, Postpolitics, and Attention Economies. *Communication, Culture & Critique,* 8, 327–333. doi.org/10.1111/cccr.12097

Hayek, F. (1979). *Law, Legislation and Liberty: A New Statement of the Liberal Principles of Justice and Political Economy. Volume 3: The Political Order of Free People.* Chicago: University of Chicago Press.

Hayek, F. (2011). *The Constitution of Liberty.* 2nd ed. Chicago: University of Chicago Press.

Hernes, T. (2014). Alfred North Whitehead. In R. Holt (Ed.), *The Oxford Handbook of Process Philosophy and Organization Studies* (pp. 255–271). Oxford: Oxford University Press.

Hessinger, P. (2015). Das Risiko des Kapitals—Nützlichkeitsarrangements auf den Finanzmärkten, Rechtfertigungsregime in der "Realökonomie"? *Soziale Systeme,* 20(1), 86–134. doi.org/ 10.1515/sosys-2015-0005

Hofstadter, R. (1964). The Paranoid Style in American Politics. *Harper's Magazine.* https://harpers.org/archive/1964/11/the-paranoid-style-in-american-politics

Hopp, W. (2008). Husserl on Sensation, Perception, and Interpretation. *Canadian Journal of Philosophy,* 38(2), 219–245.

Hui, Y. (2015). Modulation after Control. *New Formations,* 84/85, 74–91. doi. org/10.398/NewF:84/85.04.2015

Hume, D. (2004). *A Treatise of Human Nature.* Mineola: Dover.

Husserl, E. (1991). *On the Phenomenology of the Consciousness of Internal Time (1893–1917).* Dodrecht/Boston/London: Kluwer Academic Publishers.

Husserl, E. (2001). *Analyses Concerning Passive and Active Synthesis: Lectures on Transcendental Logic*. Dodrecht/Boston/London: Kluwer Academic Publishers.

Ionica, C. (2016). Halting the Production of Repression. Paradox-based Humour, or, Deleuze, Guattari, Beckett, and the Schizo's Stick. *Angelaki*, 21(2), 99–118. doi.org/10.1080/0969725X.2016.1182729

Jal, M. (2009). Umweg, or The Detour: On Marx's Theory of Radical Time. *Critique*, 37(2), 217–236. doi.org/10.1080/03017600902760711

Jansen, J. (2016). Kant's and Husserl's Agentive and Proprietary Accounts of Cognitive Phenomenology. *Philosophical Explorations*, 19(2), 161–172. doi.org/1 0.1080/13869795.2016.1176233

Johns, F. (2005). Guantánamo Bay and the Annihilation of the Exception. *European Journal of International Law*, 16(4), 613–635. doi.org/10.1093/ejil/chi135

Jolley, N. (1998). Causality and Creation in Leibniz. *The Monist*, 81(4), 591–611. /doi.org/10.5840/monist199881430

Jorgensen, L. M. (2015). Leibniz on Perceptual Distinctness, Activity and Sensation. *Journal of the History of Philosophy*, 53(1), 49–77.

Kakutani, M. (2018, June 14). The Death of Truth: How We Gave Up on Facts and Ended Up with Trump. *The Guardian*. www.theguardian.com/books/2018/jul/14/the-death-of-truth-how-we-gave-up-on-facts-and-ended-up-with-trump

Kant, I. (1992). Concerning the Ultimate Ground of Differentiation of Directions in Space. In *Theoretical Philosophy 1755–1770* (D. Walford & R. Meerbote, Trans., pp. 361–372). Cambridge: Cambridge University Press.

Kant, I. (2008). *Kant's Critiques*. Knutsford: A&D Publishing.

Kedem, N. (2011). Introduction: Prophetism and the Problem of Betrayal. *Deleuze Studies*, 5, 1–6. doi.org/10.3366/dls.2011.0033

Kieserling, A. (1999). Wer kennt Niklas Luhmann? In T. M. Bardmann & D. Baecker (Eds.), *"Gibt es eigentlich den Berliner Zoo noch?" Erinnerungen an Niklas Luhmann* (pp. 56–62). Konstanz: UVK.

Kim, J. (2015). The Social and the Political in Luhmann. *Contemporary Political Theory*, 14(4), 355–376. doi.org/10.1057/cpt.2014.53

Kirchmeier, C. (2012) Sinn. In O. Jahraus, A. Nassehi, M. Grizelj, I. Saake, C. Kirchmeier, & J. Müller (Eds.), *Luhmann-Handbuch: Leben—Werk—Wirkung* (pp. 117–118). Stuttgart/Weimar: J. B. Metzler.

Kirk, G. S. (1951). The Problem of Cratylus. *The American Journal of Philology*, 72(3), 225–253

Kleinherenbrink, A. (2015). Territory and Ritornello: Deleuze and Guattari on Thinking Living Beings. *Deleuze Studies*, 9(2), 208–230. doi.org/10.3366/dls.2015.0183

Klett, D. J. (2018). Luhmanns Humor. https://de-de.facebook.com/LuhmannsHumor

Klymenko, I. (2012). Autopoiesis. In O. Jahraus, A. Nassehi, M. Grizelj, I. Saake, C. Kirchmeier, & J. Müller (Eds.), *Luhmann-Handbuch: Leben - Werk—Wirkung* (pp. 69–70). Stuttgart/Weimar: J. B. Metzler.

Knodt, E. M. (1995). Foreword. In N. Luhmann, *Social Systems* (pp. ix–xxxvii). Stanford, CA: Stanford University Press.

Konings, M. (2018). *Capital and Time: For a New Critique of Neoliberal Reason.* Stanford, CA: Stanford University Press.

Kruckis, H.-M. (1999). Abgründe des Komischen. Schlaglichter auf Luhmanns Humor. In T. M. Bardmann & D. Baecker (Eds.), *"Gibt es eigentlich den Berliner Zoo noch?" Erinnerungen an Niklas Luhmann* (pp. 47–52). Konstanz: UVK.

Kurz, R. (2012). *Geld ohne Wert. Grundrisse zu einer Transformation der Kritik der politischen Ökonomie.* Berlin: Horlemann.

Laclau, E., & C. Mouffe (2012). *Hegemony and Socialist Strategy: Towards a Radical Democratic Politics.* 2nd ed. London: Verso.

Lærke, M. (2015). Five Figures of Folding: Deleuze on Leibniz's Monadological Metaphysics. *British Journal for the History of Philosophy*, 23(6), 1192–1213. doi.org/10.1080/09608788.2015.1019337

Lampert, J. (2006). *Deleuze and Guattari's Philosophy of History.* London & New York: Continuum.

Landgraf, E. (2013). The Physiology of Observation in Nietzsche and Luhmann. *Monatshefte*, 105(3), 472–488.

Lange, S. (2005). *Niklas Luhmanns Theorie der Politik. Eine Abklärung der Staatsgesellschaft.* Wiesbaden: Westdeutscher Verlag.

Laruelle, F. (2000). Identity and Event. *Pli*, 9, 174–189.

Lauermann, M. (1999). Abu Telfan. In T. M. Bardmann & D. Baecker (Eds.), *"Gibt es eigentlich den Berliner Zoo noch?" Erinnerungen an Niklas Luhmann* (pp. 111–117). Konstanz: UVK.

Lazzarato, M. (2006). The Concepts of Life and the Living in the Societies of Control. In M. Fuglsang & B. Meier Sorensen (Eds.), *Deleuze and the Social* (pp. 170–190). Edinburgh: Edinburgh University Press.

Lecercle, J.-J. (2002). *Deleuze and Language.* Houndmills: Palgrave Macmillan.

Leibniz, G. W. (1890). *The Philosophical Works of Leibniz.* Tuttle: Morehouse & Taylor.

Leibniz, G. W. (1989). *Philosophical Papers and Letters* (G. M. Duncan, Trans). Dodrecht: Kluwer Academic Publishers.

Leibniz, G. W. (1990). The Principles of Philosophy known as Monadology (G. Montgomery & A. R. Chandler, Trans.). In *The Rationalists: Descartes, R., Spinoza, B. de, Leibniz, G.W* (pp. 455–461). Anchor Books: New York.

Leston, R. (2013). Unhinged: Kairos and the Invention of the Untimely. *Atlantic Journal of Communication* 21, 29–50. doi.org/10.1080/15456870.2013.743325

Lettvin, J., H. R. Maturana, W. S. McCulloch, & W. H. Pitts (1959). What the Frog's Eye Tells the Frog's Brain. *Proceedings of the IRE*, 47(11), 1940–1951.

Lindroos, K. (1998). *Now-Time Image-Space: The Temporalisation of Politics in Walter Benjamin's Philosophy of History and Art.* Jyvaskyla: SoPhi.

Livingston, P. M. (2011). *The Politics of Logic: Badiou, Wittgenstein, and the Consequences of Formalism.* London: Routledge.

Luhmann, N. (1958). Der Funktionsbegriff in der Verwaltungswissenschaft. *Verwaltungsarchiv* 49(2), 97–105.

Luhmann, N. (1971a). Moderne Systemtheorien als Form gesamtgesellschaftlicher Analyse. In N. Luhmann & J. Habermas, *Theorie-Diskussion. Theorie der Gesellschaft oder Sozialtechnologie—Was leistet die Systemforschung?* (pp. 9–24). Frankfurt a. M.: Suhrkamp.

Luhmann, N. (1971b). Systemtheoretische Argumentationen Eine Entgegnung auf Jürgen Habermas. In N. Luhmann & J. Habermas, *Theorie-Diskussion. Theorie der Gesellschaft oder Sozialtechnologie—Was leistet die Systemforschung?* (pp. 291–403). Frankfurt a. M.: Suhrkamp.

Luhmann, N. (1976). The Future Cannot Begin: Temporal Structures in Modern Society. *Social Research*, 43(1), 130–152.

Luhmann, N. (1980). Talcott Parsons—Zukunft eines Theorieprogramms. *Zeitschrift für Soziologie*, 9(1), 5–17.

Luhmann, N. (1981). Kommunikation mit Zettelkästen. Ein Erfahrungsbericht. In H. Baier, M. Kepplinger, & K. Reumann, K. (Eds.), *Öffentliche Meinung und sozialer Wandel. Für Elisabeth Noelle-Neumann* (pp. 222–228). Wiesbaden: VS Verlag für Sozialwissenschaften.

Luhmann, N. (1984). The Self-Description of Society: Crisis Fashion and Sociological Theory. *International Journal of Comparative Sociology*, 25(1–2), 59–72.

Luhmann, N. (1987). *Archimedes und wir: Interviews*. Berlin: Merve Verlag.

Luhmann, N. (1988). Warum AGIL? *Kölner Zeitschrift für Soziologie und Sozialpsychologie*, 40, 127–139.

Luhmann, N. (1989). *Ecological Communication* (J. Bednarz, Trans.). Chicago: University of Chicago Press.

Luhmann, N. (1990a). *Essays on Self-reference*. New York: Columbia University Press.

Luhmann, N. (1990b). *Political Theory in the Welfare State* (J. Bednarz, Trans.). Berlin/New York: Walter de Gruyter.

Luhmann, N. (1990c). *Die Wissenschaft der Gesellschaft*. Frankfurt a.M.: Suhrkamp.

Luhmann, N. (1991a). Am Ende der kritischen Soziologie. *Zeitschrift für Soziologie*, 20(2), 147–152.

Luhmann, N. (1991b). *Soziologie des Risikos*. Berlin/New York: Walter de Gruyter.

Luhmann, N. (1991c). Das Moderne der modernen Gesellschaft. In W. Zapf (Ed.), *Die Modernisierung moderner Gesellschaften. Verhandlungen des 25. Deutschen Soziologentages in Frankfurt am Main 1990*. Frankfurt a. M. & New York: Suhrkamp.

Luhmann, N. (1993a). Observing Re-entries. *Graduate Faculty Philosophy Journal*, 16(2), 485–498.

Luhmann, N. (1993b). Ecological Communication: Coping with the Unknown. *Systems Practice*, 6, 527–539.

Luhmann, N. (1995a). *Social Systems* (J. Bednarz, Trans.). Stanford, CA: Stanford University Press.

Luhmann, N. (1995b). The Paradoxy of Observing Systems. *Cultural Critique*, 31(2), 37–55.

Luhmann, N. (1996a). Entscheidungen in der "Informationsgesellschaft." www.fen. ch/texte/gast_luhmann_informationsgesellschaft.htm

Luhmann, N. (1996b). *Die neuzeitlichen Wissenschaften und die Phänomenologie*. Wien: Picus-Verlag.

Luhmann, N. (1997a). Es gibt keine Biographie. Interview mit Dr Wolfgang Hagen. www.youtube.com/watch?v=nFhQ6SrIKVo

Luhmann, N. (1997b). Control of Intransparency. *Systems Research and Behavioural Science*, 14, 359–371.

Luhmann, N. (1998). *Observations on Modernity* (W. Whobrey, Trans.). Stanford, CA: Stanford University Press.

Luhmann, N. (2000). *Die Religion der Gesellschaft*. Frankfurt a. M.: Suhrkamp.

Luhmann, N. (2002). *Die Politik der Gesellschaft*. Frankfurt a.M.: Suhrkamp.

Luhmann, N. (2004). *Law as a Social System* (F. Kastner, R. Nobles, D, Schiff & R. Ziegert, Eds; K. A. Ziegert, Trans.). Oxford: Oxford University Press.

Luhmann, N. (2006). System as Difference. *Organization*, 13(1), 37–57. doi. org/10.1177/1350508406059638.

Luhmann, N. (2008a). *Die Moral der Gesellschaft*. Frankfurt a. M.: Suhrkamp.

Luhmann, N. (2008b). *Soziologische Aufklärung 6. Die Soziologie und der Mensch*. 3rd ed. Wiesbaden: VS Verlag für Sozialwissenschaften.

Luhmann, N. (2009a). *Soziologische Aufklärung 1. Aufsätze zur Theorie sozialer Systeme*. 8th ed. Wiesbaden: VS Verlag für Sozialwissenschaften.

Luhmann, N. (2009b). *Soziologische Aufklärung 2. Aufsätze zur Theorie der Gesellschaft*. 6th ed. Wiesbaden: VS Verlag für Sozialwissenschaften.

Luhmann, N. (2009c). *Soziologische Aufklärung 3. Soziales System, Gesellschaft, Organisation*. 5th ed. Wiesbaden: VS Verlag für Sozialwissenschaften.

Luhmann, N. (2009d). *Soziologische Aufklärung 5. Konstruktivistische Perspektiven*. 4th ed. Wiesbaden: VS Verlag für Sozialwissenschaften.

Luhmann, N. (2012a). *Theory of Society, Volume 1*. Stanford, CA: Stanford University Press.

Luhmann, N. (2012b). *Macht*. 4th ed. Konstanz: UVK.

Luhmann, N. (2013). *Theory of Society, Volume 2*. Stanford, CA: Stanford University Press.

Luhmann, N. (2015). *Politische Soziologie*. Frankfurt a. M.: Suhrkamp.

Luhmann, N., K. Hayles, W. Rasch, E. Knodt, & C. Wolfe. (2000). Theory of a Different Order: A Conversation with Katherine Hayles and Niklas Luhmann. In W. Rasch, & C. Wolfe (Eds.), *Observing Complexity: Systems Theory and Postmodernity* (pp. 111–136). Minneapolis: University of Minnesota Press.

Lundborg, T. (2009). The Becoming of the "Event." A Deleuzian Approach to Understanding the Production of Social and Political "Events." *Theory & Event*, 12(1).

Lundborg, T. (2015). *Politics of the Event: Time, Movement, Becoming*. London: Routledge.

Lundy, C. (2013). Why Wasn't Capitalism Born in China? Deleuze and the Philosophy of Non-events. *Theory & Event*, 16(3), 1–6.

MacKenzie, I., & R. Porter (2011). Dramatization as Method in Political Theory. *Contemporary Political Theory*, 10(4), 482–501. doi.org/10.1057/cpt.2010.38

MacKenzie, I., & R. Porter (2019). Totalising Institutions, Critique and Resistance, *Contemporary Political Theory*, 1–17. 10.1057/s41296-019-00336-w

Mader, M. B. (2014). Whence Intensity? Deleuze and the Revival of a Concept. In A. Beaulieu, E. Kazarian & J. Sushytska (Eds.), *Deleuze and Metaphysics* (pp. 225–249). Lanham, MD: Rowman and Littlefield.

Mader, M. B. (2017). Philosophical and Scientific Intensity in the Thought of Gilles Deleuze. *Deleuze and Guatarri Studies*, 11(2), 259–277.

Magee, J. M. (2000). Sense Organs and the Activity of Sensation in Aristotle. *Phronesis*, 45(4), 306–330.

Makin, G. (2000). *The Metaphysicians of Meaning: Russell and Frege on Sense and Denotation*. London: Routledge.

Malowitz, K., & V. Selk (2015). Angst in Bielefeld. Über ein ausgeschlossenes Gefühl in der Systemtheorie. *Soziopolis: Gesellschaft beobachten*. www.ssoar.info/ssoar/bitstream/handle/document/82272/ssoar-sopolis-2015-selk_et_al-Angst_in_Bielefeld_Uber_ein.pdf?sequence=1&isAllowed=y&lnkname=ssoar-sopolis-2015-selk_et_al-Angst_in_Bielefeld_Uber_ein.pdf

Marchart, O. (2007). *Post-Foundational Political Thought. Political Difference in Nancy, Lefort, Badiou and Laclau*. Edinburgh: Edinburgh University Press.

Marshall H., and A. Drieschova (2018). Post-Truth Politics in the UK's Brexit Referendum. *New Perspectives*, 26(3), 89–105. doi.org/10.1177/2336825X1802600305

Marx, K. (1973). *Grundrisse: Foundations of the Critique of Political Economy*. London: Penguin.

Marx, K. (2000). *Selected Writings*. 2nd ed. Oxford: Oxford University Press.

Massumi, B. (1995). The Autonomy of Affect. *Cultural Critique*, 31(3), 83–109. doi.org/10.2307/1354446

Massumi, B. (2002). *Movement, Affect, Sensation: Parables for the Virtual*. Durham, NC: Duke University Press.

Massumi, B. (2011). *Semblance and Event: Activist Philosophy and the Occurrent Arts*. Cambridge, MA: MIT Press.

Massumi, B. (2014). *The Power at the End of the Economy*. Durham, NC: Duke University Press.

Maturana, H. (1980). Introduction. In H. Maturana & F. Varela. *Autopoiesis and Cognition: The Realization of the Living* (pp. 73–76). Dodrecht/London: Reidel.

Maturana, H., & F. Varela (1980). *Autopoiesis and Cognition: The Realization of the Living*. Dodrecht & London: Reidel.

McIntyre, L. (2018). *Post-truth*. Cambridge, MA: MIT Press.

McIntyre, L., & J. Rauch (2021, January 25). A War on Truth Is Raging. Not Everyone Recognizes We're in It. *The Washington Post*. www.washingtonpost. com/opinions/2021/06/25/war-truth-is-raging-not-everyone-recognizes-were-it

Mengue, P. (2005). The Absent People and the Void of Democracy. *Contemporary Political Theory*, 40(4), 386–399. doi.org/10.1057/palgrave.cpt.9300237

Mengue, P. (2013). The Idiot in Societies of Control. *Theory & Event*, 16(3).

Mitchell, W. J. T (2020). Present Tense 2020. An Iconology of the Epoch. *Critical Inquiry*. https://criticalinquiry.uchicago.edu/present_tense_2020_an_iconology_of_the_epoch

Moeller, H.-G. (2012). *The Radical Luhmann*. New York: Columbia University Press.

Moeller, H.-G. (2017). On Second-Order Observation and Genuine Pretending: Coming to Terms with Society. *Thesis Eleven*, 143(1), 28–43. doi. org/10.1177/0725513617740968

Mouffe, C. (1993). *The Return of the Political*. London: Verso.

Mouffe, C. (2000). *The Democratic Paradox*. London: Verso.

Mouffe, C. (2005). *On the Political*. London: Verso.

Mouffe, C. (2019). *For a Left Populism*. London: Verso.

Moulard, V. (2003). The Time-image and Deleuze's Transcendental Experience. *Continental Philosophy Review*, 25, 325–345. doi.org/10.1023/A:1022687422795

Müller, J. (2012a). Gabriel Tarde (1843–1904). In O. Jahraus, A. Nassehi, M. Grizelj, I. Saake, C. Kirchmeier, & J. Müller (Eds.), *Luhmann-Handbuch: Leben—Werk—Wirkung* (pp. 265–268). Stuttgart/Weimar: J. B. Metzler.

Müller, J. (2012b). Differenz, Differenzierung. In O. Jahraus, A. Nassehi, M. Grizelj, I. Saake, C. Kirchmeier, & J. Müller (Eds.), *Luhmann-Handbuch: Leben—Werk—Wirkung* (pp. 73–74). Stuttgart/Weimar: J. B. Metzler.

Mulligan, K. (1995). Perception. In B. Smith & D. Woodruff Smith (Eds.), *The Cambridge Companion to Husserl* (pp. 168–238). Cambridge: Cambridge University Press.

Murphy, R. T. (1980). *Hume and Husserl: Towards Radical Subjectivism*. The Hague: Martinus Nijhoff.

Nassehi, A. (2008). *Die Zeit der Gesellschaft. Auf dem Weg zu einer soziologischen Theorie der Zeit*. 2nd ed. Wiesbaden: VS Verlag für Sozialwissenschaften.

Nelson, A. (1999). *Marx's Concept of Money: The God of Commodities*. London & New York: Routledge.

Nietzsche, F. (1988). *Menschliches, Allzumenschliches I und II*. Berlin & New York: Walter de Gruyter.

Nietzsche, F. (2002). *Beyond Good and Evil* (R.-P. Horstmann & J. Norman, Eds.; J. Norman, Trans.). Cambridge: Cambridge University Press.

Nietzsche, F. (2006). *On the Genealogy of Morality*. (K. Ansell Pearson, Ed.; C. Diethe, Trans.). Cambridge: Cambridge University Press.

Opitz, S. (2013). Was ist Kritik? Was ist Aufklärung? Zum Spiel der Möglichkeiten bei Niklas Luhmann und Michel Foucault. In M. Amstutz & A. Fischer-Lescano (Eds.), *Kritische Systemtheorie* (pp. 39–62). Bielefeld: Transcript.

Opitz, S., & U. Tellmann (2015). Future Emergencies: Temporal Politics in Law and Economy. *Theory, Culture & Society*, 32(2), 107–129. doi. org/10.1177/0263276414560416

Overwijk, J. (2021). Paradoxes of Rationalisation. Openness and Control in Critical Theory and Luhmann's Systems Theory. *Theory, Culture & Society*, 38(1), 127–148. doi.org/10.1177/0263276420925548

Pahl, H. (2008). *Das Geld in der modernen Wirtschaft. Marx und Luhmann im Vergleich*. Frankfurt a. M. & New York: Campus.

Palmer, J. (2013). *The World of Early Greek Philosophy*. London: Routledge.

Parsons, T. (1991). *The Social System*. London: Routledge.

Patton, P. (1997). The World Seen from Within: Deleuze and the Philosophy of Events. *Theory & Event* 1(1). doi.org/10.1353/tae.1991.0006

Patton, P. (2000). *Deleuze and the Political*. London: Routledge.

Patton, P. (2005). Deleuze and Democracy. *Contemporary Political Theory*, 4(4), 400–413. doi.org/10.1057/palgrave.cpt.9300236

Paulani, L. M. (2014). Money in Contemporary Capitalism and the Autonomisation of Capitalist Forms in Marx's Theory. *Cambridge Journal of Economics*, 38, 779–795. Doi.org/10.1093/cje/bet066

Philippopoulos-Mihalopoulos, A. (2006). Dealing (with) Paradoxes: On Law, Justice and Cheating. In M. King & C. Thornhill (Eds.), *Luhmann on Law and Politics: Critical Appraisals and Applications* (pp. 217–234). Oxford/Portland: Hart.

Philippopoulos-Mihalopoulos, A. (2011). *Niklas Luhmann: Law, Justice, Society*. London: Routledge.

Philippopoulos-Mihalopoulos, A. (2013). The Autopoietic Fold: Critical Autopoiesis between Luhmann and Deleuze. In A. La Cour & A. Philippopoulos-Mihalopoulos (Eds.), *Luhmann Observed: Radical Theoretical Encounters* (pp. 60–84). Houndmills: Palgrave Macmillan.

Philippopoulos-Mihalopoulos, A. (2014). Critical Autopoiesis and the Materiality of Law. *International Journal for the Semiotics of Law*, 27, 389–418. doi. org/10.1007/s11196-013-9328-7

Plato (1997). *Complete Works* (J. M. Cooper, Ed.). Indianapolis & Cambridge: Hackett.

Porpora, D. V. (2020). Populism, Citizenship, and Post-truth Politics. *Journal of Critical Realism*, 19(4), 329–340. doi.org/10.1080/14767430.2020.1800967

Pottage, A. (1998). Power as an Art of Contingency: Luhmann, Deleuze, Foucault. *Economy and Society*, 27(1), 1–27. doi.org/10.1080/03085149800000001

Powell, M. (2017). This Is My (Post) Truth, Tell Me Yours. Comment on "The Rise of Post-truth Populism in Pluralist Liberal Democracies: Challenges for Health

Policy." *International Journal of Health Policy Management*, 6(12), 723–725. doi.org/ 10.15171/IJHPM.2017.58

Prien, T. (2013). Kritische Systemtheorie und materialistische Gesellschaftstheorie. In M. Amstutz & A. Fischer-Lescano (Eds.), *Kritische Systemtheorie* (pp. 81–98). Bielefeld: transcript.

Procyshyn, A. (2017). Can Social Systems Theory Be Used for Immanent Critique? *Thesis Eleven*, 143(1), 97–114. doi.org/10.1177/0725513617741167

Rae, G. (2020). *Poststructuralist Agency: The Subject in Twentieth-Century Theory*, Edinburgh: Edinburgh University Press.

Rammstedt, O. (1999). In Memoriam: Niklas Luhmann. In T. M. Bardmann & D. Baecker (Eds.), *"Gibt es eigentlich den Berliner Zoo noch?" Erinnerungen an Niklas Luhmann* (pp. 16–20). Konstanz: UVK.

Rasch, W. (1997). Locating the Political: Schmitt, Mouffe, Luhmann, and the Possibility of Pluralism. *International Review of Sociology*, 7(1), 103–115. doi. org/10.1080/03906701.1997.9971226

Rasch, W. (2000). *Niklas Luhmann's Modernity: The Paradoxes of Differentiation*. Stanford, CA: Stanford University Press.

Rasch, W. (2013). Luhmann's Ontology. In A. La Cour & A. Philippopoulos-Mihalopoulos (Eds.), *Luhmann Observed: Radical Theoretical Encounters* (pp. 38–59). Houndmills: Palgrave Macmillan.

Ratcliffe, M. (2013). Phenomenology, Naturalism and the Sense of Reality. *Royal Institute of Philosophy Supplement*, 72, 67–88. doi:10.1017/S1358246113000052

Renner, M. (2013). Die Wirtschaft der Weltgesellschaft: Möglichkeitsräume für eine systemtheoretische Kritik. In M. Amstutz & A. Fischer-Lescano (Eds.), *Kritische Systemtheorie* (pp. 219–236). Bielefeld: transcript.

Richter, H. (2018). Homo Sacer Is Syrian. Movement-Images from the European "Refugee-Crisis." In H. Richter (Ed.), *Biopolitical Governance: Race, Gender, Economy* (pp. 79–98). London: Rowman & Littlefield International.

Robinson, K. (2009). *Deleuze, Whitehead, Bergson: Rhizomatic Connections*. Houndmills: Palgrave Macmillan.

Robinson, K. (2010). Back to Life: Deleuze, Whitehead and Process. *Deleuze Studies*, 4(1), 120–133. doi.org/10.3366/e1750224110000875

Roche, A. (2010). Kant's Principle of Sense. *British Journal for the History of Philosophy*, 18(4), 663–691. doi.org/ 10.1080/09608788.2010.502351

Roffe, J. (2017). Deleuze's Concept of Quasi-cause. *Deleuze and Guattari Studies*, 11(2), 278–294. doi.org/10.3366/dls.2017.0266

Rossbach, S. (2004). "Corpus mysticum" Niklas Luhmann's Evocation of World Society. In M. Albert & L. Hilkermeier (Eds.), *Observing International Relations: Niklas Luhmann and World Politics* (pp. 44–56). London: Routledge.

Rouvroy, A. (2011). Technology, Virtuality and Utopia: Governmentality in an Age of Autonomic Computing. In M. Hildebrandt & A. Rouvroy (Eds.), *Law,*

Human Agency, and Autonomic Computing: The Philosophy of Law Meets the Philosophy of Technology (pp. 119–140). London: Routledge.

Rouvroy, A. (2013). The End(s) of Critique: Data Behaviourism versus due Process. In M. Hildebrandt & K. de Vries (Eds.), *Privacy, Due Process and the Computational Turn: The Philosophy of Law Meets the Philosophy of Technology* (pp. 157–182). London: Routledge.

Sainsbury, R. M. (2009). *Paradoxes*. 2nd ed. Cambridge: Cambridge University Press.

Santucci, J. (2020). Did the Party System Change from 2012–2016? *Journal of Elections, Public Opinion and Parties*, 32(4), 836–846. doi.org/10.1080/174 57289.2020.1794884

Schimank, U. (2015). Modernity as a Functionally Differentiated Capitalist Society: A General Theoretical Model. *European Journal of Social Theory*, 18(4), 413–430. doi.org/10.1177/1368431014543618

Schmidt, J. F. K. (2012) Luhmanns Zettelkasten und seine Publikationen. In O. Jahraus, A. Nassehi, M. Grizelj, I. Saake, C. Kirchmeier, & J. Müller (Eds.), *Luhmann-Handbuch: Leben—Werk—Wirkung* (pp. 7–13). Stuttgart/Weimar: J. B. Metzler.

Schmidt, J. F. K. (2014). Aus dem Archiv. Der Nachlass Niklas Luhmanns-eine erste Sichtung: Zettelkasten und Manuskripte. *Soziale Systeme*, 19(1), 167–183. doi.org/10.1515/sosys-2014-0111

Schmitt, C. (1912). *Gesetz und Urteil*. Berlin: Liebmann.

Schmitt, C. (1979). *Politische Theologie: Vier Capitel zur Lehre von der Souveränität.* 3rd ed. Berlin: Duncker & Humblot.

Schmitt, C. (1996). *Der Begriff des Politischen*. 7th ed. Berlin: Duncker & Humblot.

Schmitz, F. (2015). On Kant's Conception of Inner Sense: Self-Affection by the Understanding. *European Journal of Philosophy*, 23(4), 1044–1063. doi. org/10.1111/ejop.12025

Schönwälder-Kuntze, T. (2009). Das zwölfte Kapitel: Re-entry into the Form. In T Schönwälder-Kuntze, K. Wille, & T. Hölscher (Eds.), *George Spencer Brown Eine Einführung in die "Laws of Form"* (pp. 194–206). 2nd ed. Wiesbaden: VS Verlag für Sozialwissenschaften.

Schrift, D. A. (2000). Nietzsche, Foucault, Deleuze, and the Subject of Radical Democracy. *Angelaki*, 5(2), 151–161. doi.org/10.1080/09697250020012250

Schütz, A. (2000). Thinking the Law with and against Luhmann, Legendre, Agamben. *Law and Critique*, 11(11), 107–136. doi.org/10.1023/A:1008939323404

Schützeichel, R. (2003). *Sinn als Grundbegriff bei Niklas Luhmann*. Frankfurt a. M.: Campus Verlag.

Sharpe, M. (2009). Only Agamben Can Save Us? Against the Messianic Turn Recently Adopted in Critical Theory. *The Bible & Critical Theory*, 5(3), 40.1–40.20 doi.org/10.2104/BC090040

Shaviro, S. (2007). Eternal Objects. www.shaviro.com/Blog/?p=578

Shaviro, S. (2009). *Without Criteria: Kant, Whitehead, Deleuze, and Aesthetics.* Cambridge, MA: MIT Press.

Shaviro, S. (2011). Transcendental Empiricism in Deleuze and Whitehead. In R. Faber & A. M. Stephenson (Eds.), *Secrets of Becoming Negotiating Whitehead, Deleuze, and Butler* (pp. 70–81). New York: Fordham University Press.

Shores, C. (2014). In the Still of the Moment: Deleuze's Phenomena of Motionless Time. *Deleuze Studies*, 8(2), 199–229. doi.org/10.3366/dls.2014.0143

Silverman, A. (1990). Plato on Perception and "Commons." *The Classical Quarterly*, 40(1), 148–175. doi.org/10.1017/S0009838800026859

Simondon, G. (1992). The Genesis of the Individual. In J. Crary & S. Kwinter (Eds.), *Incorporations* (pp. 297–319). New York: Zone Books.

Simondon, G. (2005). *L'individuation à la lumière des notions de forme et d'information*. Grenoble: Millon.

Simondon, G. (2010). The Limits of Human Progress: A Critical Study. *Cultural Politics: An International Journal*, 6(2), 229–236. doi.org/10.2752/1751743 10X12672016548405

Simondon, G. (2012). On Technico-Aesthetics. *Parrhesia*, 14, 1–8.

Simondon, G. (2017). *On the Mode of Existence of Technical Objects*. Minneapolis: University of Minnesota Press.

Singer, B. C. J. (2021). Populism and the Separation of Power and Knowledge. *Thesis Eleven*, 164(1). https://doi.org/10.1177/0725513620983685

Siri, J., & K. Möller, Eds. (2016). *Systemtheorie und Gesellschaftskritik: Perspektiven der Kritischen Systemtheorie*. Bielefeld: Transcript.

Sixel, F. W. (1976). The Problem of Sense: Habermas v. Luhmann. In J. O'Neill (Ed.), *On Critical Theory* (pp. 184–204). New York: Seabury Press.

Smith, D. W. (2009). Deleuze's Concept of the Virtual and the Critique of the Possible. *Journal of Philosophy: A Cross-Disciplinary Inquiry*, 4(9), 34–43. doi.org/10.5840/jphilnepal20094913

Smith, D. W. (2011). Flow, Code and Stock: A Note on Deleuze's Political Philosophy. *Deleuze Studies*, 5 (supplement), 36–55. doi.org/ 10.3366/dls.2011.0036

Smith, D. W. (2012). *Essays on Deleuze*. Edinburgh: Edinburgh University Press.

Snyder, T. (2021, January 9). The American Abyss. *The New York Times*. www.nytimes.com/2021/01/09/magazine/trump-coup.html

Somer, M., & J. McCoy (2018). Déjà vu? Polarization and Endangered Democracies in the 21st Century. *American Behavioral Scientist*, 62(1), 3–15. doi.org/10.1177/0002764218760371

Somers-Hall, H. (2011). Time Out of Joint: Hamlet and the Pure Form of Time. *Deleuze Studies*, 5 (supplement), 56–76. doi.org/10.3366/dls.2011.0037

Sotiris, P. (2016). The Many Encounters of Deleuze and Marxism. *Deleuze and Guattari Studies*, 10(3), 301–320. doi.org/10.3366/dls.2016.0228

Souto, C. (1999). Luhmann als Mensch. In T. M. Bardmann & D. Baecker (Eds.), *"Gibt es eigentlich den Berliner Zoo noch?" Erinnerungen an Niklas Luhmann* (pp. 154–156). Konstanz: UVK.

Speaks, J. (2013). Individuating Fregean sense. *Canadian Journal of Philosophy*, 43(5), 634–654. doi.org/10.1080/00455091.2014.925678

Speed, E., & R. Mannion (2017). The Rise of Post-truth Populism in Pluralist Liberal Democracies: Challenges for Health Policy. *International Journal of Health Policy Management*, 6(5), 249–251. doi.org/ 10.15171/IJHPM.2017.19

Spencer Brown, G. (1969). *Laws of Form*. Boston: Dutton.

Stäheli, U. (2000). *Sinnzusammenbrüche: eine dekonstruktive Lektüre von Niklas Luhmanns Systemtheorie*. Weilserswist: Velbrück Wissenschaft.

Stegmaier, W. (1987). Zeit der Vorstellung. Nietzsches Vorstellung der Zeit. *Zeitschrift für philosophische Forschung*, 14(2), 202–228.

Stegmaier, W. (2016). *Orientierung im Nihilismus—Luhmann meets Nietzsche*. Berlin & Boston: Walter de Gruyter.

Steinbacher, S. (2009, June 18). NS Zeit: Viele Fragen offen. *Die Zeit*. www.zeit.de/2009/26/L-P-Benz

Stengers, I. (2011). *Thinking with Whitehead: A Free and Wild Creation of Concepts*. Harvard & London: Harvard University Press.

Strickland, L. (2014). *Leibniz's Monadology: A New Translation and Guide*. Edinburgh: Edinburgh University Press.

Świątkowski, P. (2016). *Deleuze and Desire: Analysis of The Logic of Sense*. Leuven: Leuven University Press.

Tang, C.-C. (2013). Toward a Really Temporalized Theory of Event: A Luhmannian Critique and Reconstruction of Sewell's Logics of History. *Social Science Information*, 52(1), 34—61. doi.org/10.1177/0539018412466633

Tartar, H. (1999). Stanford University Press. In T. M. Bardmann & D. Baecker (Eds.) *"Gibt es eigentlich den Berliner Zoo noch?" Erinnerungen an Niklas Luhmann* (pp. 88–89). Konstanz: UVK.

Taylor, M., & J. Murray (2020, February 10). "Overwhelming and Terrifying": The Rise of Climate Anxiety. *The Guardian*. www.theguardian.com/environment/2020/feb/10/overwhelming-and-terrifying-impact-of-climate-crisis-on-mental-health

Ternes, B. (1999). *Invasive Introspektion: Fragen an Niklas Luhmanns Systemtheorie*. München: Wilhelm Fink.

Teubner, G. (2001). Economics of Gift—Positivity of Justice. The Mutual Paranoia of Jacques Derrida and Niklas Luhmann. *Theory, Culture & Society*, 18(1), 29–47. doi.org/10.1177/0263276012205162

Thompson, E. P. (1967). Time, Work-Discipline, and Industrial Capitalism. *Past & Present*, 38(4), 56–97

Thornhill, C. (2006). Niklas Luhmann's Political Theory: Politics after Metaphysics?, In M. King & C. Thornhill (Eds.), *Luhmann on Law and Politics: Critical Appraisals and Applications* (pp. 75–99). Oxford/Portland: Hart.

Thornhill, C. (2007). Niklas Luhmann, Carl Schmitt and the Modern Form of the Political, *European Journal of Social Theory*, 10(4), 499–522. doi.org/10.1177/1368431007075966

Thornhill, C. (2013). Luhmann and Marx: Social Theory and Social Freedom. In A. La Cour & A. Philippopoulos-Mihalopoulos (Eds.), *Luhmann Observed: Radical Theoretical Encounters* (pp. 263–283). Houndmills: Palgrave Macmillan.

Thyssen, O. (1999). Memories of Luhmann. In T. M. Bardmann & D. Baecker (Eds.), *"Gibt es eigentlich den Berliner Zoo noch?" Erinnerungen an Niklas Luhmann* (pp. 143–151). Konstanz: UVK.

Toles, T. (2017, April 10). Having Failed to Drain the Swamp, Trump Decides to Call It a Lake. *The Washington Post*. www.washingtonpost.com/politics/trump-drain-the-swamp/2020/10/24/52c7682c-0a5a-11eb-9be6-cf25fb429f1a_story.html

Toscano, A. (2008). The Culture of Abstraction, *Theory, Culture & Society*, 25(4), 57–75. doi.org/10.1177/0263276408091983

Tuastad, D. (2017). "State of Exception" or "In Exile"? The Fallacy of Appropriating Agamben on Palestinian Refugee Camps. *Third World Quarterly*, 38(9), 2159–2170. doi.org/ 10.1080/01436597.2016.1256765

Tuinen, S. van, & N. McDonnell, Eds. (2010). *Deleuze and the Fold: A Critical Reader*. Houndmills: Palgrave Macmillan

Virilio, P. (2007). *Speed and Politics* (M. Polizzotti, Trans.). Los Angeles: Semiotext(e).

Virilio, P. (2012). *The Great Accelerator* (J. Rose, Trans.). Cambridge: Polity.

von Foerster, H. (2003). *Understanding Understanding: Essays on Cybernetics and Cognition*. New York/Berlin/Heidelberg: Springer.

Voss, D. (2013a). Deleuze's Rethinking of the Notion of Sense. *Deleuze Studies*, 7(1), 1–25. doi.org/10.3366/dls.2013.0092

Voss, D. (2013b). Deleuze's Third Synthesis of Time. *Deleuze Studies*, 7(2), 194–216. doi.org/10.3366/dls.2013.0102

Voss, D. (2018). Simondon on the Notion of the Problem: A Genetic Schema of Individuation. *Angelaki*, 23(2), 94–112. doi.org/10.1080/0969725X.2018.1451471

Weber, S. (1992). Taking Exception to Decision: Walter Benjamin and Carl Schmitt. *Diacritics*, 22(3/4), 5–18. doi.org/10.2307/465262

Wehrsig, C. (1999). Gesten der Person. Zur hintergründigen Anwesenheit Niklas Luhmanns. In T. M. Bardmann & D. Baecker (Eds.), *"Gibt es eigentlich den Berliner Zoo noch?" Erinnerungen an Niklas Luhmann* (pp. 53–55). Konstanz: UVK.

Weinbaum, D. R. (2015). Complexity and the Philosophy of Becoming. *Foundations of Science*, 20(3), 283–322. doi.org/10.1007/s10699-014-9370-2

Whitehead, A. N. (1920). *The Concept of Nature*. Cambridge: Cambridge University Press.

Whitehead, A. N. (1978). *Process and Reality: An Essay in Cosmology*. New York: The Free Press.

Widder, N. (2003). Thought after Dialectics: Deleuze's Ontology of Sense. *The Southern Journal of Philosophy*, 41, 451–476. doi.org/10.1111/j.2041-6962.2003.tb00961.x

Widder, N. (2008). *Reflections on Time and Politics*. University Park: Pennsylvania State University Press.

Widder, N. (2012). *Political Theory after Deleuze*. London: Bloomsbury.

Widder, N. (2021, February 26). Forget the Virtual, What Matters Is Intensity: On the Development of Deleuze's Distinction between the Virtual and Intensity from Nietzsche and Philosophy to *The Logic of Sense*. Presented at the Royal Holloway Centre for Continental Philosophy research seminar series (online).

Wiener, N. (1985). *Cybernetics or Control and Communication in the Animal and the Machine*. 2nd ed. Cambridge, MA: MIT Press.

Williams, J. (2008). *Gilles Deleuze's Logic of Sense: A Critical Introduction and Guide*. Edinburgh: Edinburgh University Press.

Williams, J. (2009a). If Not Here, Then Where? On the Location and Individuation of Events in Badiou and Deleuze. *Deleuze Studies*, 3(1), 97–123. doi. org/10.3366/E1750224109000506

Williams, J. (2009b). A. N. Whitehead. In G. Jones & J. Roffe (Eds.), *Deleuze's Philosophical Heritage* (pp. 282–299). Edinburgh: Edinburgh University Press.

Williams, J. (2010). Immanence and Transcendence as Inseparable Processes: On the Relevance of Arguments from Whitehead to Deleuze Interpretation. *Deleuze Studies*, 4(1), 94–106. doi.org/10.3366/E1750224110000851

Williams, J. (2011). *Gilles Deleuze's Philosophy of Time: A Critical Introduction and Guide*. Edinburgh: Edinburgh University Press.

Williams, J. (2016a). *A Process Philosophy of Signs*. Oxford: Oxford University Press.

Williams, J. (2016b). What Is a Diagram (for a Sign)? *Parrhesia*, 23, 41–61.

Wimmer, R. (1999). Begegnungen mit Beratern. In T. M. Bardmann & D. Baecker (Eds.), *"Gibt es eigentlich den Berliner Zoo noch?" Erinnerungen an Niklas Luhmann* (pp. 24–28). Konstanz: UVK, 42–46.

Wirtz, T. (1999). Entscheidung. Niklas Luhmann und Carl Schmitt. In A. Koschorke & C. Visman (Eds.), *Widerstaende der Systemtheorie. Kulturtheoretische Analysen zum Werk Niklas Luhmanns* (pp. 177–197). Berlin: Akademie Verlag.

Wittgenstein, L. (1981). *Zettel* (G. E. M. Anscombe & G. H. V. Wright, Eds.). 2nd ed. Oxford: Blackwell.

Wolff, L. (2021). The Past Shall Not Begin: Frozen Seeds, Extended Presents and the Politics of Reversibility. *Security Dialogue*, 52(1), 79–95. doi. org/10.1177/096701062091296

Woodward, A. (2020, October 2). "Fake News": A Guide to Trump's Favorite Phrase—and the Dangers It Obscures. *The Independent*. www.independent.co.uk/news/world/americas/us-election/trump-fake-news-counter-history-b732873.html

Zollinger, D. (2021). Voters' Notions of "Us" and "Them" May Consolidate a New Cleavage in Western European politics. *LSE blog*. https://blogs.lse.ac.uk/europpblog/2021/11/23/voters-notions-of-us-and-them-may-consolidate-a-new-cleavage-in-western-european-politics

Zourabichvili, F. (2012). *Deleuze: A Philosophy of the Event together with The Vocabulary of Deleuze* (G. Lambert & D. W. Smith, Eds; K. Aarons, Trans.). Edinburgh: Edinburgh University Press.

Zourabichvili, F. (2017). Deleuze and the Possible: on Involuntarism in Politics (K. Aarons & C. Doyle, Trans.). *Theory & Event*, 20(1), 152–171.

Index

absorption of uncertainty, 3, 133–134, 145
abstract machines, 141, 189n6. *See also* capitalist machine
actualization, 68
Agamben, Giorgio, 88–90, 100, 120, 187nn5–6
  on 'state of exception,' 88–90, 121–122, 166–167
  on time, 89–90
Aion concept, 97–98
Althusser, Louis, 6
anarchy, institutional model of, 13
anti-immigrant propaganda, 154
Anti-Oedipus (Deleuze and Guattari), 2, 140–142, 175, 189n6
Artaud, Antonin, 34–35
autopoiesis, autopoietic and
  definition of, 114
  events and, 114–115
  function of, 55
  functional logic of, 136
  inclusion and, 131–132
  individuation and, 62–66
  in modern politics, 131, 134, 140–142, 148
  neuronal networks and, 55
  paradox of, 72
  perspectivism and, 68

  self-reference and, 55
  social systems theory and, 54–56, 68–69
  structural coupling and, 81
  of systems theory, 56, 61, 70
  time in, 76–77, 85–91
  windowless existence and, 55–56
  worldmaking, 72

Benjamin, Walter, 100, 119–122, 129, 187nn5–6
Bergson, Henri, 9, 93–94, 186n1
The Birth of the Tragedy (Nietzsche), 83–84
Bowden, Sean, 24–25, 101–102, 177, 182n2
Brown, Wendy, 153–158, 169, 189n1

calculus theory, 39, 58–59
capital
  capitalism and, 138
  conditioning role of, 160
  as filiative, 141
  forms of, 137
  money as, 137–139
  self-extensive, 143
  self-productive functionality of, 138–139
  social conditions of, 140

213

www.ingramcontent.com/pod-product-compliance
Lightning Source LLC
Chambersburg PA
CBHW020349270326
41926CB00007B/368